Archaeology Versus Metal Detecting

The Cause and the Cure

First Edition

Peter G. Spackman

First published in Great Britain in 2024 by
Pen & Sword History
An imprint of Pen & Sword Books Limited
Yorkshire – Philadelphia

Copyright © Peter G. Spackman 2024

ISBN 978 1 03610 178 7

The right of Peter G. Spackman to be identified as
Author of this Work has been asserted by him in accordance
with the Copyright, Designs and Patents Act 1988.

A CIP catalogue record for this book is
available from the British Library

All rights reserved. No part of this book may be reproduced or
transmitted in any form or by any means, electronic or mechanical
including photocopying, recording or by any information storage and
retrieval system, without permission from the Publisher in writing.

Typeset by Mac Style
Printed in the UK by CPI Group (UK) Ltd, Croydon, CR0 4YY.

Pen & Sword Books Limited incorporates the imprints of After
the Battle, Atlas, Archaeology, Aviation, Discovery, Family History,
Fiction, History, Maritime, Military, Military Classics, Politics,
Select, Transport, True Crime, Air World, Frontline Publishing, Leo
Cooper, Remember When, Seaforth Publishing, The Praetorian Press,
Wharncliffe Local History, Wharncliffe Transport, Wharncliffe True
Crime and White Owl.

For a complete list of Pen & Sword titles please contact

PEN & SWORD BOOKS LIMITED
47 Church Street, Barnsley, South Yorkshire, S70 2AS, England
E-mail: enquiries@pen-and-sword.co.uk
Website: www.pen-and-sword.co.uk
or
PEN AND SWORD BOOKS
1950 Lawrence Rd, Havertown, PA 19083, USA
E-mail: uspen-and-sword@casematepublishers.com
Website: www.penandswordbooks.com

Peter George Spackman

This single sentence I offer is an apt quote that speaks a thousand words encompassing a lifetime of wisdom.

> *"There are many ways to approach stories, The professional folklorist, the Jungian, Freudian, or other sort of analyst, the ethnologist, anthropologist, theologian, **archeologist**, each has a different method, both in collecting tales and the use to which they are put."*
>
> Dr. Clarissa Pinkola Estés (1992)

In addition, I add an apt response to offer a little something to consider.

> *"Once a story is told there will emerge many who interpret the message in their own way, to match their own thoughts, and in consequence lose an offer of guidance to a path of enlightenment, truth, and fulfilment."*
>
> Peter George Spackman (2022)

Contents

List of Illustrations		ix
Acknowledgements		x
Preface		xii
Abbreviations		xx

Chapter 1	Archaeology, In the Beginning	1
	1.1 Archaeology and archaeologists	1
	1.2 Archaeology from conception to birth	7
	1.3 Portable Antiquities Scheme	17
	1.4 Archaeology meets detectorist	26
	1.5 The public debate	43
	1.6 Topsoil and plough soil	53
	1.7 CBA Reports and extracts	82
	1.8 Murky world of Auction House and Museum	100

Chapter 2	Metal Detecting, In the Beginning	108
	2.1 Metal Detecting and Detectorists	108
	2.2 Metal detecting and media representation	120
	2.3 Contexts, stratigraphy and finds	126
	2.4 Metal detecting Rallies and Clubs	138

Chapter 3	A Metal Detectorists Guide Designed for Archaeologists	144
	3.1 A motive and an aim	144
	3.2 Permission and research	145
	3.3 Equipment	146
	3.4 Methodology none-archaeological site	152
	3.5 Recovery, recording and care techniques	154
	3.6 Insurance and representative institutions	160

Chapter 4	An Archaeologist Guide for Metal Detectorists	162
	4.1 Equipment	163
	4.2 Health and Safety	167
	4.3 Methodology	168
	4.4 Qualifications and metal detecting	173
	4.5 Finds, removal, care, recording and sampling	180

Conclusion   185
Bibliography   189

List of Illustrations

Front cover	Cellar highlighting plotted metal artefacts.	
Figure 1	PAS Institutions Databases 1–4 compilation	50
Figure 2	PAS Institutions Databases 5–8 compilation	51
Figure 3	PAS Institutions Databases 1.8 Totals	52
Figure 4	PAS Finds Recovery Methodology. Totals	52
Figure 5	Finds Recovered in Pasture by Depth	67
Figure 6	Finds Recovered in Plough Soils by Depth	67
Figure 7	Amateur Status	79
Figure 8	PAS Finds Recovery Percentages, by Method	129
Figure 9	Section showing stratification and contexts	134

Acknowledgements

The help received from the Portable Antiquities Scheme [PAS] for access to their database, for without that invaluable information this study would have been incomplete and the added substance to the arguments presented was most appreciated.

A big thank you to Nigel Ingram, Managing Director of Regton Ltd, for an honest and forthright background synopsis covering the historical information of the family and business via his personal communication, all of which gave an insight into the skill and determination associated with the birth and expansion of modern technologies. Thanks also for the fine details regarding the birth and subsequent contributions to the sale and distribution of metal detectors and the company's expert advice that is always forthcoming, not only to amateur and professional metal detectorists but also to amateur and professional archaeologists.

A vote of thanks to Peter Welch of Weekend Wanderers and members for interaction and assistance with the metal-detected artefact depth surveys taken from varied locations, incorporating not only different soil types but also a diversity of weather conditions and agricultural processes. Well done to the participants, who painstakingly entered depth details on the recording forms; credit is also due to the several individual detectorists on their own permissions who were only too eager to contribute.

My dear wife, Carol Ann, should not go unmentioned, as the many hours of understanding and sacrifice are a credit to her commitment and patience during my dedicated endeavours. She was always at hand with either a refreshing mug of my preferred fennel tea or my favourite tipple: a lovingly poured glass of cider, or 'rough cider', as our cousins in the US call it, because over there cider is no more than apple juice. Carol Ann also acted as the much-welcomed resident proofreader, an essential exercise that went a long way to helping this dyslexic author; also, thank goodness for spellchecker.

Acknowledgement to the University of Leicester for their help and understanding during periods of illness towards the vital latter months of my learning programs those many years ago.

A huge thank you to Craig Allison, owner of Crawfords Metal Detectors, who was kind enough to supply a comprehensive background covering the birth and transitional periods of Crawfords: built by hard work and determination and near 30 years of continuing business acumen with progression always at the fore, and as usual always approachable for information and advice.

Preface

This book is aimed at an audience specifically encompassing the worlds of metal detecting and archaeology, where both parties are striving for, ultimately, the same aims and objectives: discovering our historic and cultural past, and in the process gathering knowledge, leading to a better understanding of not only our heritage but also the manufacturing, distribution and stylistic attribution of small finds. Along the way, gathering evidence involves the use of different techniques, methodologies, equipment, ideologies, and skills. There are a number of differences of opinion, as there are with any subject, with no exceptions, but it is the differences that cause conflict and discontent that will be dealt with, coupled with a no-holds-barred attitude. Inevitably this will, at times, be considered rather controversial to say the least. There will be no apologies for that, but I will endeavour to offer an honest and forthright rendering of the 'state of play' before it becomes a *fait accompli*.

In the past few years there appears to be growing an overwhelming desire by one party to govern and rule over the other, and it is this that has drawn an intermediary who is passionate about both metal detecting and archaeology. Someone who is prepared to delve into the historic formation and present function of both factions to ascertain the reasoning behind any conflict, distrust and ignorance, bringing the problem out into the open where it can be analysed, categorised and discussed. But any amount of dialog is worthless unless the recipients are not only prepared to listen but also acknowledge that positive constructive action is forthcoming and applied.

The intent of this publication is to, as an experienced long-time practitioner of both sciences, look at the activities in question, past and present, and strive towards an explanation that offers an unbiased lucidity. In the process, I hope to iron out any past ambiguities borne upon the shoulders of the many, instigated by the hands and thoughts of the few, in both archaeological and metal detectorist perspectives.

From the grave robbers and mound diggers of the past, to the conception of an archaeological process and the invention of an innovative piece of electronic equipment, leading to unimaginable discoveries. A sense of elucidation should shine forth as the reader travels through the pages of informative historical background of the institutionalised thoughts and practices that tend to react almost with a chemical process to the modern world with its freedoms and progressive ideas. With a little instruction and guidance, and of course more than a little cooperation from not just the two apparent protagonists, but from different factions within archaeology and metal-detecting communities, hopefully a sense of enlightenment should prevail. My relative background: *'Involvement in Archaeology'* began at an early age, having been brought up in the market town of Hexham, Northumberland. I was surrounded by the Roman remains of Hadrian's Wall, a short bicycle ride away, and the excavations at Corstopitum Roman fort, in the early 1950s, less than two miles away. Anglo-Saxon and medieval structures such as the local Moot Hall and Hexham Abbey, in which I spent many an hour as a choirboy during the 1950s, and a fascination with all things historic. I have, since the early 1980s, worked on archaeological sites under many guises, including volunteer, supervisor and site director, finding fulfilment in helping university students, local societies and volunteers alike, whenever the need arose. I obtained a Diploma in Archaeology and followed that with a BA(Hons) degree in Archaeology and History from the University of Leicester, and have for many years held Practitioner Chartered Institute for Archaeologists [PCIfA]. That amounts to near forty years excavating and supervising on sites of all periods, from Neolithic to the Second World War, with a preference for Roman and Anglo-Saxon. I have presented lectures and exhibitions to societies and the general public on a diversity of subjects, ranging from Anglo-Saxon history to PowerPoint presentations covering 'work in progress' at archaeological excavations, as well as arranging and presenting small finds exhibitions. There has always been a fascination concerning our past cultures and their structures and artefacts; this is something that has an almost cognitive behavioural characteristic, leading to the urge to search and rescue.

Institutional bodies and publication subscriptions to which I belong, excluding local historical societies and heritage groups:

ARA	The Association for Roman Archaeology (1892)
ASPROM	Association for Study and Preservation of Roman Mosaics
BNS	Banbury Numismatics Society
CA	Current Archaeology Magazine
CBA	Council for British Archaeology (24817)
	Finds Group
	Roman Pottery Group
	Diggers Forum
CWA	Current World Archaeology Magazine
PCIfA	Practitioner Chartered Institute for Archaeologists (5722)
RESCUE	The British Archaeological Trust

My relative background: *involving metal detecting* is forty years' experience searching with local groups and attending organised rallies as well private commissions. I have conducted numerous field-walking exercises both as an archaeologist and a metal-detectorist, and detected on live archaeological sites during excavations, as part of the excavation team. I have also detected as a professional on sites undergoing archaeological investigation for the construction industry, and privately as a paid professional metal detectorist.

I have for many a year attended the organised digs and rallies of 'The Weekend Wanderers' [WWs], a Southern England-based metal detecting group that adheres to the metal detectorists' code of practice set out by the National Council for Metal Detectorists [NCMD], as well as following the rules and regulations of the Chartered Institute for Archaeologists [CIfA] and Council for British Archaeology [CBA]. As an advocate of the adage 'finds do not belong to the finder' (discussed fully in later chapters), so honesty and openness has always been my aim. Alongside educating local history and heritage groups and the public on the pleasures of archaeology, I take great care to pass on the pleasures, fulfilment and science of both archaeology and metal detecting equally as a profession and a hobby. Not forgetting the health and wellbeing benefits of these outdoor activities, and of course the opportunity for learning a great deal of historical information concerning the land, its history, its cultural heritage and its remains, and the inevitable rescue of artefacts. As a long-time member of several associations, past and present, although not at all compulsory, I eulogise the pleasures and benefits of membership to an association, official body or club, which will undoubtedly lead to an opportunity to meet likeminded people, offering a variety of pathways to accessible information, guidance, and learning. In relation to the last statement, my personal membership and publication subscriptions to relevant associations involved with metal-detecting activities are listed below:

AMDS	Association for Metal Detecting Sport (2530)
BFMD	The British Forum for Metal Detecting
FID	Federation of Independent Detectorists (21228)
MDG	Metal Detectives Group
NCMD	National Council for Metal Detecting (14411)
TH	Treasure Hunting Magazine
TS	The Searcher Magazine
WW	Weekend Wanderers Metal Detecting Club (1523)

Not to be forgotten are the opportunities to not only learn but also to pass on knowledge to whoever wishes to receive it, an undertaking that often gives more pleasure than discovering the hidden history involved in either archaeology or metal detecting. An example of this are the many times at the end of a gruelling day trowelling slimy sediments of an old ditch when absolutely nothing had come to light, or detecting a field of hard stubble without even a single ring-pull on a scorching hot summer's day, and you have your shower and relax with the thoughts of 'that was a good day' and a realisation that with either archaeology or metal detecting, it's not always all about the finds but the activity.

My two most recently published books are an expanded view of field-name interpretation, which encourages historical research, and a historical-based novel of short stories covering a multitude of historical and pre-historical time periods incorporating an anti-bullying theme. The latter is neither archaeologically nor detectorist based as such, but the plinths of early 'archaeologists' were indeed historians and antiquarians, were they not?

The main aim of this current publication is to open channels that could lead to a clearer understanding and recognition of both pathways; pathways that cross into both realms more times than one would think. *An argument* is not one body, nor should it be, setting out rules and doctrines that must be obeyed by another body, but a two-way pipeline of openminded discussion that recognises, with sincerity, the skills and professionalism of others: akin to a meaningful *Entente Cordiale*. It also aims to offer clear instructions and guidance, to educate the uneducated on the art of each other's tools, skills, and procedures, looking at every aspect from organisational preparation through to record keeping, which differs widely through the hierarchical levels of ability and doctrines. That chapter is somewhat eye-opening in that both archaeological and metal-detecting practitioners, like it or not, are subjected to the pleasures of working with both complete novices and experts alike.

In the last decade both metal detecting and archaeology have been subject to changes that, in part, are not conducive with both parties. Archaeology as a whole suffered university course closures as the subject was removed from the general curriculum, and metal detecting, which was, in the past, often the domain of a singular or small club hobbyist with one or two permissions to their names, has suffered at the hands of more and more business-oriented organisations that offer outings to multiple permissions for a fee. All points raised will be subjected to discussion in later chapters, with an ambition to leave the reader a little wiser about the diverse worlds of historical research of both archaeology and metal detecting.

The chapters that are directed specifically at the doctrines involved will offer an insight into the required skill base to operate alongside each other; *id est*, metal detectorists will be enlightened as to the methods and practices of archaeologists, and archaeologists will be enlightened as to the equipment, methodologies and skills of the metal detectorists. Neither party should approach this with an attitude of pre-programmed preconceptions, but just read, digest and most of all practise and accept alterations to their own working practices and acknowledge that change is a way of life. A dogmatic approach is not, I repeat, not, an educational methodology to be used as a coexistent approach to form a congenial recipe for openness and learning.

If there are obstacles that are solely associated with cash flow or a restricted purse, what price is our heritage, what price is our culture, and if a heritage asset is at threat by cutting corners to save money, then that should not be an option. Heritage assets are not an infinite resource and ultimately great care should be at the fore of both archaeological and metal-detecting investigations. There will be home truths that are hard to swallow and working practices that practitioners rely on but are a little questionable to say the least, but again heritage asset rescue and protection should be the key to a realistic acknowledgement of commitment. Skills, and expertise in the areas of commerce, construction, and the sport and leisure sectors, are encompassing the subjects archaeology and metal detecting in practice.

Commerce cannot be discounted in the argument as it is all too often the main driving force behind procedures and practices in the commercial archaeology and construction industries, where timescales and expenditure are regularly monitored. I am not insinuating that 'correct procedures' are not being strictly adhered to, but sometimes the minimum requirements leave a little to be desired. On the other hand, an all too often nervous secrecy seeps through the rank and file of well-meaning operatives.

An analogy that I remember well incorporated a hobby, a sport and a commercial enterprise that demanded unacceptable (personal and ethical) practices and procedures. Participating in fly fishing from an early age, I rebelled against some of the practices and procedures demanded by the local governing body. Now before you, with my cap in hand, are the confessions of a 12-year-old in the heart of Northumberland back in the late 1950s. My main hobby was fishing and I had access to the rivers Coquet, the North Tyne and the South Tyne, where the sport was game fishing. The prey were brown trout, sea trout and salmon (classed as game fish), which supplied family and relatives with a steady supply of fresh produce; along with a schoolmate, I helped catch the first salmon from the Tyne, in my hometown of Hexham, for thirty years. The fish caught were also my pocket money and I remember well that I was receiving £1 a pound for salmon and half a crown a pound for trout when sold to the local fishmongers. Using mainly homemade dry fly for the trout, one of the rules of the river was that if any coarse fish were caught, which were mainly dace and roach, they (coarse fish) should not be returned to the water and the penalty for doing so would be an instant ban. There were people in high places who preferred that only game fish were entitled to the food source and my pocket money and family food was in jeopardy. Many a pile of those beautiful silver dace and the flamboyant red flashes of the roach could be spotted and smelt in nearby bushes on the banks of such scenic rivers. The dilemma was: do I give up my pleasure and comply with barbaric rules to slaughter coarse fish? Yes, I killed trout and salmon (for food), but to needlessly kill something was cruel and inhumane, and was not something I relished. So, I changed my hunting grounds to more rural areas that were out of sight from prying eyes and put back into the river, with pride and a clear moral conscience, any coarse fish I caught. What has that to do with this publication you may well ask. Nothing but the moral is my reply.

As in most circumstances, a compromise can be reached, but when one party is domineering and the other non-submissive, the bright flame of the prospects of negotiation flicker and fade; that is when barriers are erected and unfortunately entrenchment follows. This of course is neither constructive nor productive, so before that transpires, and it is never too late, we will delve into the very different working practices of archaeology and metal detecting. These two worlds that are, at the very least, heading in the same direction, on the same footpath as it were, with the same fundamental goals of enlightenment and knowledge of our past, accomplished both by research and action, followed by a sharing of the knowledge gained. The critical question is: does someone wish to own the footpath and enforce an attitude of toll-bridge entrance by way of rules, legislation, and ownership? This would be a barrier to passage and I for one would not want that to happen, so let us see what we can do, not by opening a 'Pandora's Box', but more likely the proverbial 'can of worms'. At least the latter is a lesser evil, but both head towards unwanted outcomes, which is unfortunately inevitable, but they represent a real and present conclusion. An expectation of a banner held aloft displaying the modern idiom No Pain, No Gain, used in the modern era by US Vice President Adlai Stevenson (1952) in a presidential nomination acceptance speech in Chicago, with the words *'there are no gains without pains'* (Cohen and Cohen (1971, pp. 358–9)), which could have been an interpretation of an entry in *Hesperides*, by Robert Herrick (1650) who wrote *'if little labour, little are our gains'*, and a possible indication by Baldwin (2022), who in turn presents knowledge of the second-century Hebrew Rabbi, Ben Hei -Hei, who is associated with the ancient saying *'According to the pain, is the gain'*.

Sometimes the *'common ground'* appears as nothing more than a boggy mire, a mirage or a Will-o'-the-Wisp, but hopefully only in the minds of the few when the many will see a rising sun over fields of wildflowers coupled with the perfumes of spring. Our history, heritage and culture are strewn with the casualties caused by the inability to reach the common ground; sometimes or actually most times the inability to achieve agreement lays heavily upon the shoulders of those who govern the parties involved. So, it is my resolve not to merely inform by understandable fact and highlight the principal factors of discontent that have led to an apparent impasse of, some would say, irreversible magnitude, but the information supplied and suggestions offered could indeed lead to a positive outcome, even if the only achievement accomplished is meetings and then perhaps the creation of an acceptable state of working equilibrium and understanding. The information gleaned from this study was, to me as an archaeologist and an avid metal detectorist, both educational and enlightening.

Abbreviations

ACP	Approved Code of Practice
AKA	Also Known As
ALGAO	Association of Local Government Archaeological Officers
AMDS	Association for Metal Detecting Sport
AMP	Agricultural Management Plan
ARA	Association Roman Archaeology
ASPROM	Association for Study and Preservation of Roman Mosaics
BBC	British Broadcasting Corporation
BC	Before Christ
BFMD	British Forum for Metal Detecting
BM	British Museum
BNS	Banbury Numismatic Society
BSc	Bachelor of Science
CA	Current Archaeology
CBA	Council for British Archaeology
CIFA	Chartered Institute for Archaeologists
CLIC	Cancer and Leukaemia in Childhood
CORN	Cornwall
CSCS	Construction Skills Certificate Scheme
CTRL	Channel Tunnel Rail Link
CWA	Current World Archaeology
DCMS	Department for Digital, Culture, Media and Sport
DEFRA	Department for Environment, Food and Rural Affairs
DGPS	Differential Global Positional System
DMV	Deserted Medieval Village
DNA	Deoxyribonucleic Acid
DQC	Driver Qualification Card
DUR	Durham
Ed	Editor
Edn	Edition

FID	Federation Independent Detectorists
FIFA	Federation of International Football Association
FLO	Finds Liaison Officers
FTE	Full-time-equivalent
GNSS	Global Navigation Satellite System
GPS	Global Positional System
Ha	Hectare
HAMP	Hampshire
HF	Heritage Finds
H & S	Health and Safety
IARCH	Iron Age & Roman Coin Hoards
IED	Improvised Explosive Device
IOW	Isle of Wight
LED	Light Emitting Diode
LIN	Lincoln
MOLAS	Museum of London Archaeology Service
NAGPRA	North American Graves Protection
NAM	National Army Museum
NCMD	National Council for Metal Detecting
NHMF	National Heritage Memorial Fund
NMS	Norfolk Museum Services
NPPF	National Planning Policy Framework
PAS	Portable Antiquities Scheme
PC	Politically Correct
PCIfA	Practitioner Chartered Institute for Archaeologists
PI	Pulse Induction
PIM	Pulsed Induction Meter
PPE	Personal Protection equipment
PPG15	Planning Policy Guidance 15
PPG16	Planning Policy Guidance 16
PPS5	Planning Policy Statement 5
RFERL	Radio Free Europe Radio Liberty
RUH	Royal United Hospital
SAL	Society of Antiquaries London.
SCC	Suffolk County Council.
SCCAS	Suffolk County Council Archaeology Service
SMA	South Midlands Archaeology

SRP	Soil Resource Plan
STM	Society Thames Mudlarks
SUR	Surrey
TH	Treasure Hunter
TS	The Searcher
TT	Time Team
TAMDM	The Archaeology and Metal Detecting Magazine.
TV	Television
UFO	Unidentified Flying Object
UK	United Kingdom
UKDFD	United Kingdom Detector Finds Database
ULAS	University Leicester Archaeological Service
UNESCO	United Nations Educational, Scientific and Cultural Organization
USA	United States of America
USN	United States Navy
USS	United States Ships
VLF	Very Low Frequency
VOL	Volume
WILT	Wiltshire
WMA	West Midlands Archaeology
WSI	Written Scheme of Investigation
WWII	World War Two

Chapter 1

Archaeology in the Beginning

1.1 Archaeology and archaeologists

It is of benefit to delve into the backgrounds, the roots, of both archaeology and metal detecting as it is important to investigate the evolution of the methods, codes of practice, guidelines and ruling bodies. In a modern environment we appear to have one discipline in decline and the other in ascendancy, but all will come to light in due course.

In the beginning, but not as we know it today, as with most, if not all subjects, whether leisure based or academically taught, today's advance in technology comes with its own innovations that often require changes in rules and working practices.

King John became the first monarch to act as an early archaeologist (Hodgson (2015, p. 45)), or should we read that as 'treasure hunter', by searching the old Roman town of *Corstopitum*, modern-day Corbridge, Northumberland in 1201 AD. King John appeared to be on the right track as years later a hoard of solid silver paraphernalia, presumably from a nearby temple to Apollo or as suggested by Higham (1993, p. 51), buried by a high-ranking officer, was found in the adjacent River Tyne in 1735; one surviving tray known as *The Corbridge Lanx* is on display in the British Museum. Then some 700 years after the attempts of King John, a staggering coin hoard was uncovered during excavations in 1911 AD under the floor of a building on the site of the *Corstopitum* (Corbridge, Northumberland) settlement, comprising 162 Roman-period gold *aurei* (Bland *et al.* (2020, pp. 214–215)).

For many centuries, the searches for the truth of past human evidence were stifled by religious beliefs, predominantly the belief that humans did not exist before the year 4004 BC; the year of estimation for the writing of *Genesis* is suggested by Andrew Steinmann (2019, p. 2) of being between 1450 BC and 1400 BC. Three thousand or so years later, we see the emergence or a kind of 'hatching' of a more tolerant or learned society eager for the expansion of knowledge and ultimately a truth that is not encumbered by the shackles of past doctrines.

2   Archaeology Versus Metal Detecting

Historian and genealogist John Leland 1503–52, when given the distinguished title of King's Antiquary, showed that even the monarchy had encouraged an interest in antiquities as a political means to create, what Roskams (Excavation 2001, p. 22) described as an *'ideology of nationalism'* is open to debate. Leland is now known as *'Father of English History Societies'* on account of being a stickler to detail. William Camden 1551–1623, a noted historian, developed from an early age a passion for antiquarianism even to the extent of learning Anglo-Saxon and Welsh languages as an aid to the interpretation of placenames. Camden's Britannia, first printed in 1585, was another example of attentive organisational ability and according to Britannica (The Editors of Encyclopaedia, Online), Camden's skills laid the foundation of regional archaeological societies with a realisation that there were a number of early antiquarians who also deserved the title of founder of history and archaeological societies. Dr William Stukeley 1687–1765, an antiquarian, physician, clergyman and archaeologist, was, in retrospect, one of the forebears of archaeological investigations, as John F.H. Smith (2022, p. 1) gives Stukeley the title 'Father of British Archaeology'. An enthusiastic mound digger, Stukeley was probably most famous for his archaeological work and investigations concerning the ancient sites of Stonehenge and Avebury. Although most interpretations could be called dubious, as Lloyd and Jennifer Laing (1982, pp. 19–21) suggest that Stukeley was more than a little obsessed with the thought that Druids were responsible for prehistoric monuments such as Stonehenge, he nonetheless laid the grounds for thorough archaeological excavation techniques. In 1753 William Stukeley was recognised as a leading figure of the age and welcomed as a trustee and helped to set up the British Museum. Among other subjects, he penned a score of books incorporating the subjects of archaeology, antiquarians and historians. William Stukeley travelled far and wide exploring and recording new interpretations of history along with historic monuments. An indication of Stukeley's work is shown in Renfrew and Bahn (2000, p. 20), where we can see a part page of Stukeley's handwritten notes and sketches. Because of Stukeley's interest in practices and *'presumed'* monuments of Druids, the relationship of the serpentine avenue of Avebury seen by Stukeley and the similarity to ancient serpent mounds in North America all associated with earth energies is discussed in Bord (1982, pp. 237–38). Others worked just as enthusiastically in their own locality and an example of this is one William Dugdale 1605–86, who meticulously compiled historical records;

records of which many would have been lost or forgotten without his ambition, culminating in the quite monumental publication '*The Antiquities of Warwickshire*' (Dugdale, 1656, Vol. 1). That work, or usually copies of, is now in the regime of a myriad of heritage and history societies the length and breadth of the country, whereas Dugdale devoted a large part of his life to the county of Warwickshire. We see several individual antiquarians affording virtually a lifetime to personal study and another example is Alfred Beesley 1800–47, who dedicated his life to compiling all things historic about the market town of Banbury and Banburyshire; the pinnacle of this study was '*Copious Historical and Antiquarian Notices*' (Beesley, 1841), leaving behind a legacy of procedural exemplarism.

There were also the compilers, such as Henry Spelman (1562–1641), who gathered orderly accounts of medical and church records, and Encyclopedia Britannia (2021) enlightens us that Spelman was possibly responsible for the first systematic compilation of church documents and in the process contributed a certain methodological guide to data recording, becoming a noteworthy compiler extraordinaire. Then emerged the age of the collectors, such as the almost hoard-like mentality of Elias Ashmole (1617–92), who amassed curiosities and historical artefacts, as MacGregor (2001, p. 15) relates that Ashmole favoured books and manuscripts with a penchant for collecting coins, but it was the inheritance from the estate of John Tradescant, a collection of note in 1678, that encouraged Ashmole to bequeath the collection to the University of Oxford, eventually leading to the opening of one of, if not the first, museum in the UK open to the public in 1683, which was proudly set at the centre of the city of spires, Oxford. During this period, more and more people, as was their want, travelled abroad with the sole purpose of obtaining artefacts whether by sale or by excavating with apparent intent to own. They, the collectors of the day, were the hierarchy of society; one excellent example was Thomas Howard Earl of Arundel (1585–1646), who in the early seventeenth century toured Italy in search of ancient artefacts and even took to the spade to extract cultural artefacts to adorn houses or private collections, and amassed a collection of more than 700 paintings and numerous sculptures and Greek marbles, later to be donated to the Oxford University in 1667 known as the Arundel marbles (*Encyclopaedia Britannica*, 2022). These marbles were either looted from Greece in antiquity or much copied by successive Roman Emperors.

Most of the scholars would have been members of the College of Antiquaries, initially founded in London in 1586 but lasting less than thirty years as James I abolished the society in 1614. It took more than a century before the society was again reconstituted in the year 1707 and succeeded in being honoured with a royal charter from George II in 1751. These are brief histories of the initial foundation years of the society, now called Society of Antiquaries London (SAL, 2022), which remained gender specific until Catherine Downes became the first female to enter the hallowed grounds of the society. In a recent YouTube seminar, Madeleine Pelling (2021) recalls how Catherine Downes in 1786 proved as meticulous as many of her counterparts and found the mosaic drawings from the Roman Villa at Pit Meadow near Warminster in the county of Wiltshire, which were later deposited with the SAL. According to Pelling (2021), Downes had become '*a rare example of woman's contribution to eighteenth century institution*'. It is of note that archaeologists, in those early days of archaeological history, were considered by scholars of the day to be purely amateurs. Less than twenty years later in 1805, William Cunnington (1754–1810), another one of the early archaeologists honoured with the title of 'Fathers of Archaeology', could be found excavating near to Stonehenge (Renfrew and Bahn 1991, p. 21) alongside Richard Colt Hoare (1758–1838), who had excavated hundreds of mounds in southern England. Unfortunately, Cunnington passed away in 1810, but not before leaving a legacy of pioneering archaeological investigation (for whatever purpose). Later antiquarians, such as Augustus Henry Lane Fox (1827–1900), also known as either Pitt Rivers or General Pitt-Rivers (Renfrew and Bahn (1991, p. 31), offers such superlatives as '*impeccably*' and '*organised*' when referring to both excavations and post-excavation reports, and this appears to be a turning point when Pitt Rivers' methodological practice of total recording was accepted as a guide. During the latter quarter of the eighteenth century, Pitt Rivers spent many seasons excavating sites and, as Laing and Laing (1982, p. 34) add, with a caring for both the '*mundane and the beautiful*', resulting in a set of reports being published between 1887 and 1898 covering excavation at Cranborne Chase. These excavations were in the southwest of England and Bowden ((1991 in Greene, 1983), Revised 1995, pp. 61–2) admires the completeness of Pitt Rivers' reports, especially his detailed accounts of both excavations and recovered artefacts alike. A substantial proportion of Pitt Rivers' collection of anthropological and ethnological artefacts, which formed a base for the now successful Pitt Rivers Museum, was obtained from donations; researcher Alison Petch (2005) provides examples of many hundreds of artefacts that were either gifted or purchased between 1884 and 2008.

Early twentieth-century archaeologist Sir Robert Eric Mortimer Wheeler (1890–1976), known simply as Mortimer Wheeler, emerged as a significant cog in the wheels of archaeology, spending many years post-First World War investigating monuments around southern England. One of his most recounted excavations was Maiden Castle. Wheeler, according to Roskams (2001, p. 13), was an advocate for detail, encompassing all areas of the archaeological process; one could say that he introduced a more formal approach and at the very least, a template for others to follow. Mortimer Wheeler developed and preferred box-excavation coupled with total control. We can see a progression of the box-excavation technique between the Maiden Castle excavations of the late thirties in Roskams (2001, pl. 2, p. 14) and the post-Second World War box-excavations at Arikamedu, India during 1945 (Chadha (2002, Figure 2, p. 387)), and further evidence of that technique is presented by P. Barker (1993 cited in Greene, 1983, third Edn. 1995, pp. 64–5) with thirty-six meticulously excavated boxes by Wheeler during the 1951–2 seasons at Stanwick, Yorkshire, which demonstrate that Wheeler had perfected that particular technique. Wheeler's remarks concerning the importance of 'a written record' are highlighted by Salway (1981, p. 226) in connection with validity of a written source and bolstered by Chadha (2002, p. 388), who emphasised Wheeler's advocacy that regular publication is as important as any systematic excavation. Included in Chadha's conclusion (2002, p. 396) is a telling sentence that refers to Wheeler's style of archaeology but tells us more than is meant: *'Wheeler's intervention ... formed a disciplinarian discourse that resulted in a widespread domination of the past as a cultural category'*. With any archaeological procedure there must be some sort of discipline, whether it be individual, colleague or authoritarian based, but when refering to *'widespread domination of the past'* it becomes uncannily apparent that this could be a description for an archaic proactive ideology that infests the archaeology of today and the asserted efforts to enact the domination; times have changed and methodologies have moved on, but the procedural legacies of some of the founders of modern-era archaeology appear to be a little deep rooted. According to Cunliffe (1988), there has, historically, been rifts in archaeological practices concerning classicists versus prehistorians, which lives on, but Wheeler, who was classics trained, incorporated both methodologies as Cunliffe (1988) suggests Wheeler studied the indigenous cultures wherever possible, prehistoric or otherwise, as part of a study ethic.

Barrington Windsor Cunliffe (1939–present), better known as Barry Cunliffe, developed standards, techniques, and methods that brought or dragged archaeology firmly into the twentieth century. One of the practices that Cunliffe advocated involved the study of landscapes around excavated monuments. As Phillip Barker (1977, p. 33) notes, the technique employed by, and with reference to, Cunliffe (1973) transformed archaeology from a near antiquarian pastime mentality that was practised by notable individuals to a constantly developing science. Cunliffe brought his skills and knowledge to the University of Southampton as Professor of Archaeology and in 1972 as Professor of European Archaeology at the University of Oxford, and the list of some of the many achievements are highlighted by The British Academy (2022). Cunliffe was still penning great literary works, taking the opportunity to pass on his vast knowledge not just of excavation, but also his deep understanding of ancient peoples of the world, such as '*The Oxford Illustrated History of Prehistoric Europe*' (1994) and '*Britain Begins*' (2012). I can only describe Barry Cunliffe as a '*Great Oak in the Archaeological Landscape*' (Spackman, 2023), which is in no way meant as a reflection of age, but to represent a powerful steadfast influence in the fields of archaeology, history and anthropology.

Andrew Colin Renfrew (1937–present), more often known simply as Colin Renfrew, is a contemporary of Barry Cunliffe, both of whom held, according to Jesus College Cambridge (2022), on separate occasions, the post of Professor of Archaeology at the University of Southampton. Quite a prolific writer, and any archaeologist's library most likely contains at least one copy of a publication, which cover a diversity of topics, and they would be hard pressed not to have referenced Renfrew in an essay or a dissertation. Two books that I have opened many times that show a certain diversity concern the origin of Indo-European Languages (Renfrew, 1987), and the other, a must-have for any archaeologist, historian, and interested enthusiast, centres on the theories and practices of the archaeological process (Renfrew and Bahn, 1991); with 640 pages of sheer bliss, it is in my top ten. There are few areas of anthropology and archaeology from prehistory to the present that have not been blessed by the pen of Renfrew, and there is an obvious passion in his work, including an avid contribution to the provenance and

Archaeology in the Beginning 7

ownership of cultural antiquities from the UK and beyond, a subject dear to my heart (see chapter 3 (this publication) and Renfrew (2000)). One can come across the depth of knowledge of Renfrew with an example such as an insight into the subject of socio-political systems and the emerging cultural complexities involved (Renfrew, (1996)), and many more. There are of course a multitude of authors who have influenced, by theory, practice, and foresight. the associated sciences of the archaeological process, and it would take a whole volume to honour their efforts. My modest collection of 1,400 volumes are but a few names that bear witness to the modern foundations of archaeological studies such as: Richard Buckley, Aubrey Burl, Clive Gamble, George Holmes, Henrietta Leyser, Frank Stenton and Harold Taylor; an apology to the 1,300+ I have not mentioned, as those listed are a random selection from my shelves and in no way represent any hierarchal importance. This is a good indication of the many veins of archaeology that supply the arteries with knowledge, which feeds the hungry head, most of which the layperson would not associate with that of an archaeologist in the truest sense, and a meaningful use of words by Wheeler (1962, p. 5. In Wood, E. 1963), *'At no previous time have so many critical specialists been at work in so many and various fields'*, is an indication that sixty years ago rapid expansion was prevalent; just imagine how big the beast has now grown. These archaeologists, mostly pioneers, were at the beginning of their careers during the latter half of the twentieth century, often stepping into unknown territories of application, technique and theoretic exploration, and it was with fortitude, knowledge, and skill that Cunliffe and Renfrew, two eminent professors, paved the way for a more modern archaeology: a wider, more complex presentation incorporating such subjects as radio-carbon dating, language roots, and deoxyribonucleic acid [DNA], the almost constant advances in the expanding sciences involved in the all-encompassing title of archaeology.

1.2 Archaeology from conception to birth

Archaeology, as we know it, did not exist until the mid-nineteenth century when overwhelming evidence supplied by geologists and historians could no longer be ignored, and the once thought origin of humanity in the year 4004 was thrown, well and truly, out of the window. During the nineteenth century, the influence of early antiquarians and archaeologists can be seen in the birth of historical and archaeological societies; one example is the Kent Archaeological Society and their publications of '*Archaeologia Cantiana*'. In my own library I have issues of Vol. V and Vol. VII (Brent, 1863 and 1868). An excellent example is the meticulous record keeping concerning excavations of an Anglo-Saxon cemetery at the hamlet of Sarr in the county of Kent, and the exquisitely drawn illustrations (in colour) of finds from Grave 4 at the Sarr/Sarre site (Plate I and Plate II) by Messrs F.W. Fairholt and F.G. Netherclift in Vol. V (Brent, 1863). The many volumes of the Kent Archaeological Society printed more than 150 years ago are, indeed, a showcase and indicative of advances, learning and the transmission of knowledge in those years gone by. The Kent Archaeological Society in 1857 was founded only thirty-three years after the word '*archaeology*' earned its place in the annuls of the world-renowned Collins English Dictionary in 1824. There are obvious signs that the contributors continued to heed the earlier works and possibly influenced later antiquarians and archaeologist such as Cunnington and General Pitt Rivers *et al*. The influence of Pitt Rivers is also noted by Sheppard Frere (1967, p. 321), who praised the reports by Pitt Rivers from excavations on farmsteads such as Woodcutts and Rotherley. Today we can find '*archaeology*' described simply as, '*the study of man's past by scientific analysis of the material remains of his cultures*' (Collins, 2014, p. 102). Onions C.T. (1985, p. 48) suggests, in the equally respected The Oxford Dictionary of English Etymology, a meaning referring to study of prehistoric matters. Interestingly, neither interpretation gives the slightest indication of exploration by excavation or even delving beneath the soil by any means.

There are at present more than 6,000 memberships, not counting affiliates from the worlds of archaeological, history and heritage groups and individuals listed with the CBA (2021, p. 8), and more not listed who contribute towards a database of collective knowledge, however large or small. These societies and individuals have for many decades, if not centuries, been the mainstay of the supply of archaeological and historical knowledge to the public, along with the more accessible, world-famous Time Team, a programme that Tim Taylor (1999, p. 6) describes as '*one of television's most popular programmes on archaeology*'. Time Team ran for more than twenty years as a weekly TV series (Channel 4, 1994–2014), interspersed with the occasional special. These would have been, for the vast majority of the UK populous, their first encounter with and insight into the fascinating world of heritage and historical knowledge extraction. I recall one of the last excavations to be honoured by Mick Aston, who was much more than an archaeologist, and remember well, spending almost an hour sitting on a bench during the Burford Priory dig in the warm sunshine and chatting about all things archaeological. When I mention heritage, I refer of course to either land or artefacts that someone has proven heritage ownership, which in the case of artefacts is a rare occurrence indeed. It is these artefacts that are rescued from the earth in their hundreds week after week by metal detectorists and an untold number by professional archaeologists and amateur archaeologists, and the fact that it is everyone's right and entitlement to have access to the post-excavation information regarding artefacts or heritage assets. Not to infer that access to the actual dig site is made available to the public sector, just the dissemination of heritage and historical information. Many of the larger excavations provide public viewing platforms or educational open days; after all, whose heritage is it? The archaeologists, the landowners, the metal detectorists, the contractors, or the nation as a whole? Land and property are of course subject to inheritance, but there are few people who can lay claim, by heritage, to artefacts recovered from their land. I fully realise that archaeological units may be themselves governed by the constraints of the small print encountered in contracts and freedom of information clauses, but if a metal detectorist or a member of the public is expected to record a notable find with the PAS as standard practice, within 14 days depending upon whichever class of find is involved, which in turn gives information freely accessible to professional archaeologists, amateur archaeologists, metal detectorists and the general public alike, one would expect reciprocal activity from the world of commercial archaeology and archaeology as a whole.

    The Chair of the CIfA Stephen Carter (2022, p. 13) presents the Annual Review, which included the updated membership statistics showing that there are 4,397 members registered with the institute, but Aitchison, K. *et al* (2020, 1.1), looking at profession profiles, estimate that there are approximately 7,000 personnel employed in all areas of the archaeological processes in the UK. However, not all belong to the recognised prominent professional organisation CIfA, which indicates that with a membership of 4,397, which of course is subject to slight daily fluctuations, there are upwards of 2,500 unregistered with that particular organisation, professional archaeologists, and many thousands more unregistered amateur and volunteer archaeologists working on commercial, private and community-led sites. In the archaeological sector it is not compulsory to belong to a professional body, although presumably advantageous for a job application and the proverbial 'career ladder'. Interesting that metal detectorists are often mentioned as being 'amateur metal detectorists' because they do not belong to an official body (which most do); so, I wonder if 2,500 archaeologists who are not registered with CIfA belong to an official body, or are they too classed as amateurs? There are arguments emanating from the world of archaeology for all metal detectorists to come under the umbrella and government of archaeological hierarchy and their archaeological regulations, and for the metal detectorists to pay an annual fee for the privilege of holding official membership cards, which also entails attending fee-paying educational classes. Membership of one particular organisation that surfaced as recently as 2018 required metal detectorists to attend a number of paid courses based on archaeological principles in the hope of a non-specified qualification that would allow a metal detectorist to work alongside archaeologists on an archaeological site; whether as a paid participant was not forthcoming. This will be discussed in detail in a later chapter.

Archaeological publications of the early twenty-first century began to mention metal detectors as an aid to finds recovery, with Roskams (2001, p. 223) suggesting pre-excavation searching but only to highlight and flag any metal objects located and as a spoil heap artefact rescue tool. The problem with the latter is that the artefact would already be out of context; both these procedures are discussed in full in later chapters. Looking back even just twenty years ago, a metal detector used officially on an archaeological site could still cause *'eyebrows to be raised'* (Roskams 2001, p. 108) and exhibit deep-set rifts from the *'old school'*. Yes, when these machines and their operators first came on the scene they were indeed used to, they hoped, recover items of worth, and quite understandably even people who took up this healthy hobby to enjoy the countryside and all its wonders, and who were happy just to come home with a good horseshoe, were tarred with the very same brush as pure treasure seekers. Has the archaeological and heritage faction forgotten the millions of artefacts recovered from sites abroad, by archaeologists, now housed in most of the major museums of the world, some awaiting cultural repatriation. Are these not the spoils of treasure seekers beneath a guise of archaeologists who plundered the tombs and treasures of ancient civilisations?

A look at a general selection of archaeologically related publications from the early years gives us an insight into the thought development regarding the use of metal detectors and metal detectorists both in an archaeological scenario and as a hobbyist activity.

A brief mention by Ian Riddler and Richard Sewart (1994, pp. 101–106) in the Archaeological Site Manual published by the Museum of London Archaeology Service [MOLAS] does give an insight into the importance or lack of the use of metal detectors and detectorists, or as they call them 'detector operators'. Pages 101–106 of the manual refer to 'Some Further Guidelines on Finds Retrieval Methods', which does show a certain awareness of the technology, but as with other dedicated archaeological publications it lacks commitment to full detection leading to the full benefits of complete survey, and appears to give an air of non-committal to acceptance. A repeated instruction regarding various site types refers to testing of spoil with a metal detector but does request full detection on insitu roads and insitu tessellated floors, but there is a recognition of the importance of fill detection of grave fills. A rather interesting final sentence contains information on metal-detecting personnel:

'*Metal detecting can be carried out by site staff, a MOLAS detector operator or members of the Society of Thames Mudlarks along with a statement that the Site/finds and liaison supervisor will provide metal detectors*'. Again, we see here that the metal detector is predominantly seen as a spoil heap search tool and there is an ominous non-mention of a detectorist from a bona fide metal-detectorist association, for whatever reason.

Interesting to note is that the total number of words dedicated to metal detectors and their operators amounts to just seventy in a monumental publication of more than 600 pages dedicated to archaeological theories and practice by Renfrew and Bahn (1991). I believe that this small but informative paragraph must be read in its full context before any comments about the archaeological profession and the thought processes involved in those early years of a somewhat nervous acknowledgement of the rise and rise of the metal detectorist. '*Metal detectors can be of great value to archaeologists, particularly in providing quick general results and locating modern metal objects that may lie near the surface. They are also very widely used by non-archaeologists, most of whom are responsible enthusiasts, but some of whom vandalise sites mindlessly and often illegally dig holes without recording or reporting the finds they make*'. (Renfrew and Bahn, 1991, third edition, 2000, p. 104).

Truthful in context and more than thirty years later the statement is still valid, but the description given in the last sentence is what people reflect upon and is embedded in the mindset of all who have read it. Those thieves indeed use metal detectors as a tool to steal and have little in common with the hobby or the hobbyist, apart from the easily available equipment. By the time this third edition was on the shelves, the acceptance of their (metal detectorists) importance by the British Museum [BM] and PAS was well established and metal detectorists had enjoyed more than forty years of progress and dedication, and established themselves as a source of knowledge and expertise. Yes, there are bad apples in every barrel; again, as an archaeologist this vandalism, by the few, is not tolerated, and as a metal detectorist I loathe the association with said thieves and vagabonds, just like every crime against society and the nation. Thankfully, the text does not mention the dreaded word 'public', who according to a multitude of publications are responsible for finding all these millions of artefacts; 'public' both as a definition and label is discussed fully in section 1.3 below. Realising that this edition was published more than twenty years ago and today's estimate is a little difficult to establish, but if the figures from the National Council for Metal Detecting [NCMD] website are anything to go by, the 30,000 detectorists who are mostly represented by NCMD (2023) would seem, on paper, a rather conservative figure. That figure purports to be the membership and therefore there would be a number of non-members, giving a feasible total of metal detectorists in the UK at 40,000, but it is difficult to offer more than an estimated guess. The figure of 40,000 is also given by Michael Lewis and Steve Burrow (PAS, 2022) in the opening page of the Christmas Special Newsletter of the newly formed Association for Metal Detecting Sport [AMDS]. Dobinson and Denison (1995, p. 4) state 300,000 as the number of instances of detectorist activity in the 1980s, which could be construed as an estimated figure of actual detectorists, but more likely refers to, as stated, the instances of activity. Presuming a detectorist participates in a, very conservative, two sessions a year, multiplied by the ten years of the 1980s, gives us a figure of twenty-four, then divide Dobinson and Denison's (1995, p. 4) figure of 300,000 by twenty-four, and this equates to just 12,500 active metal detectorists and even less if the detectorist ventures out three times a year, meaning the figures do not make sense. This is not a nit-picking exercise on my part but merely highlighting the limit of positive information available, or should that be non-information, from not only archaeological publications but also the media as a whole. I reiterate my first comments that I am offering an unbiased argument that, in places, is maybe a little hard to swallow, but my fingers point in both directions and the world of the metal detectorist will be given equal consideration with praise and chastisement freely forthcoming. So let us analyse those seventy words that, unfortunately, helped lay some of the seeds from which grew a reputation; one that reflects the adage 'tarred with the same brush'. The first statement, *'Metal detectors can be of excellent value to archaeologists'*, is of course one hundred percent true, but as I have seen on countless occasions, it is not just the metal detector who is of immense value, but essentially the actual purpose it is employed for coupled with an operator who possesses the experience plus a skill and knowledge base that accompanies an experienced metal detectorist. Similarly, one of the main tools of an experienced field archaeologist would be a simple non-technical trowel, which would be, in my opinion, absolutely useless and indeed damaging in the wrong hands, as we will find out in a later chapter. With the second part of the first sentence, *'locating modern metal objects that lay near the surface'*, I wonder what happened to the historic and pre-historic finds laying near the surface; surely the archaeological world must have known from the, in those days, 30,000 metal detectorists and the PAS, established in 1998, that more than ninety percent of finds discovered by metal detectorists are recovered from a depth less than 75mm. This is a layer the archaeologists call the 'topsoil'; the very soil that a professionally qualified archaeologist would take off with a spade or bulldozer and throw onto an unstratified spoil-heap without batting an eyelid. As an archaeologist for many a year, I have practised that during archaeological excavations, searching and recording topsoil pre-disturbance as a stratified level and layer recorded with a context of 001; this makes a lot more sense when it comes to recording finds, etc. than simply ignoring a true layer and recording as unstratified or unnumbered simply as either topsoil or plough soil. The final comment in that small but telling paragraph by Renfrew and Bahn (1991, 2000) cannot be either denied or condoned by any means, but there are thieves and vagabonds in any form of life and occupation; even archaeologists have their share of greedy and unscrupulous personnel. I will not dwell on this subject too long, but if there is bad press and published remarks regarding metal detectorists, my balanced and unbiased offering must include a counter argument and one that can justifiably enlighten the reader with a very small offering of offenders in the world of archaeology, without actually naming the unfortunate beings; to name and shame on both sides is not my intent, but balanced information is my prerequisite accomplished by giving clear examples, which are to be found on later pages.

One of the earlier reference books, which was a must, in its day, as a primary of British archaeology, and prepared with conviction by Lesley and Roy Adkins (1982) interestingly under a title of *'Methods of Locating Sites and Surveying'*, does not give a single mention of metal detecting as an 'archaeological technique', even though from the outset it was realised that one of the new archaeological site discovery techniques was, and still is, by a detectorist and the use of a metal detector. What is stated, though, is an instrument called a *pulsed induction meter* [PIM] and that *'the instrument is of little use in detecting anything other than metal'*, continuing with a sentence that brought a smile to my face: *'and thus of extremely limited use in the detection and interpretation of sites'* (Atkins, L and Adkins, R. 1982, p. 208). The PIM, an early type of metal detector, is fully explained along with other types of metal detectors, their uses, functions, and operational abilities in later chapters of this publication.

A mention of *'Treasure Hunters'* can be found alongside the comment *'the extraction of metal objects for their own sake has little place in archaeology'* (Clark 1990, reprint 2001, pp. 121–2), which then goes on to suggest that under archaeological control, detectors can be useful in site survey for locating relevant artefacts and adds that *'detectors are useful in locating metal objects that end up on the spoil heaps'*, and infers that on sites that are under time constraints where archaeologists do not have time to do the job properly they [metal detectors] *'may be of some help'*, which is a positive but rather understated offering from a technical work displaying the title *'Seeing Beneath the Soil'* and concerning an apparatus that has accounted for more than ninety-six percent of the 1.5 million entries on the British Museum's Portable Antiquities Scheme's department (PAS, 2022). In contrast, the publications from Finds Liaison Officers [FLO] who work for the PAS are, in my opinion, outstanding, informative, and truly open in their opinions regarding metal detecting and the metal-detecting community as a whole, not to mention instigator and curator of one of the largest, if not the largest, artefact databases covering finds recovered by non-archaeologists. Details of artefacts recovered by means of archaeological procedures are not easily available even by fellow archaeologists, unless the items are classed as treasure and appear on show in a museum; don't forget that finds excavated by an archaeologist are rarely recorded on the PAS-operated database as only 0.03

percent have been recorded by archaeologists, compared to 96.39 percent by metal detectorists; see Figure 4 in this publication.

Professor Mick Aston does give a rare, from the archaeological community, balanced offering in Robinson and Aston (2002, pp. 148–53), although the first mention by Robinson and Aston (Chapter 5, p. 60) infers that the metal detector is unpacked and used as a last resort when the archaeologist, portrayed in text, was unable to uncover any clues to what was going on in an excavated posthole. Credit is of course due for the fact that a metal detector was mentioned at all within an archaeological context. The understanding of metal-detecting finds, and associated contexts, is a little misguided in so much that the description supplied by Robinson and Aston (2002. p. 152) contradicts itself; the passage below is of course a true statement and the Gordian coin relates to a fictitious excavation of a posthole where the coin was located in a lower context/level, but the issue is with the bold text between brackets (see below): *'The coin of Gordian you found in your trench isn't important just because it's old, rare, or looks nice. Its valuable because it can tell you about the archaeology in your garden. (If a hundred coins like it were handed over to a local museum along with an assortment of belt buckles, scabbard ends, strap ends and brooches, all without a detailed context or provenance, they would not be archaeology. They'd be a historical mishmash lying around wasting storage space')* (Robinson and Aston (2002)). That remark does nothing but confuse the use of the meaning implied, in so much that numerous published archaeologists have referred to metal detectorists' finds as archaeological finds (Lewis (2015b, p. 2, 2016, p. 127), Shopland (2005) *et al*). Robinson and Aston (2002) clearly state that finds with no context are not to be classed as archaeology, so surely finds without contexts cannot be archaeological finds but are historic and heritage artefacts. The inferred meaning, I suspect, attempts to offer, perhaps, a dig at metal-detectorist practitioners and their hobby, but the majority of finds that are voluntarily recorded by the detectorist fraternity are recorded with context and findspot information. The entry in Robinson and Aston (2002) above strongly infers the possible proceeds of metal detecting and presumably finds handed into museums and the PAS are all without contexts, but surely the vast majority 96.3 percent of finds recovered and saved from further destruction and decay by metal detectorists (PAS, 2020) are from what archaeologists call topsoil and plough soil, both of which are commonly discounted by said archaeologists as out of context. So yes, the 1.5 million metal-detecting finds handed into the PAS

16 Archaeology Versus Metal Detecting

by metal detectorists do have a context, 'context 1' topsoil or plough soil, which are also layers. Meredith Laing (2013, p. 4) echoed the concerns of Bland (2004) that metal detectorists are responsible for problems of context destruction, which, maybe, could have been avoided by an updated Treasure Act back in the 1960s – 1970s. With regard to that suggestion, whatever contexts were the subject; the only context searched by metal detectorists are plough soil and topsoil, which are not destroyed during the detectorist artefact recovery processes and clearly from context 1. As Hirst (2018) clearly states, '*context is the place where an artefact is found*', so according to that simple but factual statement just how can any artefact be out of context, except for those missed by archaeologists during excavation, which end up on the proverbial spoil-heaps and in so being are definitely out of context unless we as archaeologists give spoil-heaps a context, which is unlikely. Bad media, or should it be a certain lack of respect, inadvertently or otherwise because of a long history of misinformation, does nothing to honour the good name of the vast majority of the conscientious metal detectorists. The comments of archaeologist Paul Barford (2016, p. 31) are a little confusing when referring to metal detectorists, but may become clear in analysis: '*In the British Isles, the most common user of metal detectors on archaeological sites and assemblages is by hobbyists engaged in collecting artefacts for personal entertainment and profit*'. When referring to archaeological sites, is Barford (2016) suggesting that metal detectorists are conducting their hobby activities on archaeological sites that are scheduled sites or actual archaeological sites with archaeologists actively engaged in excavations? If so, the detectorists would be classed as illegal nighthawkers, but if the sites are neither of these and the hobbyists have the landowner's permission, the metal detectorists are legally participating in their enjoyable hobby. What Barford (2016) means by '*assemblages*' in conjunction with archaeological sites can only be open to conjecture because if they are a collection of sites, they are all archaeological sites and again if not scheduled, there is no problem if the metal detectorists have obtained landowner permission. As far as collecting finds for entertainment is concerned, after a day's metal detecting there would be joyous laughter heard echoing around the countryside as groups of metal detectorists compared the finds as pouch after pouch are emptied and the ring pulls, chocolate wrappers and human detritus are proudly shown. The entertainment to a metal detectorist is the birdsong and comradery, and the profits are new friends and participation with a knowing realisation that the search is indeed the entertainment. Even a TV advert promoting the benefits of one of the UK's leading building societies aired repeatedly during 2022 quite blatantly mentions the antics of an, albeit fictitious, metal detectorist who searches a beach and acquires someone's trousers with money, etc. in the pockets, much to the annoyance of the owner, and is truly indicative of a thief at work and is unfortunately a tasteless representation of a metal detectorist using a detector, giving a definite false impression to the viewing public and, I envisage, unfounded remarks such as, 'look out, there's a metal detectorist about'. Comments of professional archaeologists are heeded and will be included as seen fit even when they appear to be derogatory in content.

1.3 Portable Antiquities Scheme

The PAS, founded in 1997, has been under the management of the British Museum since 2007, offering a means of recording finds, the vast majority by metal detectorists, a limited amount by members of the public, and very rare entries from archaeologists, with an aim to encourage best practice. The scheme was, and still is, welcomed by the metal-detectorist community and as mentioned earlier, more than 1.5 million finds have now been voluntarily logged with the PAS, for all to see, for the benefit of the nation, our heritage and historical research. It was ten years earlier in 1997 that the Treasure Act 1996 became law, which covered items that came under the term of treasure under the act, but there was no provision for items that did not match the criteria required for treasure, and that was and is the purpose of PAS: to provide the means and wherefores to record these interesting but not essentially valuable artefacts. Of note is that the archaeologists Pearce and Worrell (2015) still expressed concern that some artefacts may not have been recorded, although that statement is most likely correct as the PAS scheme is voluntary, unless items fall under the current version of the Treasure Act. Again, there are hundreds of thousands of artefacts recorded by metal detectorists, in fact well over 1.5 million, of which metal detectorists account for 96.39 percent of metal finds, easily filling any category concerning metal finds entered on the PAS databases; see figures 1, 2, 3 and 4 below. The concerns of the archaeologists Pearce and Worrell (2015) that some finds, no mention of what find types, are not being recorded by metal detectorists are noted, but I will add that archaeologists do not, normally, record any finds that are uncovered by themselves, voluntarily or not, with the PAS, as we can see from the vast databases of finds of the PAS Spackman (2023, Fig. 4), which shows that archaeologists have recorded 0.03 percent of the estimated 1.5 million finds against 96.39 percent recorded by metal detectorists; however, the archaeological profession wants everyone else to follow the correct procedures and record recordable finds on the PAS databases. I and many other metal detectorists have, in the past, approached museums with notable, but non-treasure, finds and have been informed that there was, at the moment, no facility to either store, conserve or display the artefacts. In reality there is, and has been for many years, decades in fact, a huge problem regarding a lack of storage facilities that have been a national concern with museums, but on occasion when artefacts, classed as treasure, were handed to a museum, suddenly a space appears, which is quite understandable but unfortunate. One could ask, as many a detectorist has, what has an archaeologist got to do with the actual hobby/sport of metal detecting, unless, of course, the detectorist is working alongside an archaeologist on an archaeological site and would then be classed officially as an archaeologist. The British Museum PAS have their own guidelines for recording and deposition, which no doubt are adhered to by the PAS team. The PAS was in 1997 created as a pilot scheme to cater for the ever-rising numbers of metal-detector enthusiasts as the hobby advanced in the field of technological innovation and expertise of detectorists in the art of recovering our past heritage by uncovering an ever-increasing number of finds. That statement is confirmed in a paper by archaeologist Tom Brindle (2008, p. 54), who states that the '*Portable Antiquities Scheme was established to promote understanding of the importance of finds made by metal detector users*', but does not mention members of the public in conjunction with a metal detectorist, so we can therefore conclude that a member of the public is indeed in a different category; a category not used by PAS in their databases but one that is constantly used, all too frequently, by media and archaeological academia when the wording should be metal detectorist. The association of metal detectorists as members of the public is unconstructive and a possible attempt to discount the importance of metal-detectorists' contributions to our historic, heritage, and cultural information base; public as a descriptive is dealt with fully in a later chapter. This coincided with the much-needed Treasure Act (1996); this act covered the more valuable finds that were declared as treasure and by law had to be declared within a fourteen-day window. The pilot scheme was soon justified in its operation, and in 2003 attracted support from the National Lottery Fund and later by the Department for Digital, Culture, Media and Sport [DCMS], giving an opportunity for expansion of the scheme and providing the gateway to more and more detectorists to record the fruits of their endeavours; I may add that the vast majority of finds are worthless bits of rubbish and the declared artefacts were and are mostly of little monetary value, but of great importance to the history and heritage of past peoples, art and technological advances. The PAS, has, since 2007, been under the management of the British Museum and has made great inroads regarding the recording and conservation of the many hundreds of thousands of historic finds that have passed through their hands and, according to the PAS databases, the vast majority from metal detectorists; the PAS also offer advice for conservation, which is freely available online. There have been ripples of discontent regarding both the PAS and the up-to-date version of the Treasure Act (1996). The discontent emanates from a number of stakeholders such as the National Council for Metal Detecting, NCMD (2023), which highlights a number of concerns but agrees that an updated Treasure Act is needed. The updated laws are not due to come into force until 30 July 2023, by which time any disagreements should hopefully be ironed out amicably and can be read at leisure (DCMS 2023).

The practice of archaeology as a profession is well recorded and covers a multitude of associated professions involving specialists and their own essential skills, including, but in no way a full list, geophysics, anthropologists, environmentalists, scientists of many disciplines, finds specialists, ceramic specialists, field archaeologists, landscape archaeologists, illustrators, archivists, archaeometallurgy, ethno-archaeology, environmental archaeology and forensic archaeology, to name but a few. Both the dictionary and etymological description fall short, by a long way, in offering a truly descriptive narrative of what archaeology really involves. There were and still are, as archaeologists can confirm, a fairly large number of the general public who think that archaeologists dig up fossils and dinosaur bones; of course, that could happen, but it is not the aim of an archaeologist, unless the bones are shaped, decorated, worn, or arranged by humans, and a fairly clear dictionary definition: '*archaeology – archeology the study of man's past by scientific analysis of the material remains of his cultures*' Collins (2014, p. 103), Etymology '*archaeology – ancient history, antiquities XVII; study of prehistoric matters*' Onions, (1966, p. 48). The mention of science in the above dictionary description deserves its own explanation and I share the definition for good measure; Collins English Dictionary (2014, p. 1772) *'Science - the knowledge so obtained or the practice of obtaining it'*. One wonders if the above description fits that of a metal detectorist and their researching, conserving, and recording of our country's historic and heritage artefacts of past lives and cultures; a statement sincerely meant for contemplation. As far as provenance and the PAS, it would appear that grid references of 4, 6 and 8 figures are the most popular, but grid references are governed somewhat in respect of security of findspots, which are sometimes shortened or on rare occasions withheld to honour the wishes of landowners or stakeholders; so Robinson and Aston (2002) will be pleased to see that the 1.5 million finds recorded voluntarily through the PAS organisation by the general public are, in fact, mostly the results of dedicated metal detectorists and are well referenced. To note, the figure of 1.5 million heritage finds recorded above does not include all the finds presented by metal detectorists, as Michael Lewis (2016, p. 131) informs us that PAS staff are unable to record everything received and the finds were therefore subjected to selective recording, meaning that the final figures would otherwise have been, at the very least, a little higher. Covering the benefits of the PAS, Lewis and Burrow (2022) inform the readers that the FLOs are usually the first port of call by metal detectorists to record their finds and reiterates comments made six years earlier by Lewis (2016, p. 131) that the FLOs *'must be selective when recording finds'* (Lewis and Burrow (2022, p. 1)). That statement could presumably affect results purporting to artefact statistics, but there is no mention to which recovered artefacts are to be left out of the recording procedures of the well-established PAS, or are the recovered artefacts left to the personal discretion of individual FLOs? It is of interest that both archaeologists and metal detectorists are not required by law or rule to record any non-treasure finds on the British Museum PAS website, but it is the metal detectorists who voluntarily contribute without anonymity and will no doubt continue to regularly enter many thousands of records annually on the PAS databases. Detectorists have two recording avenues readily available: the PAS and the UK Detector Finds Database [UKDFD], both of which are willingly used by metal detectorists to report finds. Both the PAS and UKDFD databases are readily used by archaeologists, historians, and authors not as a means of recording archaeologists' finds, but to take advantage of the information therein as research tools, most often for personal gain, i.e. for publication information. Looking at available data from the PAS website for January –

December 2020 from Norfolk Museum Services [NMS], of the 4,952 finds that were recorded, 4,642 are by metal detectorists and only 4 finds from the use of a metal detector during controlled archaeological investigations; the latter record does not, unfortunately, stipulate whether the controlled detector user was an experienced detectorist or an archaeologist amateur or otherwise using a detector. It would be beneficial, I believe, to develop or promote a level of standardisation of an acceptable universal code or term when referring to 'small finds' recovered by metal detectorists; at the moment there are numerous descriptions for these items. An archaeologist would refer to them as 'small finds', or just plain artefacts; media tends to refer to them using more eye-catching and headline-grabbing narratives involving the terms 'gold', 'silver', 'treasure', 'hoard', and the like. The term 'archaeological artefacts' is in itself more than a little misleading and is often used by archaeology-based academia as if to promote a sense of ownership by proxy for and on behalf of the archaeological profession, even if found by a metal detectorist. Detectorists prefer non-archaeological terms in conversation by prefixing 'finds' with the period of manufacture, *id est* Iron Age, Roman, Saxon, Medieval, or even the period followed by type, *id est* Bronze-Age Axe, Roman Brooch, Medieval Coin, etc. In presentations or more formal settings, terms such as 'portable antiquities', 'historic artefacts' or even 'heritage artefacts' are frequently used, but very rarely, if at all, would the term 'archaeological' come into play unless structural evidence is involved and excavated by an archaeologist. Expressions used by Michael Lewis (2016) from the British Museum and PAS are: 'material culture' (Lewis (2016, p. 130)), 'archaeological finds' (Lewis (2016, pp. 127, 130)), 'finds' (Lewis (2016, p. 13)), 'detector finds' (Lewis (2016, p. 13)). As an archaeologist, I have always used the term 'small finds', which are then duly recorded on a small finds register, and in forty years have never heard the term 'archaeological finds' used on or off site, or for that matter on archaeological reports, and the term seems to have appeared with the formation of the PAS and possibly used to placate the world of archaeology. Otherwise, lo and behold the metal detectorists who account for 96.39 percent of PAS finds would appear to take the credit, but then the PAS would have been seen as a wholehearted supporter of metal detectorists. Fig. 4 (below) shows that 99.9 percent of finds recorded with the PAS have been found by the mysterious 'members of the public' when in fact 96.39 percent were found by metal detectorists; two words that are omitted from the PAS introduction (see below). But once the databases are consulted, the wording 'metal detectorists' appears and detectorists are deservedly credited with their efforts towards the overall total; so those finds are recorded as metal detector finds for all to see and research at leisure. The original aims of the PAS, which is jointly run by the British Museum and Amugueddfa Cymru National Museum Wales to encourage the recording of archaeological objects found by members of the public in England and Wales, are outlined below. The aims stated are indeed as clear as day, but are they not directed at archaeology and archaeologists? The very same profession and professionals who have accounted for only 0.03 percent of entries on the PAS database. Do the aims reflect the actual intent of encouraging metal detectorists to enter their more important finds on the PAS database, which account for 96.39 percent of entries, or does the wording appease the major stakeholders by the inclusion of so many dominating archaeological connotations?

The aims of the PAS (Michael Lewis, (2015b, 2)) are to:

- Record **archaeological** finds to advance **archaeological** knowledge.
- Promote best **archaeological** practice.
- Raise awareness of the importance of recording **archaeological** finds.
- Increase public participation in professional **archaeology**.
- Support museum acquisitions of **archaeological** finds.

The aims are indeed clear in presentation but appear to be rather opaque in meaning; this warrants, I believe, a response as Lewis (2016, p. 130) does inform the reader that the *'stakeholders in the project will have clear views on which aims are most important'* and one aim comes to the fore: *'public engagement'*. That single statement is the probable cause of the repeated use of the term *'members of the public'*, a phrase that is all too often used instead of, or in lieu of, metal detectorists. Members of the public as a statement is unused by the metal-detecting community and is treated as more than a bugbear. Is it because members of the public are perhaps used as an appeasement for the benefit of stakeholders, which appears somewhat to shackle the freedoms of the PAS; not as an expression but more of a cracked kernel that, rather than protects, smothers the true and deserving title of a metal detectorist? To address the list of five aims presented above by Lewis (2015b, 2), may I suggest a more apt and truthful narrative, a more politically correct interpretation of the PAS aims, which in turn is probably less than would be expected in a stakeholder's portfolio:

- Record *metal-detected* finds to advance *cultural and heritage* knowledge.
- Promote best *metal-detecting* practice.
- Raise awareness of the importance of recording *metal-detected* finds.
- Increase *metal detectorists'* participation in professional *archaeology*.
- Support museum acquisitions of *metal-detectorist treasure* finds.

To support the above, I refer to Figures 1, 2, 3 and 4 below, which are eye-opening if you acknowledge the PAS database or the interpretation of the wording of the PAS aims supplied by Lewis (2015b, 2). Michael Lewis, who heads the PAS and is a legend in the field of archaeology, does suggest that for '*most archaeologists the fundamental importance of the PAS is that it logs archaeological finds that might not otherwise be recorded to advance knowledge*'; well, that has certainly been achieved in spades, as it were, through the '*discoveries of ordinary people – not professional archaeologists – meaning that the public is transforming our knowledge of the past*' (Lewis (2016, p. 130). Hear, hear, I say. But unfortunately, it is neither the public that is responsible for this transformation, as the public is responsible for just 1.2 percent, nor for that matter archaeologists, who have contributed a total of 0.03 percent of the recorded finds. It is the metal detectorists who are responsible for 96.39 percent of entries, so this is a simple call for credit where it is justly due; I believe this is called respect. Lewis (2016, p130) gets a little carried away with the very next short sentence: '*This is community archaeology in its truest sense*'. Is this an attempt to kidnap metal detectorists and place them safely under the wing of the mothering swan, archaeology, and should metal detectorists now assume the suggested official title of a community archaeologist (Lewis, 2016, p. 131) instead of metal detectorist and discard that incorrigible millstone laid upon the necks of an estimated 30,000+ detectorists (Copping, 2007, in Hamerow, Hinton and Crawford. 2011, p. 1033)? Indeed, would the regular members of the archaeological profession agree with the learned professional Michael Lewis (2016) in instantly creating 30,000 new community archaeologists? These newly enlisted community archaeologists could then record all the 1.5 million metal-detected small finds on the PAS database under the title of archaeologists, and lo and behold the total recorded finds for archaeology would jump from a miserly

0.03 to 96.42 percent overnight and finds for metal detectorists would miraculously disappear from 96.39% to zero; the problem for archaeology and the archaeological profession would forever be solved!

The first listed aim is acknowledged in one of the immediate paragraphs (Lewis 2016, p. 131) with the following statement: *'This data is used in many ways, most importantly as a resource for professional archaeologists and researchers to better understand the historic environment'*. This is all echoed by the myriad of dissertations, papers, publications, and lectures, not counting the academic achievements gained upon the backs of the, often chastised, metal detectorists. There are literally hundreds of publications generated from the information directly connected with the recorded metal-detecting finds. I have no intention of listing them all, but a handful of examples should suffice: Iron Age and Roman Coin Hoards in Britain (2020), well written by a whole gaggle of eminent archaeologists of the highest calibre, including Bland, R. Chadwick, A. Ghey, E. Haselgrove, C. Mattingly, D. Rogers, A. and Taylor, J., with information from PAS databases of metal-detected finds recorded by detectorists; very little acknowledgement of the contribution of metal detectorists, but the main credits were to the PAS databases from which the information was gleaned. This did give the impression of purposely using PAS in lieu of and at the expense of the main contributors to the multiple databases, and they are none other than the thousands of conscientious bands of obliging metal detectorists who have, in often appalling weather, rescued a multitude of artefacts and spent time and energy either self-recording or recording through an FLO the very finds that archaeologists are profiting from through publication with a very small sample shown below.

50 Finds of Early Medieval Coinage, by John Naylor (2021), archaeologist, who is the National Finds Advisor for Early Medieval and Later Coinage, part of the PAS, and compiled by using PAS databases and metal-detected finds.

King Alfred's Coins: *The Watlington Viking Hoard*, (2016) jointly by Gareth Williams, a historian, numismatist, and archaeologist, together with John Naylor after this hoard was found by metal detectorist James Mather and recorded with the PAS.

The Watlington Hoard, (2022), which again involved archaeologist and coin advisor John Naylor and Eleanor Standley, who is Associate Professor of Medieval Archaeology in the School of Archaeology and Curator of Medieval Archaeology in the Ashmolean Museum. The hoard was located by a metal detectorist, and is now housed in the Ashmolean Museum, Oxford.

After intensive examination, the information gleaned has transformed the understanding of ninth-century coinage and the hoard contains many rare types of mainly Alfred the Great (Wessex) and also Ceolwulf II (Mercia), and gave an insight into the great Viking army of the period. The above gives an indication of the valuable information that is openly available by exploring the PAS databases and the contribution, not by archaeologists, but by the heritage and historic finds rescued by metal detectorists (see Figures 1, 2, 3 and 4 below). Hundreds of thousands of small finds all dutifully recorded, by metal detectorists, with the PAS, whose expertise is responsible for the processing of amazing amounts of artefacts, all of which enabled the use of information to write hundreds of books, present thousands of lectures and talks, and endlessly discuss new and fresh information that would otherwise not be available without the enormous contributions by all metal detectorists.

Referring to the 'balanced' argument offered by Robinson and Aston (2002), an enlightening paragraph entitled 'Archaeologists with dirty hands' is welcoming as a sincere attempt to highlight the fact that there are bad apples on most trees:

'It's up to archaeologists to set an example. Most of them will go to any lengths to record their work fully then publish it. But the sad truth is that this hasn't always been done, even on some of the most important sites in Britain. Sometimes twenty or thirty years go by and there's still no full report. Even worse, sites have been excavated by professional archaeologists and the records and notes and even the finds have been lost'. It goes on to inform the reader that *'it's difficult to point the finger of blame at others when its own house isn't yet completely in order'*, Robinson and Aston, (2002, p. 152). Robinson and Aston (2002, pp. 148–149) add that *'it is not just the valuable finds that matter but the actual provenance'*, and go on to bombard metal detectorists for not recording finds and selling finds on the open market, but does not take note of the Portable Antiquities Scheme (PAS, 2022) databases (see results) (Figs. 1, 2, 3 and 4 in this publication) when 96.39 percent of finds on that database are from voluntary recording by metal detectorists and the lack of recording by archaeologists shown to be 0.03 percent using figures from the PAS database (2022). As for selling finds, I believe that if the transaction was illegal, the said detectorists would be open to lawful procedures and there are, unfortunately, instances of illegal activity with both archaeologists and metal detectorists being prosecuted.

1.4 Archaeology meets detectorist

Detecting practitioners have over a short time evolved and have become prolific recorders, expert finds identifiers, as well as proficient researchers, keeping records that would match any from the worlds of antiquaries and archaeologists, and in doing so not only gained but also shared knowledge to equal if not surpass scholars of the day. This was a time when metal detectorists and their copious finds recovery rates left archaeologists in their wake and the time that archaeologists may have felt, for whatever reason, somewhat threatened; perhaps there was/is an underlying thought ethic that history, heritage, and artefacts belonged to the realm of archaeology. A great proportion of the reference books regarding metal finds and finds identification, which can be found on both metal detectorists and archaeologists' bookshelves, stem from the foundations of a metal detector practitioner's meticulous record keeping; and are a must for any archaeological finds specialist, researcher, or indeed the archaeologist. As I have witnessed on numerous occasions, on archaeological sites where detectorists are employed, they, detectorists, are usually the first people consulted with regard to initial identification of metallic finds. With regard to identification of metal finds, there are a number of informative publications, notwithstanding the Detector Finds series of seven volumes by Bailey (1992–2011), covering all manner of strange and wonderful metal artefacts highlighting the wealth of information made public along with other specialist publications used by both archaeologists and detectorists. One of the most comprehensive and stunningly displayed 'small finds' references, in publication, encompasses the four editions of Benet's small finds, covering a multi-era timeline by Paul Murawski (2000, 2003). Brett Hammond (2014) and Aaron Hammond (2021) and the more specific Benet's two-volume set of finds by Brett Hammond (2015, 2016), which are period specific from medieval and Roman periods. Of course, metal finds publications are not confined solely to the realm of the metal detectorist, nor am I inferring that that is the case; indeed, in my own library archaeological reports outnumber those based entirely upon the findings of metal detectorists' endeavours. But what is glaringly noticeable is a leaning towards a near denial by authors, not of the finds themselves and their obvious kinetic historical information, but of the fact that a detectorist was responsible for recovering the vast majority of the artefacts in the first place, and I do not mean items recovered by employment on archaeological excavations. Showing more than 400 artefacts covering most historical periods and a much-needed publication at that time, Michael M. Cuddeford (1992) is not alone in declining to give credit and highlighting this, intentional or not, practice that is rife to this day. Because of my interest in numismatics, among many other subjects, a book published in 2020 caught my eye and it was one of those 'must have' publications and a fascinating subject to boot: *Iron Age & Roman Coin Hoards in Britain*, [IARCH] Roger Bland, Colin Hazelgrove, Adam Rogers *et al*, (2020). This is a well-researched, in-depth, much-needed, comprehensive, and informative study as well as a joy to read. Covering more than 360 A4 pages, we find again the unfortunate statement '*as many hoards are found by members of the public*' (Bland, Hazelgrove, *et al* 2020. p. 2), this mysterious, almost mythical phantom of the misty, muddy, mirk that creeps eerily through the countryside as a sort of Will-o'-the-Wisp. An archaeologist has a title, a metal detectorist who steals an artefact is given the title metal detectorist, but the tens of thousands of honest, enthusiastic and conscientious metal detectorists who have contributed, via PAS, to the majority of entries – 96.39 percent of metal artefacts in the PAS database, which in turn contributed to the main body of Bland *et al* (2020) and their own database – are called, questionably, 'a member of the public'. One can imagine the majority of detectorists fuming at the passage above with reference to the term 'public', discussed fully in a later chapter in this publication, and many a hackle standing proud on the nape, but one can begin to understand the often negative response from the world of archaeology in almost denying the existence of a section of the populace who are dedicated historical research practitioners, i.e. metal detectorists, and are outnumbering practising archaeologists actually registered with CIfA by 7–1. One wonders why and can only conclude that this is a blatant attempt at a denial of respect, provenance, correct reference, acknowledgement, and worthy praise for metal detectorists even when they, metal detectorists, and the product of detecting form a major part of a publication. Concerning the recording of methods of discovery, a telling graph (Bland et al, (2020. Fig. 2.1, p. 18)) does give credit to metal detectorists and eerily the 'members of the public' have melted into the mists, and shows that metal detectorists accounted for the recovery and recording of 850 hoards from the 1970s up to 2000 AD – roughly 70 percent. Since then, 185 hoards have been recovered and recorded by metal detectorists, equating to 90 percent, with archaeology responsible for just 18 hoards, which reflects current trends that are still rising sharply in favour of the detectorist and the recovery of 'at risk' portable antiquities. Of course, this is not in any way a competition, just acknowledgement of accomplishment coupled with an understanding that archaeologists are, at the very least, feeling anxious and threatened that as far as finds are concerned, the limelight shines elsewhere. There are problems regarding findspots and their recorded location (Bland et al, (2020, p. 23)), acknowledging that most archaeologists pre-twentieth-century were not forthcoming with acceptable finds locations and even many locations of twentieth-century hoards pre-metal detecting era could not be pinpointed to an acceptable level. In the twenty-first century we find that the vast majority of Iron Age and Roman hoards have been rescued by the metal-detecting community and duly recorded with PAS, along with many other period-specific artefacts and hoards, and as far as hoards are concerned metal detectorists have followed the relevant codes of practice and informed PAS and FLOs, who are fully aware of the need to professionally excavate the findspot. Grid reference and location identification problems confronted by IARCH (2020, p. 73) are addressed to all interested parties alike – archaeologists, metal detectorists, contractors and FLOs – by requesting at least an eight-figure reference to be recorded at the outset. This in turn is problematic in so much as there are quite frequently counter requests from the relevant stakeholders with concerns about security and health and safety [H&S] issues, and the general consequences of full grid references. IARCH found that the PAS is overstretched at times with the sheer volume of finds that they, PAS, personally deal with on a day-to-day basis, and does give praise to perseverance under an almost constant in-tray. Any report of finds to an FLO by metal detectorists is duly entered on PAS databases, resulting in a summary published annually. As for archaeologists, Bland, Haselgrove *et al* (2020, p. 327), in researching pre-publication of IARCH, do echo concerns in the apparent non-systematic recording process of hoards by archaeologists, and reiterate '*although they should be under the Treasure Act*'. By far the worst were the attempts to uncover the hoards and their details from developer-funded archaeological excavations, which are spread over thirty years (Bland, Haselgrove *et al*, 2020, p. 327); the above excavations of course are conducted by professional archaeologists and there is a suggestion that '*budgetary constraints*' may be an underlying cause, but that suggestion in itself should not be an excuse.

An earlier publication by Suzie Thomas and Peter Stone (2009) opens in the 'Foreword' by Lord Redesdale with the thought that archaeologists distrust those outside of academia (House of Commons, (2008)), and goes on to inform the reader that *'most metal detectorists have no professional training'*, but fails to suggest which or what professional training does the Right Honourable Gentleman refer to? That brings to mind the few days spent with a group aptly named Oxford Blues Metal Detecting Club, a private members-only club that presumably contains an academic or two. Rupert Redesdale (2008) suggests that *'the main problem is that both archaeology and metal detecting is based on hard work with little reward'*. In reply, most of the many hundreds of metal detectorists I have conversed with enjoy the sport/leisure activity, in the main for the comradery, education and exercise, and that is their reward, whether it be rain, snow, wind or shine, and most definitely not for the monetary gains. I agree that metal detecting can be, at times, a hard day's work, but you will have to go a long way to find a detectorist who moans about the effort for little reward, as any finds are a bonus with the reward being the countryside and comradery and the vast majority of metal detectorists are not out-and-out treasure hunters *per se*. So, Lord Redesdale, hard work is definitely not a problem for a metal detectorist, who literally takes hard work in their stride. As far as archaeology and archaeologists are concerned, I can confirm that their work is at times hard graft, but is it, or is it not, paid work? Like any good chef would say, if you can't stand the heat, get out of the kitchen. Archaeology as a profession can also be rewarding, if you enjoy what you're doing and there is or should be a sense of achievement at the end of every day. It brings to mind the worldly remarks of professional musical wizard Bill Wyman, who has been an avid metal detectorist for well over thirty years *'Metal Detecting is not just for anoraks and eccentrics; it's probably the best and most enjoyable way of learning about history'* Wyman (2014). Bill Wyman has also co-authored an extremely interesting book covering an unfolding story of Britain's historic past as a timeline of unearthed artefacts (Wyman, and Havers (2005)). I agree that archaeology, not necessarily archaeologists, assume that the profession owns all artefacts, so much so that they label artefacts found in the soil as archaeological finds, whether or not they were found by an archaeologist and it is their learned right to be the ones who claim that privilege, but as we shall see later the very same archaeological academics, as a general procedure, discount and remove the very layers from which metal detectorists recover a large percentage of our, what metal detectorists rightly call, historic, cultural, heritage artefacts; finds that the everyday archaeologist calls 'small finds'. Just in case the archaeological academia and archaeologists do not already know, all artefacts legally belong to the landowner, notwithstanding the rules of the Treasure Act of course, and any find kept by a metal detectorist is with agreement with the landowner. The most telling comment by Lord Redesdale (2008) refers directly to archaeology with regard to evolution: *It could be argued that studying the ideological difference between the two groups gives a clear picture of fault lines that run through the practice of archaeology...* ' What an enlightening remark. As an archaeologist I totally agree, but also must add that as a metal detectorist of forty years, there are still a few hairline cracks within the hobby, but the fault lines mentioned by Lord Redesdale are a little more concerning and will be a much harder task to repair. What did bring a smile to my face concerned a conscious effort by metal detectorists to break down the barriers set by archaeologists, which would be of more benefit to the world of archaeology; an asset so far unused or rebuffed was the comment from Peter Addyman (in Thomas and Stone, 2009. p. 59): '*but how many archaeologists could afford to give the necessary hours, days, or weeks of 'free' consultancy to make this work*'; a quick and concise reply is, not as many free hours as metal detectorists have spent over four decades assisting archaeologists, and *Dei Gratis* to boot. The reason for the smile is, as a detectorist thirty-six years ago I was like every other detectorist: always on the lookout for pastures new, pardon the pun, when I was asked to detect some ground about 20 miles away and I eagerly agreed. Having given out quite a few well-designed business cards over the previous months explaining exactly what was involved in the hobby of metal detecting and the service that was offered, these brought interest from landowners for the purpose of locating missing tractor parts, wedding rings, etc., leading to permissions to search. On the business card were the words *'No charge for landowners for recovery of lost items.'* Well, I arrived at this new venue and met the person I had spoken to, who I followed to the search area – the vacant football stadium and ex-ground of Aylesbury Football Club. My task was to detect the football pitch and excavations on said pitch. In reply, I explained that if I am employed by a firm or local authority to detect, I have an hourly charge and expenses, to which the person replied that my card states no charges for landowners and we now own this land, which is earmarked for development. I duly honoured my word and spent two full days on the land and reworded my business card; accordingly, during the conversation I was informed that metal detectorists are just too eager to find new land and that our company uses them all the time and all as volunteers and we do not need to pay anything. On another occasion, myself along with six members of a local metal-detector group were commissioned by a well-known archaeological company to search land that was earmarked for large landscaping before the formation of flood defences. Again, this was on a volunteer basis. The reason given was we did not carry a Construction Skills Certification Scheme [CSCS] card, so I showed my CSCS card and informed the head archaeologist that we would carry out the work but next time a payment would be required. The reply was, 'We can always get a metal detectorist, they're two a penny.' It was quite obvious that metal detecting was part of the archaeological company's instructions, either in the Written Scheme of Investigation [WSI] or a planning consent that must be adhered to, but the archaeologists appear to be intent not to actually employ metal detectorists. Although I possessed all the official health, safety and construction skills documents as well as being a qualified archaeologist, this particular company appeared to be a little loathe to actually have a detectorist on their books. The outcome was our group skilfully and professionally detected, mapped, and recorded all finds, and needless to say we never heard from that company again, as detectorists are two a penny. I am not gullible, but as recently as 2021 and again approached by one of the mainland's largest construction company's archaeological units to work under the guise of their commitment to community involvement, this time we took their own H&S tests and purchased the appropriate high-visibility clothing and other protection equipment with the thought that this might lead to an opportune pathway for paid work, the outcome of which is discussed in a later chapter. So it would appear, on the surface, that some but not all paid archaeologists and archaeological institutions are still using both volunteer amateur archaeologists and volunteer metal detectorists to meet commitments, and in some cases taking what could be deemed as advantage of free labour; a somewhat harsh statement, yes, but unfortunately all too truthful as I am only one among others who have experienced this, both as an archaeologist in the community and as a metal detectorist working with professional archaeologists and local historical and archaeological societies. One of the archaeological forerunners on the small screen was of course the much loved but never forgotten and recently resurrected Time

Team, who actually paid a daily rate to metal detectorists, including expenses and an ample meal; I still have my last cheque from Time Team from Burford Priory, aired 2010, in a frame. An indication and acknowledgement of the positive use of metal detectors in the hands of a knowledgeable skilled detectorist and not just to mop up the vital metallic finds that mechanical excavators and manual excavators alike have deposited on spoil heaps; the latter of course are finds that have been distanced from both their stratified position and their contexts missed by skilled professional archaeologists. Back to the comment, above, by Peter Addyman in Thomas and Stone (2009. p. 59), who referred to consultancy time, which is perhaps a clear indication of the intended meaning: that metal detectorists were expected to be trained by archaeologists. This scenario was perhaps the likely outcome, but fails to elucidate what was on offer and how that consultation would be of benefit; presumably it would cover training in archaeology, which would be of benefit on an archaeological site. In reply, it would also be of great benefit to archaeologists to be the recipient of training from a metal detectorist, which will be discussed in a later chapter, and no doubt consultation time and expenses could be arranged. In normal practice, a metal detectorist would gladly share their knowledge and practical expertise with any interested party, which according to Addyman (2009) should be classed as a consultancy. The point raised by Addyman (2009) concerning consultancy is that in my bibliography there are numerous references that emanate from archaeological sources and I cannot recollect any of the publications that mention metal detectors or detectorists, either quoting or referencing a single metal detectorist in their bibliographies, so presumably none of the scholars found it necessary to actually consult a metal detectorist with possibly a realisation that a metal detectorist is indeed a 'specialist'.

This brings to mind one of the subjects concerning finds of treasure that is a bone of contention: when a non-archaeologist, not necessarily a metal detectorist, finds an artefact classed as treasure, a certain percentage, in most cases, of its worth would be paid to the finder, but an archaeologist who finds treasure is not entitled to any remuneration. This is interesting because as soon as a metal detectorist is working on-site, paid or unpaid, alongside archaeologists, they are automatically classed as an archaeologist and therefore also entitled to no reward whatsoever, nor hold title to any finds whether treasure or not; this subject is again dealt with in a later chapter alongside the news of pending new organisations peddling certificates and courses

Archaeology in the Beginning 33

that would enable metal detectorists to work alongside archaeologists. I and many other detectorists have for many a year been working alongside archaeologists who only require our skill, knowledge, and professionalism; one does not require certificates to play a musical instrument, just skill and knowledge, as is the case with numerous other occupations. Not a subject to dwell on, but how would all the archaeologists and media like to be called amateur motorists if they drive a vehicle? Some might laugh at that, but there is no difference to calling a metal detectorist an amateur metal detectorist as professional drivers hold documents to show that they are professionals and everyone else is undoubtedly an amateur as just having a driving licence does not make a professional driver.

A publication that I have recommended to my volunteers and first-year students as an excellent basic guide and manual for dealing with finds and finds processing (Shopland (2006, p. 49)) dedicates just fourteen words highlighting uses and benefits of a tool for locating metal finds in a publication of more than 150 pages: *'It may be beneficial to use a metal detector to check the area first'*; a definite understatement as the text was used in connection with grave excavations. What would have been of great benefit was to have informed the target reader, an archaeologist, of the type, not just the make, of metal detector used, such as a pin-pointer or scuba-tector, instead of the more common long-handled metal detectors; specific types of equipment and their uses and benefits are discussed in later chapters of this publication. Another more comprehensive and informative book, by the same author, with a subject matter of archaeological finds and identification, illustrates many of the metal finds recorded with the PAS by metal detectorists, but does not give a single reference to either a metal detectorist or the use of a metal detector as a well-known method of recovery (Shopland (2005)). One could easily assume that this was an oversight concerning finds from England or an act of censorship and non-recognition of metal detectorists, their equipment, and skills; unfortunately, much larger archaeological publications follow the same method of exclusion and acknowledgement. I acknowledge that there is a single mention of 'metal detector' (Shopland, 2005, p. 8), or should that be less of a complimentary mention and more of a reluctant inclusion regarding Scotland and their own finds procedures and what appears to be a dig at (pardon the pun) the wonderful and much-needed contributions of the PAS, coupled with a near arrogant use of the PAS finds database without clear reference to the monumental contribution of the metal-detecting community. However, Shopland (2005, p. 8) does enlighten the reader that the PAS undertakes procedures that the PAS certainly does not provide, *id est*, '*PAS is responsible for the recording of all archaeological objects found by members of the public*', and gives a good overview of frequently found items (Shopland, 2005, p. 8). This statement does raise some points that need addressing and a certain clarification: (a) Apparently there is a clear distinction between an archaeologist and a metal detectorist, but where is the corresponding distinction between both parties and members of the public? Members of the public do find on occasion an item with a link to our shared heritage and historic past, and the PAS clearly differentiates in their vast databases of recovered finds by accrediting metal detectorists accordingly; (b) One doubts very much that the PAS or any museum for that matter would accept all archaeological objects found, as Shopland (2005) specified, nor accept responsibility for the recording of all objects found, nor does the PAS stipulate in their guidelines or vast web-based databases that that is the case. I can only presume that Shopland (2005, p. 8) misinterpreted somewhat the aims and procedures of the PAS, which do not stipulate that they, the PAS, are responsible for recording all finds; although Shopland (2005, p. 8) does mention the method and procedures of Scotland Treasure Trove and the practice in that country, unlike the PAS, to record all finds, regardless of whether they are metal-detecting finds or an archaeological excavation, Shopland (2005, p. 8) unfortunately does not differentiate, leading to apparently misleading published information.

The metal-detectorist community have voluntarily either self-recorded on the PAS website or handed items to official FLOs employed by the PAS who then record the finds. If the metal detectorists were requested to send every find that they unearth, treasure or not, to the PAS, I doubt very much that the finds would be accepted. On average, to find a single 'recordable' artefact on an average field or plot of land of twenty acres over 400 items, my research could be of little worth both monetarily and historically and include foil sweet wrappers; shrapnel from drinks cans; copious amounts of modern rusty nails, bolts, horseshoes, tines, barbed wire; and unfortunately, in the last few years, an increased amount of green waste; need I complete an almost endless list of the detritus involved, which include discarded broken twenty-first-century dentures and hair pins and anything else from aerosol cans to broken zips. As a conservative estimate, 448,500,000 items of rubbish have been removed from the ground, items that would otherwise pollute the earth and cause countless animals, both domesticated and wild, unnecessary pain and injuries; not to mention the numerous vehicles that would end up with less breakdowns due to lumps of metal damage. As an example, just over twenty years ago I was approached by a farmer whose tractors were constantly succumbing to punctures and at a few hundred pounds per tyre was becoming less than affordable; during the resulting four days in the field, half a hundredweight of metalwork was removed including old ploughshares and the main culprits: more than thirty tines from harvesting, bailing and haymaking equipment. Archaeologists themselves practise various methods of discarding artefacts, sometimes up to 90% of all finds from a site as a methodological sampling strategy, a practice discussed in detail in a later chapter. Talented Professor Alice Roberts (2021) speaks volumes in a couple of sentences presenting a fascinating short TV series for the British Broadcasting Corporation [BBC] with archaeology-based programs aimed at a wide audience of viewers. During the introduction to the first episode, the narrative could easily be described as somewhat glorifying the archaeological experience and Roberts (2021) gives more than an impression of seeking treasure; unmistakably a deliberate act of motivating practising archaeologists and volunteers, and in turn raising viewers expectations with, *'There's still a wealth of archaeological treasure just waiting to be found, that's why each year up and down the country our archaeologists dig down searching for fresh discoveries ------ unearthing priceless artefacts'* (Roberts, A. 2021).

Metal detectorists have, in many media avenues, been labelled as treasure hunters in a derogatory sense and lately coming under attack from the anti-detecting lobby by inferring that some organised rallies, in their advertising literature, had given the impression that paying detectorists could find treasure, such as including in their advertising tempting snippets of nearby notable artefacts or features. I believe that is called marketing expertise nearly matching those introductory comments of episodes 2 and 3 (Roberts, (2021)), both of which have the same introductions as the first episode. In episode 3, during excavations at the medieval Richmond Castle in Yorkshire, Professor Alice Roberts utters a few telling words of wisdom and a rather good advertising ploy targeting both the working volunteers and the viewers with the now famous words giving an insight into the promised emotional high, exploding forth volcanically with the next trowel stroke, *'Nothing sparks more excitement than recovering small objects that have lain hidden for centuries'* (Roberts, (2021). Now that is a quote that could well be used as an answer to a question that has been directed at, over the years, many a detectorist, which is: Why do you go out in all weathers, often at great expense and most frequently producing fruitless results? 87 percent of more than 500 questioned mirrored the above statement by Professor Alice Roberts, for whom I personally have great respect and admiration; shame about the somewhat deliberate glorification concerning the activities of professional archaeologists; the latter statement should be referred to the anti-detecting lobby for their learned comments regarding excitable advertising. Is this really the point of archaeology and archaeologists, to search for, in the words of Alice Roberts (2021), *'archaeological treasure'* and *'that's why our archaeologists dig down searching for fresh discoveries'* by *'unearthing priceless artefacts'*? One could ask just who the real treasure hunters are and what may we ask is the real purpose of archaeology, because surely archaeologists are not trained or geared to follow in the footsteps of treasure-hunting grave robbers of the past.

The archaeologist and Time Team regular Helen Geake presented a video with the enigmatic title Archaeology vs. Metal Detecting, with particular reference to the late Professor Mick Aston, with whom I had the honour of meeting on one of the last Time Team programs at Burford Priory. An inspirational and inspiring person, always eager to pass on any part of his vast knowledge to anyone who had pleasure to converse. Mick Aston was, to begin with, totally against metal detectorists and this thought was, back in the 1970s, virtually unanimous among other prominent archaeologists and archaeological institutions, a thinking that was prevalent in the 1990s and still evident in some quarters even today. Back in the 1970s the now normal doctrine of all evidence is useful was acceptable, but apparently not if the evidence came from the hobby of metal detecting. This near stubbornness to acknowledge any benefits of detectorists and their magic wands stemmed, according to Geake (2020), from the fact that finds *per se*, particularly of precious metals glittering gold and shimmering silver and bronze, were not usually discussed and thought of as maybe not politically correct unless the artefacts were fashioned from flint, bone or of a ceramic nature; proper archaeology, such is the beast. One very good example of this type of behaviour was given in this lecture by Geake (2020), who mentions that while working for an organisation the archaeologist in charge refused point blank to allow the use of a metal detector, even by an archaeologist, giving the reason that if an archaeologist used one of those machines for that project it would legitimise the activity. This was on an archaeological site where the project was specifically designed for the purpose of dating ditches using datable evidence found in the ditches and was geared for metal detector use, as a means to accomplish the job in hand.

So here we see the drawbridges raised, to protect the treasures of the kingdom ruled by the archaeologists from the invading metal detectorists, who are acting as saviours of heritage and history for the sake of the nation. Sounds like the opening scene from one of King Arthur's escapades, but this denial to accept recognition did nothing to offer a platform for discussion and therefore detectorists were taboo and treated as social lepers; the untouchables in the eyes of archaeologists. It was a point in time and space that a realisation of a rift between, on one side the seemingly staid archaeological hierarchy standing firm, akin to a Saxon Shield Wall, backed by an army of loyal but apparently silent ranks who may unfortunately, and I mean that with sincerity, in this day and age of equality and freedom of speech, as a consequence of non-compliance, possess the knowledge that their very livelihood, career progression and even peer repercussions are at stake. Yes, I am fully aware that this statement is not meant to suggest that this sort of thing takes place in any modern-day institution and that freedom of speech is somewhat muffled. Having experienced, first-hand, that very situation on more than one occasion, I can only offer sympathy to those who have to weigh up the pros and cons with a realisation that the decision is yours and yours alone. I can only mention the many media-publicised instances of whistle-blowers, those who speak out and therefore go against the grain (*Collins English Dictionary*, 2014, p. 2253), again much like pilots and military personnel with regard to any unidentified flying object [UFO] sightings. So, the adage of stand up and be counted appears to have been replaced by the more Victorian sit down and be quiet with regard to the acceptance of metal detectorists. On the other side are the metal detectorists, a group of like-minded individuals who outnumber archaeologists at least four to one, legally enjoying a hobby/sport that happens to entail the rescuing of cultural and historical artefacts from top and plough soils. Is this an obstacle created by archaeologists? I'm not so sure as I have conversed, openly, with fellow archaeologists over many years and there is a prevalent philosophical opinion that as long as we, archaeologists, do our jobs to the best of our ability, this is of the most importance and the use of modern equipment of any sort that could be an aid to interpretation and therefore learning is considered a great asset and that is from the grass-roots of the profession. Is that last statement indeed indicative of the rift being in isolation in the hierarchal chambers of archaeology and academia? Helen Geake (2020) mentions that Group Captain Knocker, a notable archaeologist, while working on an archaeological site in the county of Norfolk in 1951 became one of the earliest archaeologists to use a mine detector/metal detector on site. With a reference to looting, Geake (2020) gives as an example the magnificent Mildenhall Treasure that was actually uncovered by the plough in 1942 and ploughman Gordon Butcher, who contacted his then boss Sydney Ford and they dug out around thirty-four items so thinking they were pewter, including a lidded bowl topped by a Triton blowing a conch shell (Potter, 1983). Ford kept them on a mantlepiece for years until in 1946 the dishes were recognised by a visitor as being made of silver and of national importance, making them Treasure Trove and therefore crown property. This, I suppose, was a case of ignorance to the existence of the Treasure Act and the correct procedures, but the point here is why did the presenter not inform the audience that there was not a single metal detectorist involved? This lecture was given with the title Archaeology vs Metal Detecting, so as an example of looting, it involved neither an archaeologist nor a metal detectorist, so it was unfortunately rather misleading in context with metal detecting. Another example on the same theme, Geake (2020) referred to the Hoxne Hoard, this huge hoard found by a metal detectorist, which was reported immediately to the landowners, who arranged a full and successful excavation the following day by Suffolk County Council Archaeology Service [SCCAS], uncovering many artefacts such as the magnificent six highly decorative gold bangles (Phillips (1996, p. 22); again there was no looting involved at all. This in itself raises the question why introduce the audience to these great discoveries as examples of looting without imparting the fact that these hoards did not involve looting, and along with a further mention of identifying looted artefacts from Africa, Asia, and other continents without a mention of the involvement or actually non-involvement of metal detectorists or indeed archaeologists, museums, and dealers. There was no mention of the hundreds of thousands of artefacts removed by archaeologists, now in nearly every museum or private collection in the world, that are now subject to a repatriation process and the by-product of hundreds of years of looting by persons in the name of archaeology. A mention of Nighthawkers was short, sharp and to the point, although it would be essential to impart the information and not hide the fact that it does happen and I wholeheartedly agree that the actions of a few bad apples is certainly detrimental to the good name and reputation of thousands of dedicated detectorists. What I will say is that those responsible are nothing more than thieves who have equipped themselves with technological innovations enabling the illicit practice of stealing our heritage and historical artefacts. It is enlightening that some sixteen years ago English Heritage commissioned one of the UK's most active and respected archaeological units, Oxford Archaeology, to conduct a detailed survey encompassing the deplorable problem of Nighthawking. The survey took three years to publication by Historic England (2009) and involved widespread consultation with many hundreds of heritage agencies and interested stakeholders beginning with an informative explanation of what exactly is Nighthawking. *'Nighthawking is the theft by a few of the heritage of the many. Regardless of the numbers of sites affected by Nighthawking, the heritage is a finite resource. The real value of heritage is not financial but lies in the information it can provide about our history and origins. The knowledge belongs to everyone and the most significant consequence of Nighthawking is this loss of knowledge'.* A very important point raised concerned the unlawful searching and removal of finds from scheduled monuments, and I can only reiterate that these people are nothing more than thieves using specialised equipment to locate metal artefacts from both scheduled and non-scheduled sites by ignoring the laws of trespass; they are not metal detectorists *per se*, but robbers, vandals, plunderers, and thieves. In November 2006, Oxford Archaeology was commissioned by English Heritage to undertake a comprehensive survey with consultation of 400+ agencies, all heritage related, on the subject of Nighthawking. The survey, which was conducted by professional archaeologists, led to the publication of the full results by Historic England (2009) and are obtainable for all to read; but one short entry does deserve an inclusion as support to the argument. *'Nighthawks are not to be confused with responsible metal detectorists. It is clear that many metal detectorists follow good practice guidelines, record and/or report their finds, abide by the Treasure Act (1996) and are valued contributors to archaeological understanding. This report uses the general term 'Nighthawks' to refer to those who illegally metal detect. Its use is intended to emphasise the distinction between illegal metal detectorists and law-abiding metal detectorists. It is not meant to imply either that the activities of Nighthawks are restricted to hours of darkness, or that law-abiding metal detecting can only take place during the day'* (Historic England, 2009). Oxford Archaeology does add *'that*

Nighthawking must not be confused with responsible metal detectorists' and that there is clarity between the two and that detectorists are indeed '*valued contributors to archaeological understanding*', but I must add that metal detectorists are not always acknowledged, credited, or even referenced in academia. This was not the first survey on the subject, but the earlier attempt by the CBA in 1995 was extremely limited, so after a gap of more than twenty years this new and comprehensive survey into theft by nighthawkers was more than welcomed by both archaeologists and the metal detectorist fraternity alike. To say that metal detectorists are stealing artefacts at night is surely a pointed insinuation that labels all metal detectorists with the same crime and is a bit like saying that a thief broke into a jeweller's case using a trowel so the crime was committed by an archaeologist, and heaven forbid to suggest a safe cracker using a stethoscope to listen to the clicks of the dial is none other than a Doctor of Medicine! Of course, there are instances involving archaeologists, detectorists, members of the public and professional grave robbers to name but a few that survive by thieving and looting, but archaeologists are professionals and as such carry a work-related title and earn the right to be given, if they steal, the headline, '*Archaeologist found to be a thief*'. Metal detectorists, on the other hand, according to many learned archaeological authors and archaeology-based practitioners, give reference to a metal detectorist who recovers and reports finds as a 'member of the public', and appear to purposely go out of their way to use that epithet. Now that gives us a certain dilemma in so much as, is a metal detectorist a detectorist or member of the public? Only an archaeologist, the Department for Environment, Food, and Rural Affairs [DEFRA], DCMS, English Heritage, and the PAS can address that question, and a metal detectorist will wait with, as Shakespeare intended in the Merchant of Venice, '*bated breath*' for a reply. In a closing statement, Helen Geake (2020) conveys what is deemed in the world of archaeology as an unfair situation with reference to Teresa Hall, an archaeologist who did extensive field walking in and around the Parish of Shapwick and on this particular occasion in 1998 found a single Roman coin. Helen Geake (2020) then points out the '*unfair situation*' when some years in the future metal detectorists located, in the same field as the archaeologist found the single Roman coin, the largest hoard of Denarii, at that time and according to the short report from the National Heritage Memorial Fund [NHMF] consisting of 9,238 Roman Denarii, and the NHMF (2000) duly granted a substantial award for, among others, conservation, research and education.

Helen Geake (2020) did mention that the reward would have covered the whole archaeological programme of investigations in that village and states that the detectorists acted 'unethically', but did not explain what or why it was unethical and that they, archaeologists, would train detectorists to act ethically. This leaves me with more questions that I will address because the question of no reward for the archaeologist is a cause of disagreement, especially when this situation became known via an accessible media presentation, which has been viewed more than 15,000 times. The extract from the National Heritage Memorial Fund (2000) shows that a grant was awarded for the purposes stated and is not the reward payment to the metal detectorists. The archaeologist involved must have obtained permission from the landowner to conduct the field-walking exercise and all finds were presumably correctly collected, recorded, and stored, but the point is, was this field part of an officially sponsored archaeological investigation or a private research exercise? It would be of interest to ascertain if the single silver coin, found by field-walking, was reported to the PAS or voluntarily self-recorded on the PAS database; if it was, the coin could have been classed as part of the hoard, found later, especially relevant if the metal detectorists were asked to search the field as part of the field walk programme, or was the single coin in an entirely different position? The two metal detectorists must also have had the permission of the landowner to enter the land and search for 'artefacts', which turned out to be a very fruitful exercise in what can transpire from using diverse exploration methods, and the result of the diligent search by metal detectorists was both a previously undiscovered villa and a hoard of truly national importance coming to light. Now this raises another particularly important subject that I have encountered before: if a detectorist is employed on a designated archaeological site, the metal detectorist is then classified as an archaeologist and therefore not entitled to any reward whatsoever. That is or should be understood by an archaeologist; it is the same for diamond miners, gold miners: all minerals or objects of value or not are the property of the finder unless a written agreement proves otherwise. The Treasure Act I will discuss in a later chapter as special rules then applies, which is exactly what happened in this case. One point to highlight is that for decades metal detectorists have been approached by archaeologist professionals and amateur archaeologists, history, and heritage societies, as well as contractors private and commercial, to search on sites but on a completely voluntary basis. We can only presume that some establishments did not wish to be seen to employ metal detectorists as this would have given a detectorist a professional status, or that there was a pool of more than willing detectorists only too happy to be offered a chance to search somewhere new. Having experienced both many times, even from nationwide contractors and on behalf of local councils, but one of the first organisations to offer payment and travel expenses was our much beloved Time Team [TT]. I still have my first cheque as an artefact of acknowledgement. The remark concerning unethical, which was unreservedly directed at the two detectorists, refers to being corrupt and immoral, but if the detectorists had permission and the archaeologists did not agree with it, that is an argument between the archaeologist and the landowner; if the archaeologist was annoyed with the Treasure Act, take it up with the government as I am not privy to why the accusation was fermented against the detectorists on the public domain, but any reward would not have been paid out if there was any indication of unlawful behaviour; it would of course be of interest to know if metal-detecting surveys were commissioned by the Shapwick project. The last remark by Helen Geake (2020) that I will address before I move on is the suggestion that the reward money would have paid for all the investigations in the village over the years; that may indeed be true and in some cases the landowners and the finders have waved their lawful rights to a reward under the Treasure Act (1996) and given it to the museum so the museum did not have to pay for the artefacts, so even if that had happened the private local archaeological enterprise would still not have benefitted; if by chance that did happen, would the monies have been used to pay the archaeologists for their involvement or would all the many hundreds of volunteers who also sacrificed their time and energy have received due recompense? There was no mention of the landowner having given their rightful share back to either the Somerset Museum or to the community. That is personal choice and my remit is not to delve into personal arrangements and legitimate choices but to highlight the portrayal of archaeologists with regard to metal detectorists in both the workplace, publications, and media, digital or otherwise. Not all treasure cases result in the finder or landowner receiving a monetary reward. Lorizzo (2021), reporting on the Arts Minister Lord Parkinson's speech outlining the continuing success of the PAS, informs us that in the first five months there were 54 treasure cases in 2020 where either or both the finder and the landowner had waived their right to a reward and Lord Parkinson, who launched the PAS report of 2020 at the British Museum, praised those persons for their generosity, which in turn allowed the museums to obtain the treasure finds at no expense. This equates to, on average, more than four waivers of treasure rewards per month and a positive indication that the Treasure Act (1996) is functioning correctly by offering the opportunity of choice to the main contributors: metal detectorists.

1.5 The public debate

A word about 'members of the public', which is one term commonly used as a synonym for metal detectorists that conveys a rather concerted effort to limit acknowledgement of a detectorist's contribution. This has echoes of military and aviation departments, whose personnel could not mention the words UFO for fear of ridicule or worse. The 'general public' is also a term that neither gives credit where it's due nor is it a truthful of definition. Cambridge Dictionary Online (2022) gives a definition that should enlighten: *'general public or ordinary people translate to persons that do not belong to, or are members of, a 'particular organisation' and who do not have a special type of knowledge'*. The vast majority of the metal-detecting community possess both specialist knowledge and membership of an organisation, which in itself surely removes them by definition from the category of members of the public, general public, public at large, and public. The media tend to, as is their want, use 'treasure seeker', 'treasure hunter' or even the derogatory epaulet 'amateur metal detectorist' when headlining a notable find. Archaeological publications have in the past refrained to mention, as if they were forbidden by their own occupation or peers, to use such two words as metal detectorist in combination: shades of an infamous character, namely one 'Thane of Cawdor', and a certain Shakespearean play.

There are many examples of this denial to recognise metal detectorists and metal detecting, especially in the world of archaeology, even in today's modern world of apparent misty equality. For example, a media report relevant to this argument can be found among the BBC news pages (2021) informing us of the one millionth archaeological discovery recorded found by a member of, you guessed it, the public. The artefact, which came from Lincolnshire, was a copper-alloy pendant recovered near Binbrook. That in itself gives an impression, because of the word 'archaeological', that archaeologists were responsible for the one millionth find and the words 'member of the public' signifies someone who does not belong to a particular group; it shows nothing less than an audacious assumption that everyone who is not an archaeologist is a member of the public. Is not a detectorist a member of a 'particular group'? That should be recognised as such and the words 'archaeology' or 'archaeological', when used in context with metal-detected finds, are replaced by the more politically correct 'heritage finds' or 'historically important finds' and then associated to the particular group responsible, usually a metal detectorist. This article continues with a very complimentary message from none other than the Arts Minister, Lord Parkinson (2021), referring to this mysteriously elusive group, the public. Just in case the BBC comment of the one millionth find is questioned, an article by Michael Lewis (2013), head of the PAS, entitled *'Portable Antiquities Scheme records the one millionth find by a member of the public'*, reveals that the now famous one millionth PAS artefact was a Roman coin from a hoard recovered in the county of Devon; again, the wording does not give credit due to the metal detectorist who found the hoard of 22,000 Roman coins and who immediately contacted the local PAS's FLO. The problem of which find was the one millionth find does not concern this study, but the simple answer is that one refers to the one millionth find to be logged included hoards containing thousands of artefacts, which are recorded as a singularity giving us the one millionth recorded and at the same time 1.5 million artefacts. What we are really interested in is the entry of member of the public, which does need addressing and recognition should be given to metal detectorists who are, according to PAS database records, accountable for 96.39 percent of finds, and nor does the PAS have a category that refers to the illusive group members of the public but does have a category titled 'Other', which accounts for just 1.29 percent of finds recorded on the PAS; we can only presume that these are the members of the public that are unfortunately repeatedly praised by archaeologists and their representatives, who do have their own category and, according to the British Museum Portable Antiquity Scheme, are responsible for 0.03 percent of recorded finds (Spackman (2023, figure 4) refers). 'Members of the public' is a phrase that is nothing less than a thorn in the foot for metal detectorists and highlighted by Peter Spencer (2022), who refers to the quote by Arts Minister Steven Parkinson (2021): *'I am delighted those one million records of archaeological finds made by the 'public' have now been logged...it shows the important role we all can play in protecting and cherishing our heritage.'* A truly encouraging retort, but unfortunately not one mention of a metal detectorist and again a mention of this mysterious branch of society, the public, who do not actually take credit but it is purposely forced upon them. But in the adjoining report by the British Museum-based PAS themselves, it does state that of the items found the previous year, 91 percent of artefacts were found by metal detectorists. An analytically presented in-depth study by Laing (2013) into the Treasure Act 1996 also enters into the public debate, as Laing (2013, p. 6) offers public, public at large and the general public in differing contexts, *id est* in reference to the aims of the PAS (Laing (2013, p. 6)), which are to advance knowledge by recording archaeological objects found by the public. Laing (2013, p. 6) continues with what an outcome of that knowledge should be and puts forward that the public at large should benefit from recording and research into the artefacts. Of note is that archaeological objects are now called artefacts, therefore losing the inference that artefacts belong to archaeology and archaeologists. There is a suggestion that the success of the PAS lays within its educational role, both with finders and the general public (Laing (2013, p. 7)), so here we have three distinct categories of public, to which I will add a fourth: the previously mentioned and most commonly used members of the public (Pearce and Worrell, 2015. Lewis, 2016. Marshman, 2016. Bland, Hazelgrove, *et al*, 2020) as an exceedingly small sample of publications using the vague term 'public'. The use of 'public' in any reference to metal detectorists is not only misleading to all involved but also has and still is used instead of a clear reference to metal detecting or metal detectorists, and appears to stand out as an erroneously deliberate indication of an attempt of non-recognition of metal detecting and metal detectorists. This gives the impression that the words of Michael Lewis (2013), who is Head of Portable Antiquities Scheme and Treasure at the British Museum, fell upon the proverbial barren ground and failed to find neither the attentive ears nor eyes of the media and most importantly the archaeological community when he (2013) remarked that it was important to '*Acknowledge the positive contribution made by metal detectorists and other public finders across the country*', and goes on to add, '*No matter how small, or fragmentary, these finds are all part of the great jigsaw puzzle of our past*', a sentence that still insinuates that metal detectorists are public finders. So here we have to thank Michael Lewis (2013) for even a mention of a detectorist, but at the same time wonder why there is an underlying tendency to discount detectorists as a recognised group and insist on categorising metal detectorists into the group of 'public', which is in fact not a category used by the PAS database.

An in-depth study of Roman signet rings and intaglios by Ian Marshman (2016) raised interesting facts relating to the public debate, the first of which may seem to be a minor issue. Marshman informs the reader that his study benefitted from *'finds recorded by the PAS'* (Marshman, (2016, p. I)), which surely could read finds recorded on the PAS mostly by or on behalf of metal detectorists. This is followed on the next page by an unfortunate omission in the acknowledgements of any mention of one of the main contributors to the PAS database, a database so often used by authors, researchers, archaeologists, detectorists, and members of the public alike, and that is none other than the humble and least mentioned metal detectorist. The voluntary contributions presented by metal detectorists to the PAS outweigh the total entries by all other categories many times over, and Lewis (2013) gives an indication of the scale of academic research that would not have been available without the information from metal-detectorist finds. The number of 422 projects, generated from detectorist finds, is most impressive, including fifteen large-scale research projects and an astonishing eighty-seven PhDs (Lewis (2013)), so again credit should have been given where it is due; as an update concerning the number of academic projects that have used the databases of the PAS, the latest listed total is a staggering 887 projects, for which the breakdown is freely available from the PAS (2022). Marshman (2016, p. 50) consulted another well-known metal-detectorist database, UKDFD, but in the very next line infers that all the finds on that database were by members of the public when informing us that, in Scotland, the process of recording finds by members of the public is different, which is an insinuation that all the finds are from members of the public. When referring to archaeologists, Marshman (2016, p. 51) points out that their, archaeologists, information regarding small finds varies significantly over time. Interesting to note that one of the main complaints by archaeologists is that metal-detected finds lack contexts, but Marshman (2016, p. 54) reflects on the conclusion that research into archaeological records was often hindered *'even in recent publication by a failure to refer to context numbers or phasing in the published small-finds report… or to include a full context list to allow researchers to find this information themselves'*, noting that there is no mention of archaeological finds but use of the common and normal archaeological term 'small finds'. Again, Marshman (2016, p. 54) gives reference to archaeological excavation reports that '*unfortunately a considerable number of excavated objects were from unstratified contexts*'. Here we have a cause of disagreement as to what is actually being referred to: was it (a) a historical context (datable) or (b) a physical context (place occupied in the landscape), or as the text mentions (c) unstratified (not in a layer)? Datable layers usually contain some sort of *in-situ* evidence that relates to a particular period in time. Physical context is where an artefact is found. Unstratified simply implies as, not being a layer, this is a term at times misused and abused and often given as a title for topsoil, plough soil and overburden, as I argue that all of these are layers and therefore a context worthy of respect; in reality, unstratified is or should be in the eyes of archaeological processes something of a rarity and should refer to spoil-heaps.

Members of the public as a description to identify a class of contributors responsible for the million-plus finds recorded by the PAS is at the very least misleading to the public, metal detectorists and archaeologists alike, and it appears that it is purposely used on a regular basis in certain circles to avoid a mention of metal detectors and metal detectorists. Michael Lewis, who heads the PAS and is a legend in the field of archaeology, does suggest that for '*most archaeologists the fundamental importance of the PAS is that it logs finds that might not otherwise be recorded to advance knowledge*'; well, that has certainly been achieved in spades as it was through the '*discoveries of ordinary people – not professional archaeologists – meaning that the public is transforming our knowledge of the past*' Lewis (2016, p. 130). Hear, hear, I say. But unfortunately, it is not the public that is responsible for this transformation as the public is responsible for just 1.29 percent of the recorded finds and metal detectorists are responsible for 96.39 percent (see Figure 4 below), so this is a simple call for credit where it is justly due. I believe this is called respect. Interesting that the Director of the British Museum in the foreword of the PAS Annual Report (2021) does relate that it '*was another successful year for the Portable Antiquities Scheme, with 45,581 archaeological finds made by the public*' (Fischer (2022, p. 3)), so there is still a stubborn resistance to identifying a metal detectorist by the archaeological hierarchy. Another extremely valid point of note is the fact that metal detectorists who self-record their finds on the PAS database have their recorded finds prefixed by 'PUBLIC', meaning that 1,681 self-recorded finds, instead of being credited to metal detectorists, are transformed into public (PAS (2021, p. 9)). A rather strange situation, because by self-recording, the detectorists are lessening the workload of FLOs, and we are enlightened, quite categorically, by Fischer (2022, p. 3) that *'there might be as many as 40,000 active metal-detectorists in the United Kingdom'*. This anomaly could be classed as a misinterpretation of acknowledgement as some individual detectorists have, according to the PAS, self-recorded more than 1,000 finds on the databases (PAS (2021, p. 9)). This is not the case for the PAS who, in their extensive databases, the FLOs have given credit to finds that were located by the use of a metal detector by giving a separately named group. Almost an acceptable heading, but the heading refers to the machine, metal detector, and not the operator, as in metal detectorist, whereas any find found by the process of archaeology is headed archaeologist entered by an archaeologist and not archaeology nor the tool used, *id est* a trowel. Figures 1, 2, 3, and 4 below offer an insight into the statistical records that I obtained from a random collection of eight of the databases of finds recorded by the seventy-plus institutions and entered by representatives of said institutions on the British Museum's PAS databases. The evidence shows an overwhelming number of entries are from the activities of metal detectorists, 96.39 percent, compared to entries by archaeologists, which equate to 0.03 percent (see figure 3 and pie chart figure 4 below). On the PAS database there is no mention of the public on their Institutional Databases, and the PAS does give a figure of 96 percent of finds made by metal-detectorists (PAS 2021, p. 5). The rest of the seventy databases of institutions forming the PAS are openly available to the public, archaeologist and metal detectorist, and make interesting reading. One can now begin to understand why there is an ingrown unwillingness in archaeological circles to admit openly that for the last few decades the rank and file of the metal-detecting community have contributed to this monumental collection of our heritage artefacts, which would have remained in the topsoil at the mercy of chemicals and the environment; and let us not forget the value of historical information unveiled by the dedicated artisans. In many parts this now easily accessible information has rewritten history itself, not to mention the many publications written on the backs of metal-detecting finds. Let us see the end of 'archaeological' as a descriptive prefix to finds recovered by non-archaeologists, as only archaeologists recover archaeological finds; a metal detectorist recovers heritage finds, historic artefacts, portable antiquities, cultural artefacts, or in the words of archaeologists themselves simply small finds. Looking back into the not-so-distant past, only archaeologists, professional or otherwise, found artefacts during excavation and called them archaeological finds, then along came local history and heritage groups and societies who conducted field-walking exercises and organised small excavations, and carried on the tradition of using archaeological terms by calling finds archaeological finds; this shows a clear connection between professional archaeologists and amateur archaeologists. Then along came metal detectors and their detectorist commanders, who have taken finds recovery to an entirely different level, almost like a breath of fresh air, and in the process created a new avenue for research regarding the historical and cultural heritage of not just the UK, but most countries and civilisations of the world we live in. It is a true statement, is it not, that metal detectorists are not archaeologists and the consensus of opinion among the metal-detecting community is that they (metal detectorists) do not wish to become either amateur or professional archaeologist, just proficient metal detectorists, even though they would be classed as archaeologists as soon as they officially work on an archaeological site. As stated, the choices were completely random as I felt that manually listing every one of the seventy-plus institutionally entered datasets would not unduly alter the final outcomes and would probably show even more of a shift towards a higher metal-detectorist percentage of entries. To illustrate this, I refer the reader to the entries from Durham [DUR] (see Spackman (2023, figure 1)) regarding their entries for finds located during field-walking activities of 1,306, but the average for the 7 other random institutions stands at 81, so that single institution raised the average from 81 to 234 when the mean would have shown low 90s. Of course, if anyone wishes to while away the hours, days, or even weeks studying PAS databases, have fun as the PAS website, unlike archaeological reports of the construction industry, is an open source of information and I personally would have relished a graph that encompassed all seventy-plus institutional datasets. Unfortunately, it appears to be much like many other enterprises and turned out to be a task that was not within the set timescale; however, I believe sufficient data was gleaned by researching the more than useful PAS databases to produce an accurate, explanatory and a most enlightening set of information obtained from an up-to-date database. It also offered the opportunity, to the powers that be, to rethink the use of the word 'public' and persuade themselves that the cat is out of the bag, and all is clear that metal detectorists and archaeology as a whole would clearly benefit from the truth: that a metal detectorist is just that and not a lost entity that can be corralled into a group called either

50 Archaeology Versus Metal Detecting

Random snapshots PAS Institution Breakdown of Reported Finds (1)

Year	Institution	Metal Detector	Other	Archaeologist	Fieldwalking	TOTAL
2016	LIN	2163	3	1	2	2169
2017	LIN	5198	8	1	2	5209
2018	LIN	2106	2	7	0	2115
2019	LIN	1504	11	2	0	1517
2020	LIN	1328	6	1	1	1336
Totals		12299	30	12	5	12346

Year	Institution	Metal Detector	Other	Archaeologist	Fieldwalking	TOTAL
2016	WILT	4837	28	0	0	4865
2017	WILT	8601	80	0	177	8858
2018	WILT	2700	139	1	5	2845
2019	WILT	1928	16	1	0	1945
2020	WILT	1058	67	0	1	1126
Totals		19124	330	2	183	19639

Year	Institution	Metal Detector	Other	Archaeologist	Fieldwalking	TOTAL
2016	CORN	2674	10	1	5	2690
2017	CORN	676	13	0	97	786
2018	CORN	492	2	0	9	503
2019	CORN	445	8	1	24	478
2020	CORN	1343	9	1	11	1364
Totals		5630	42	3	146	5821

Year	Institution	Metal Detector	Other	Archaeologist	Fieldwalking	TOTAL
2016	DUR	521	16	0	515	1052
2017	DUR	524	2	0	1	527
2018	DUR	629	12	0	324	965
2019	DUR	860	8	0	151	1019
2020	DUR	5044	0	0	315	5359
Totals		7578	38	0	1306	8922

Figure 1. Figure 1. Data collected from PAS database. (*P. Spackman, 2022*)

Random Snapshot PAS Institution breakdown of reported finds. (2)

Year	Institution	Metal Detector	Other	Archaeologist	Fieldwalking	TOTAL
2016	KENT	1959	17	0	8	1984
2017	KENT	1496	11	0	5	1512
2018	KENT	1393	4	0	36	1433
2019	KENT	1069	77	1	26	1173
2020	KENT	715	4	1	1	721
Totals		6632	113	2	76	6823

Year	Institution	Metal Detector	Other	Archaeologist	Fieldwalking	TOTAL
2016	HAMP	1260	29	0	1	1290
2017	HAMP	1116	105	3	0	1224
2018	HAMP	1547	27	0	75	1649
2019	HAMP	5264	52	0	27	5343
2020	HAMP	955	55	0	0	1010
Totals		10142	268	3	103	10516

Year	Institution	Metal Detector	Other	Archaeologist	Fieldwalking	TOTAL
2016	SUR	3327	19	0	29	3375
2017	SUR	3091	40	2	17	3150
2018	SUR	1333	11	0	0	1344
2019	SUR	2408	24	0	5	2437
2020	SUR	1819	79	0	0	1898
Totals		11978	173	2	51	12204

Year	Institution	Metal Detector	Other	Archaeologist	Fieldwalking	TOTAL
2016	IOW	1554	15	0	0	1569
2017	IOW	1179	16	0	0	1195
2018	IOW	1117	13	0	2	1132
2019	IOW	1191	14	0	0	1205
2020	IOW	320	4	0	0	324
Totals		5361	62	0	2	5425

Figure 2. Data collected from PAS database. (*P. Spackman. 2022*)

Total Finds Per Sample Institution.

5 Years	Inst.	M. D.	Other	Arch.	Fieldwalking	Totals
2016-20	LIN	12299	30	12	5	12346
2016-20	WILT	19124	330	2	183	19639
2016-20	CORN	5630	42	3	146	5821
2016-20	DUR	7578	38	0	1306	8922
2016-20	KENT	6632	113	2	76	6823
2016-20	HAMP	10142	268	3	103	10516
2016-20	SUR	11978	173	2	51	12204
2016-20	IOW	5361	62	0	2	5425
Totals		78744	1056	24	1872	81696

Figure 3. Data condensed from the eight sample institutions. (*P. Spackman. 2022*)

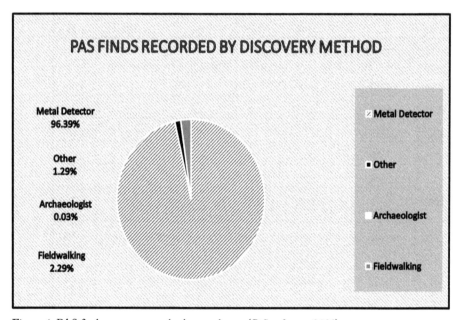

Figure 4. PAS finds, recovery methods at a glance. (*P. Spackman. 2022*)

'a member of the public' or 'an amateur' and as such expect respect as, at the very least, 'an experienced amateur' as previously discussed or something that would be universally welcomed and identifiable as a metal detectorist. Detectorists working alongside archaeologists on commercial sites do not, in normal circumstances, take reference of anything described as trash when usually a very high percentage of items are complete trash, and as a norm an archaeologist will only give a grid reference to recordable finds classed as 'small finds' by most organisations and archaeologists. Although artefacts were located by a metal detectorist on commercial sites, there appears to be a possibility that the recording of the aforementioned 'small finds' was subsequently recorded by the archaeologist on the PAS system as found by members of the public or by an archaeologist, but this would be difficult to validate.

1.6 Topsoil and or plough soils an anomaly in question

The above contexts are, to a detectorist, in normal practice, the layers of exploration and are also well known as the levels from which most of detector-located finds emerge. They therefore warrant a topic for more detailed discussion, especially as it is often used almost as a *fait accompli* when it is applied in archaeological narrative as unstratified and overburden and therefore mostly discounted as being archaeologically of little importance.

There are many more publications including books, manuals, instruction guides and leaflets that parrot the same archaeological instructions concerning topsoil and subsoil clearance, but the examples above serve to stress one of the most crucial points of concern with reference to these layers. The results of an initial sample survey (Spackman, 2021) regarding the depth of artefacts recovered were enlightening, to say the least, with 83 percent of finds including surface finds recovered by metal detectorists in Depth (1) between surface and 75mm on plough soil, and 87 percent of finds from the same depth on pasture. A more in-depth study was clearly warranted (Spackman, 2022) to produce a reliable set of data from which realistic and honest conclusions could be drawn incorporating Depth (2) the level between 75mm and 150mm, which should cover most metal-detecting limits, requiring of course two separate graphs.

Survey charts were handed out to a variety of metal detectorists, both individuals and groups, at a variety of locations over two months during the spring of 2022 and again over a one-month period in autumn. These results did not exactly mirror the not-so-comprehensive data of the much smaller survey of 2021, echoing the essential advantages of conducting the largest possible survey within timescales and work ethic. There was an expectation that the time spent searching either pasture or plough soils, the latter of course includes harvested crops stubbles, would seasonally fluctuate due to availability and type of crop. What did show is that plough soils are overwhelmingly the choice for the vast majority of detectorists in the area of the survey (see Figures 5–6, Topsoil and Plough soil). Considering that the counties of the survey are agriculturally active, it was not a surprise. What is interesting is when there is a standard practice in place and included in guidelines and procedures relating to archaeology and archaeologists to remove the top layer by spade and/or a machine with, of course, the correct bucket attached. On grassland or pasture, when commercial archaeology is involved, the turf is removed with a recommended 50mm (Morris, 2021, Step 8, version 2) of topsoil attached and stacked neatly nearby, allowing the archaeologist closer access to any archaeological layer. The removed turf along with its topsoil is given the layer name of topsoil and a context number of (1), but as far as archaeological value goes, turf and topsoil is discounted as an archaeological entity and kept for the purpose of replacing when excavation comes to an end after backfilling has been accomplished. In practice, unless the excavation is on a cricket pitch or bowling green, normal grassland, and pasture slabs of removed turf, would be, on average, a depth of between 50 and 75mm. There is no need to replicate each and every archaeological unit's relevant passage referring to the procedure of clearing and removal of these layers as there is a definite standardisation across the profession as well as obligatory guides of educational and training institutions that have archaeology included in their syllabi. The first example refers not to the issue of the practice of machined removal, but highlights the actual thickness of the turf, plus attached topsoil removed during archaeological excavation; the fact that the operative was an amateur is irrelevant as the supervisor was indeed an experienced archaeological professional – see example (a) below. This is a subject that was discussed many years ago and looking back twenty years ago, there is a mention that refers to the plough-zone and which according to Addyman and Brodie (2002, p. 180) who, in citing Gregory and Rogerson (1984), informs the reader that *'substantial amounts of artefacts fall victim of pre-excavation surface stripping'*. So, in those in-between years, what has happened is that the subject has most likely been the subject of debate and a realisation of the importance of top and plough soils, and all they contain, was in fact paramount to the understanding of the landscape's hidden historical past; something that metal detectorists had known from the outset. Now years have passed and although archaeologists understood the importance, we can still see the same old practices destroying on a daily basis the county's cultural heritage. Indeed, it may boil down to resources or financial restraints – both important factors in the world of commerce, but should not be an excuse not to fully explore land before construction.

Example (a) Concerns the actual recommended thickness of turf when a site is opened, which is, according to Morris (2019, p. 8), 5cm, but in a recent episode of Channel 4's The Great British Dig at West Derby investigating the location of a Norman motte and bailey fortification, presented by Hugh Dennis (2022, Series 2, Episode 5), seven minutes into the programme turf was duly cut, in trench three, by a local volunteer using a garden lawn edger and removed by spade, which is all correct, but the edging tool's blade had a depth of at least 9cm. Although under supervision by a professional archaeologist and the slabs of turf removed, this could give the wrong impression because the recommended depth is 5cm. The slab looked thick and heavy and the archaeologist had some difficulty trying to lift the large slab of turf and soil; the camera pans away before the struggle is completed. There was no explanation why these turf slabs displaying thicknesses of at least three times the recommendations were presented to the viewer, leaving multitudes of professionals and amateur archaeologists alike receiving, unfortunately, misguided expectations of turf depth. Most of the smaller trenches were opened in the gardens of residents with a much larger trench in the adjacent park dug by machine, and at no time was there any indication that any trench was subjected to a metal-detector search conducted.

Example (b) An example of zealous turf removal from the Iona Research Group (2018) during a manual de-turfing of a trench due to be excavated and is, in forty years of excavation experience, the thickest slabs of turf ever seen on an archaeological site. Estimated from the on-site photographs, the removed turf is given a conservative thickness of 150mm and the weight of such a slab should have been highlighted on any risk assessment; the resulting turf heap is also worth a visit to their web page.

Example (c) An excellent example of a project guide to best practice initiated with the backing of a Heritage Lottery Fund was by Oxford Archaeology, initially as a five-year project to assist more than twenty Cambridgeshire

56   Archaeology Versus Metal Detecting

local history and archaeological societies. The outcome was the formation of a much-needed and helpful umbrella organisation duly named Jigsaw Cambridgeshire and accompanied by a Jigsaw Cambridgeshire Best Practice Users Guide (2016), which includes an excavation guide by Gilmour (2016, p. 5); the guide was presented as a basic guide for the benefit of mostly community-led enterprises. Nick Gilmour is a learned professional archaeologist with firm links to East Anglia, having gained an MA in Archaeology from the University of Cambridge. The two paragraphs in question specifically relate to open-area excavation and are in no way concerned with the practice of 'test-pitting', where the norm is one square metre or even one x two metres and excavated by trowel from ground level down, but to the descriptive methodology for open-area trench excavation: a method that is generally used for trenches larger than a small test pit.

> *'This requires a machine to remove topsoil and subsoil layers down to the top of the archaeological layers…Machining will only be required when undertaking* an open area excavation project' (Gilmour, 2016, p. 5).

Example (d) Also that of a leading university and in the field of archaeology, the University of Leicester, an institution that houses an archaeological unit of repute, University of Leicester Archaeological Services [ULAS]. It was in 2012 that a certain King Richard III, who in 1485 met demise at the Battle of Bosworth Field and in so doing became the last Plantagenet King, was unearthed in a Leicester car park under the directorship of one Mathew Morris, a project officer with a long history of archaeological expertise, who had joined ULAS eight years earlier. Like the Cambridgeshire project above, Mathew Morris created a similar basic but more detailed instruction document. This gives a guideline of a recommended turf thickness of 5cm, perfect for a slab of turf (Morris, M. 2019, Version 1 and Morris, M, 2021, Version 2 just to show continuity of information in what is an excellent basic guide):

> *'De-turfing your test-pit (Step 8, p. 8) If your test pit is located in a grassed area then you will need to take the turf off before you can start digging deeper. To do this, use a sharp spade and lift off 5cms thick turf.* (Morris, M. 2019) *Digging your test-pit (Steps 9–12, p8) Once you have removed the turf, you will need to start digging'* (Morris, M. 2019). In either case there is no

mention of metal-detector use with reference to any layers removed before commencement of digging either before or after de-turfing.

Example (e) The importance of topsoil as a stratified layer, which in the past would be and still is, on most archaeological sites, a level an archaeology practitioner would be, as informed by the eminent archaeologists Renfrew and Bahn (1991, p1. 05), discounted, and removed by shovel or on larger sites by bulldozers without regard or respect for finds in that layer. In the past, topsoil was considered unstratified and hence devoid of archaeological information, and subjected to removal mechanically and quickly without investigation. Renfrew and Bahn (1991) do continue to state that this practice changed when advances in technological development needed vital chemical information and geochemical analysis from the once discounted top layers, which could then be archaeologically used to locate the presence of phosphate (phosphorus) used as a requirement during certain agricultural procedures, but there is no information of the methods used to remove those layers after chemical analysis, nor any indication of depth of removal.

Example (f) The major excavations of the Forum-Basilica at Silchester. Britannia Monograph Series No15 (Fulford M. and Timby J. 2000, p. 8) states that *'Excavation began in 1980 with the removal by machine of the plough soil and backfill to just above surviving walls.'* This practice is in a number of guides to excavation and a general practice with regard to commercial archaeology, and again no mention of a metal detector being used before or after plough soil removal.

Example (g) The use of machines to excavate near 1,000 square metres in the moat of the Tower of London, which is a United Nations Educational, Scientific and Cultural Organization [UNESCO] World Heritage Site as well as a Scheduled Monument, shows exactly what can happen as a result of excavating by machine. The machines dug and deposited tonnes of excavated soil, encapsulating hundreds of historical finds that had lain in the soils of the moat, straight onto large spoil heaps (Sandy, 2022). The remarks of Alfred Hawkins (2022), Assistant Curator of Historic Royal Palaces for the Tower of London, during the after-dig interview are informative and presented in an article by Sandy (2022, pp. 46–47): *'During the construction phase of Super-bloom we excavated over 1,000 square metres of spoil within the moat',* and enlightened the readers to the fact that *'Due to the scale and timeframe of the project, this spoil could not be assessed archaeologically, but fortunately the mudlarks, using metal detectors to recover metal artefacts... gave us a way to find and retain artefacts that would not have been possible otherwise'*.

Example (h) An excellent description from the pen of a professional and well-respected archaeologist who held the position of Lecturer of Archaeology at the prestigious University of York. Steve Roskams is author of Excavation (2021), a must-have for the professional archaeologist and enthusiast alike. The publication follows the changes in theory and practice in the field of archaeology as well as presenting aspects of all things archaeological. Both procedures below offer substance to my argument, credibility, and acknowledgement that archaeological practices have and always did have obvious flaws in their critique of metal detecting as a whole. The extracts below are to be found in Chapter 5, Excavation in Practice: Preparations on Site (Roskams, 2001).

'When starting an excavation, one may have to engage in activities which are anything but archaeological to reach the point where 'the real archaeology' begins. The removal of overburden, whether the substantial buildings or concrete slab that cover an urban site, or the turf covering a green field in the countryside, is an essential preliminary'. (Roskams, 2001, p. 93). The enlightenment of possible artefact destruction continues with a very telling statement: *'the bulldozer's main role is on those extensive rural sites where it has been decided largely to ignore the topsoil as an archaeological horizon. In such situations the top of the 'natural' stratigraphy is usually the point at which archaeological strata are deemed to start'*. (Roskams, 2001, p. 94). That sentence in itself is rather frightening as some considerable depth could be removed to reach an archaeological stratum; I have actually come across plough soils more than 50cm in depth and regularly encountered soils in excess of 30cm.

It is unfortunate that after many hundreds of years of archaeological excavations, meaning excavations by archaeologists, that they, archaeologists and archaeological institutions, are still in discord with whom they consider destroying the nation's heritage by rescuing artefacts from the very top-soils and plough soils that archaeologists and institutions quite happily, openly, and regularly remove, with little respect to the artefacts that are in these levels; all without full benefit of exploration by metal detectors used by experienced operators. There may be cries of financial restraints, workforce issues, time constraints and equipment shortage [see example (h) above]. Everyone can understand all those situations, but that should not be an excuse to badger the very people who are saving artefacts forged by the people, for the people; therefore, metal detectorists are, in reality, protecting our heritage by rescuing millions of portable antiquities from certain destruction by plough, the farmer, and bulldozer, the developer and archaeologist. We must not forget the thousands of acres or hectares of land that have, over the years, been subject to vandalism by proxy at the hands of those great ground-removing bulldozers and mechanical diggers, not forgetting pre-industrial procedures of removing all topsoil by spade. There is a realisation that on many thousands of excavations where the top layers were removed, somewhat unceremoniously, the soils and turf were indeed kept neatly to one side and replaced on closure of the excavations; well bravo: all those millions of finds in the layers that archaeologists themselves use the term 'do not matter' have been put back, albeit all trim and proper, but with *in situ* small finds included. This practice has continued through the years to modern-day excavations, even back to 1980 when the excavation was reopened on the site of the Forum-Basilica in Roman Silchester, which began with the removal of topsoil by machine (Fulford and Timby, 2000, p. 8). In this substantial publication of more than 600 pages there is no mention of a metal detector, or the use of. There is an interesting remark referring to the 1880 excavations of Revd. J. G. Joyce and the imbalance in the variety of coins handled by Joyce's four old men, compared to 1980s' efforts, described by George C. Boon as *'the greater care in searching for coins in the recent excavations'* (Boon, in Fulford and Timby 2000, pp. 127–179). Interesting because the wording includes a telling 'searching' as against superior excavation techniques; it would be of great interest indeed to confirm if a metal detector was used as a 'searching' tool and, if so, why was that procedure not documented? Many, many of those sites were, in the early years, scheduled as protected areas of archaeological importance, but is the, protection, for the archaeology, that which lay below the layers of what archaeologists class as levels of unimportance, but those unimportant levels still harbour untouched artefacts that are extremely important but now lay *in situ*, corroding into an inexcusable, inevitable inexistence.

Topsoil management on building and construction sites tends to follow the same procedure with regard to the use of machines ((DEFRA, 2009) 'Construction Code of Practice for Sustainable Use of Soils on Construction Sites' refers). This DEFRA publication highlights the importance of soil management and the need for an acceptable '*Soil Resource Plan*' [SRP], which is good news for the environment and on the surface the plan works as a sustainable resource, but also mentions that stockpiles of topsoil need not necessarily be on-site and could even be sold off or used elsewhere. Not at all particularly good for top-layer finds, but there are no instructions pertaining to full metal-detecting inspection of either top or subsoil levels. Full inspection as there are very few metal artefacts that by their very nature are large enough to otherwise be found by generally used archaeological processes, which themselves use the aforementioned machine-stripping techniques, but even so recovery during that procedure would represent an exceedingly small minority of recordable small finds.

The issue of soil management was clearly outlined during the Channel Tunnel Rail Link [CTRL] programme as Section 1, which ran 74km through the county of Kent through agricultural (Foreman (2018)) land, which accounted for more than 800 hectares (800ha), the removal of which was covered by a Code of Construction Practice. This code incorporated an Agricultural Management Plan [AMP]. When suggested plans of using derelict pits to dispose of surplus excavated soil were incorporated, this included a Schedule of Standards and Soil Handling Techniques, and among other advice a recommendation that said topsoil should be no higher than three metres and subsoils no higher than five metres. The point in question is again, why are archaeologists concerned about metal detectorists legally recovering artefacts from topsoil when archaeologists and construction corporations treat topsoil as either a resource or a commodity, although managed according to guidelines? Historic England does state that before beginning work on a construction site, the practice of stripping the topsoil from all areas that will be disturbed by construction activities or driven over by vehicles should prevail.

Another method that requires the use of machine excavation, according to archaeologists and archaeological contractors, is to remove topsoil and is aptly named 'Strip and Map'; this process is advertised by a number of archaeological contractors. It is used mainly where large areas of land are subjected to excavation and described as being used because '*it is often much more cost-effective than full excavation*' (L-P Archaeology (2022)) by a contractor who possesses more than thirty years of experience with commercial archaeology and is a Registered Organisation with [CIfA]. Stripping refers to the removal of topsoil, typically with a mechanical excavator, and any suspected archaeological features would then be cleaned by an archaeologist, who would take the responsibility for removing loose material. After this, the mapping process takes place where the remains are duly photographed, drawn, and described. Any finds or features would then be located using Differential Global Positioning System [DGPS] technology (L-Archaeology 2017) or another system. Of interest are other services offered by this experienced contractor, as well as numerous other professional archaeological bodies, and a popular activity of many a local history and heritage group: 'Field Walking' and 'Walkover' surveys; both procedures will be discussed in full in later chapters and are cited here to show a documented lack of using or mentioning any made-for-purpose metal-detecting equipment used during field-walking and walkover surveys.

Another active and well-used archaeological contractor is Cotswold Archaeology, which, as one of their professional services, offer Strip and Map, of which their involvement in the extension of Philpot Quarry is an excellent example. Three hectares of topsoil were subject to Strip and Map and according to the excavation report by following all the correct procedures and guidelines to the letter (Brannlund and Howard, 2013). There was no mention of a metal-detector survey before or after the completion of Strip and Map over 3ha of land, but Cotswold Archaeology were professional enough to document the use of metal detectors on the spoil heaps; whether the detectors were operated by paid employees or volunteers from a metal-detectorists' group was not forthcoming. There are few archaeological contractors that admit to using metal detectors on either their websites or advertising literature, but those who do offer evidence of embracing the technological innovations and benefits of having in their geophysics armament a supply of metal detectors. Cotswold Archaeology [CA] openly admit to using this type of equipment at a site in Congleton, Cheshire back in 2015 (Cotswold Archaeology Ltd. Report, 15140). Cotswold Archaeology continued to provide a complete range of services and on Parkfield Farm, Lower Hamswell, South Gloucester in 2017 with a metal-detection survey, which they undertook to fulfil Condition 6 for planning permission. Later in the same year, CA were invited to conduct a metal-detector survey on the important 1798 battlefield at Vinegar Hill in County Wexford, Southern Ireland. Another example of a major player in the field of archaeological contractors are Allen Archaeology, who from 2017–18 conducted metal-detection surveys as part of an archaeology contract on behalf of a wind farm construction. The following year, 2019, Allen Archaeology (2019) fulfilled another metal-detecting contract with a survey of the Sheriffmuir (1715) Battlefield site near Dunblane, Scotland. As a further example, Humber Field Archaeology also offer field-walking and metal-detecting surveys. The contractors mentioned are mere examples of archaeological practices that have encompassed metal detectors as respected, essential members of their already advanced technological geophysics cache of machines, but little is said that the use of metal detectors or detectorists involved the use of volunteer metal-detectorist groups, or do they in reality employ or have on their staff dedicated metal detectorists? It would appear that some use of metal detectors is solely to honour governing factors such as the compulsory compliance with conditions set during the planning processes. There are of course others, but many more are loath to admit to associating with a metal detectorist; among them are contractors that do use them on site but, for their own reasons, deny by proxy that they do, almost re-enacting St. Peter's refute.

The treatment of topsoil came to the fore during a major survey by Oxford Archaeology (2009) for English Heritage when it was acknowledged by one of the recommendations offered that '*The treatment of topsoil during commercial excavations needs reviewing at present it is typically machined away as overburden without any systematic examination for artefacts).*' A customary practice is to have the resulting spoil heaps searched by metal detectorists when again the artefacts are already out of the ground, and if a spoil-heap is more than the maximum detectable depth then this is an almost fruitless exercise, but it may tick a few boxes in so much that a detectorist was used or community involvement was fulfilled. The recommendations highlighted in the Oxford Archaeology Survey (2009) continue with a telling statement that the archaeologists '*by appearing to disregard this resource in their own working practices, archaeologists stand open to charges of hypocrisy when they try to prevent responsible detectorists [exploiting the artefactual resource in the topsoil]*' (Historic England 2009). Although I agree wholeheartedly with that statement from Oxford Archaeology, the word '*exploiting*' is harsh and antagonistic as the meaning of exploiting includes such derogatory words as unethically, unjustly, unfair and in a cruel way (Collins English Dictionary 1991, p. 692). May I suggest a modicum of modification with something nearer to the truth, *id est* rescuing, or simply recovering artefacts from the topsoil would complement metal detectorists and their efforts and the dedication involved. So, I can only wonder why or what the report is insinuating. Could it be suggesting that all metal detectorists are abusers and misusers, especially after the incredibly positive and complimentary findings of the 2006–9 survey? In retort, would it not then be correct to accuse the commercial archaeologists of exploiting the legal commitments of a cash-strapped construction industry? Of course not; I would not bow so low as to enter into a tit-for-tat philology, which would be rather petty, and will in no way resolve a somewhat trying situation. There are regulations and guidance in place concerning the removal of both topsoil and subsoil, their storage and conservation, but no guidance for the recovery and protection of artefacts that could have been recovered from the soil by metal detectorists before stripping. Turf cannot be sieved along with other soil removed as its very nature renders that particular task an impossibility, with a realisation that any artefacts within that level would no longer have an exact location and carries a high percentage of probability that it, the turf, would be replaced anywhere, if at all, within the excavated area and, as previously documented, could even be taken off site. SCC Requirements for Archaeological Excavation (updated March 2023) state that if the excavation is to begin by mechanical removal of topsoil down to the subsoil horizon, the procedure '*must be under the control and supervision of an archaeologist and that the topsoil should be examined for archaeological material*'; that is normal practice during machining to enable the archaeologist to halt progress and inspect any anomalies uncovered with the knowledge that during machining it is unlikely (but not impossible) that metal artefacts would be located. SCC (2021) indicates that there should be in place provision for hand excavation when required '*which must include metal detector survey and on site sieving to recover smaller artefacts*', that statement of course is a little ambiguous as it could refer to spoil, and as already stated artefacts that are not in situ are of little archaeological value, but even the mere mention of a metal detector being used on site is somewhat reassuring.

It would appear that both on paper and in the field, there are major concerns with regard to prospective finds that metal detectorists have recovered from the top layers of soil, something that is generally acknowledged throughout the hobby and validated by research: that turf and topsoil contain the greatest volume of finds. On some, but definitely not all, archaeological sites, excavated soils are deposited on spoil heaps where they are scanned by a detectorist – if there is a detectorist on-site of course. Larger commercial and construction sites appear to gather said soils into monumental mounds, sometimes transported away from the original site altogether, either way giving little or no chance of finds recovery, and even if the heaps were detected by a metal detectorist there is no way to identify a find spot and the depth of a spoil heap would prove an obstacle to even the most sophisticated and advanced metal-detecting machines. I have come across spoil heaps that could easily be mistaken for ancient Bronze Age burial mounds as wheelbarrow after wheelbarrow or machine bucket after machine bucket were used to build up large heaps. There is often a sense of pride among archaeologists when looking back at well-constructed and managed spoil heap. Informative and telling words by the eminent Roman finds specialist Nina Crummy (1983, reprinted 1995) not only highlight the observations of an extensive career concerning archaeological finds but also put a fly in the ointment of one of the major complaints directed at metal detectorists by the world of archaeology. That is the accusation that artefacts, when recovered by a detectorist, are removed from their original contexts and or stratigraphy: *'Readers should bear in mind that for most cases the date of the context provides a terminus ante quem for the date of the loss or deposition of the object concerned. This is because most finds have been redeposited in antiquity, perhaps several times, as the result of various disturbances'* (Nina Crummy, 1983, reprinted 1995, p. 2). Now that is truly a statement to note and digest and a statement I applaud, not because it is the truth, but that it emanated from an archaeologist with many years of experience quite a few rungs above my humble self. Nina Crummy (1983, reprinted 1995) follows that comment with eight well-chosen words: *'Objects found in their primary contexts are rare'*. Artefactual primary contexts are an exceedingly rare occurrence for a detectorist, but it is not unknown, and primary contexts are normally in the realm of archaeology and the archaeologist who works at deeper depths beyond the range of metal detectorists. This would infer that the constant hounding and rather unsuitable rhetoric directed at the metal detectorists who are rescuing artefacts from non-primary contexts, which are top-soils, plough soils, and spoil heaps, is that they are acting in an inappropriate manner, and the unsavoury rhetoric directed at the archaeological processes of removing said contexts by spade, mattock or machine, which inevitably in the process removes, unintentionally or not, unrecorded artefacts. Actually, unintentionally would need explaining, as I cannot imagine that after forty years of metal detectorists being lambasted by the world of archaeology for actually saving millions of artefacts from those very contexts, the same critics do not shower the world of archaeology with the same energetic derision; see also figures 5 and 6 below.

The information gathered gives the ongoing arguments against metal detecting more than a little knock. When looking at the evidence associated with the worlds of commercial archaeology and the construction industry with reference to topsoil management, the arguments supporting the pro-lobby for legitimate metal detecting are significantly strengthened by the survey results, which give credence to the hobby as a whole. The results from permanent pasture show that 60 percent of the metallic finds recovered came from Depth 2, 75–150mm against just under 40 percent from Depth 1, 0–75mm. Artefacts in pasture tend not to migrate far from areas of deposition due to the fact that the area has not been under the plough – apart from the results of animal activity being caused by the burrowing species in the UK: rabbits, hares, foxes, moles, badgers, and puffins, to name but a few, of which I have seen some excellent examples of artefact migration. Also, a certain amount of migration would take place on natural slopes as gravity and natural water drainage would move smaller artefacts downhill from their original positions. I recall being called out by a developer who was concerned that the recently stripped two acres of topsoil that had left subsoil exposed had been the victim of nighthawkers after spotting thirty to forty small shallow holes spread over quite a large area of the sight. As nighthawking in itself is rare, I was genuinely concerned because that area had not yet been metal detected and that particular exercise was earmarked for the day after topsoil removal. On inspection, I could see evidence of claw marks and identified the thief as none other than *Meles-meles* or the Eurasian badger, and the missing artefacts were terrestrial invertebrates in the form of earthworms, resulting in happy badgers, happy builders, contented archaeologists, and elated detectorists. With plough soil, artefacts are in a constant seasonal rotation, with the same artefact, over a number of years, migrating in all directions, hence the popularity of ploughed fields as one year there would be little to recover but the following season many more artefacts coming to light. It is an interesting scenario when detecting surveys are carried out as an aid to pre-construction or archaeological investigations, particularly on plough soils as the results can change from year to year. Even the crop itself, as it grows, lifts items upwards and even above the ground surface, and many a ring has been recovered with a stalk of wheat or another crop growing through it and the artefact is found well above the surface; I wonder what the context layer of that artefact would be as it cannot be classed as a surface find. An encouraging article by Alastair Hacket (December 2022), which appeared in an issue of a newly formed online magazine, echoes the concerns resulting from the activities of professional archaeologists and the construction industry. The article does outline the fact that there are others who are enthusiastic in presenting matters effecting the loss of a valuable resource, our heritage and cultural material, all by the archaeological processes involved in the aforementioned stripping of topsoil and an extremely limited involvement of experienced metal detectorists.

At the time of publication, I have been unable to verify the claims of Hacket (December 2022), so there is, unfortunately, no quote in my publication of the quite important details surrounding the apparent findings of Alister Hacket's (2022) facts and opinions. The main problem being that verification relies on the original documents being available from the Association of Local Government Archaeological Officers [ALGA]. The up-to-date results of both plough soil and pasture results conducted by Spackman, (2021, 2022) are more strikingly defined and clearly show that out of the 28,764 finds, 81.4 percent, or 23,407, were recovered from Depth 1, 0–75mm, and 17 percent, or 5,357, from Depth 2, 75–150mm. The previous smaller survey of 2021 showed that the Depth 1 percentage was 82 percent and therefore an acceptable difference, with a fluctuation of only 1.6 percent, is more than satisfactory.

Now we can see that the vast majority of metal-detectorists' finds were rescued from the topsoil and there is no proof that the percentage of finds will deviate more than a fluctuating acceptable figure, with the realisation that some individual areas may differ drastically from the average. To note, not all of these finds were of PAS-recordable significance and that all metal items were listed in the survey including cans, nails, and parts thereof. An enlightening article in Treasure Hunting magazine (May 2022, pp. 31–37) entitled 'Moat Larking' the Tower of London, by Jason Sandy, concerns one of the most well-known United Nations World Heritage Sites as well as a Scheduled Monument. Sandy has been involved with and a long-time member of the Society of Thames Mudlarks [STM], which had dealings with Stuart Wyatt FLO working for the PAS London as the society records their finds with the PAS from mudlarking up and down the Thames at low tides.

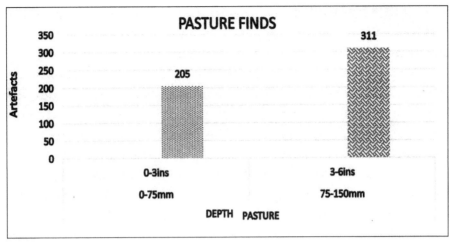

Figure 5. Pasture Depth Survey, results. (*P. Spackman. 2022*)

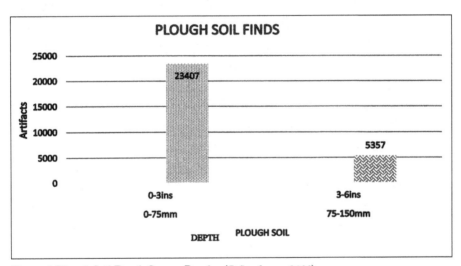

Figure 6. Plough Soil Depth Survey, Results. (*P. Spackman. 2022*)

It was Wyatt who contacted the Thames Mudlarks and Sandy to take part in a 'Mudlarking the Spoil' exercise, assisting the archaeologists of L-P Archaeology before the landscaping of the Tower Moat to accommodate millions of wildflowers in readiness for the Queen Elizabeth II celebrations. A metal detector was loaned to Sandy by a major metal-detector supplier, but Nick Stevens from the society did own a metal detector and appears to be the most experienced of the two with regard to use, not only because Nick is frequently mentioned and photographed in action throughout the three separate articles submitted by Sandy to the Treasure Hunter monthly magazine, issues May, June, and August 2022, but also Stevens, according to the photographs, appears to show an economical operator presentation and stance. A little unfortunate that Jason Sandy, in an excellent profile by MacPherson (The Chiswick Calendar, 2019), earned the title of Jason Sandy 'Thames Treasure Hunter', and his home now hosts a cabinet of curiosities. 'Treasure hunter' is a term that is a cause of disagreement with both archaeologists and dedicated detectorists alike; archaeologists often label detectorists as 'treasure hunters' and detectorists have for decades attempted to discard that derogatory epithet, but I suppose that Sandy may prefer 'mudlarker' instead of metal detectorist as it gives a more acceptable and PC title. Jason does inform the reader that on the Society of Mudlarks' open days mudlarking on the banks of the Thames (not the Tower of London), members of the public have also found some *'incredible artefacts'*; this is a clear indication that members of the public are classed as a separate group other than STMs. This practice was terminated in 2017 (Sandy, May 2022). These annual open days were part of the Festival of British Archaeology and all finds discovered were handed to an FLO from the Museum of London, who in turn recorded them on the PAS database. So, we have before us two mudlarkers and a PAS official FLO meeting with Building Curator, Historic Royal Palaces, Alfred Hawkins, who conveys the importance of using metal detectorists during the archaeological survey and uses a telling phrase: '*We are doing some mudlarking in the spoil that has been excavated out of the moat as part of the construction phase. The moat is an incredibly sensitive place, but the mudlarks offer us a way to do this project while also protecting that archaeological sensitivity.*' (Sandy, May 2022 p. 33). He was referring to the task for which they were allocated and it is somewhat discerning because, after 20-plus years, yet again the idea that a metal detectorist, or in this instance, seasoned mudlarkers, is only useful for finding artefacts that are regularly missed by archaeologists and ending up on spoil heaps; the Tower of London Superbloom Project is a classic case. With regard to protecting the archaeological sensitivity, I do believe that the archaeological sensitivity and its integrity were both destroyed when the mechanical diggers ripped through sensitive layers of the history of one of the most important sites in the country, but I suppose the correct regulation bucket size was used during a rather destructive process. Quoted by Sandy (May 2022, p. 36), Alfred Hawkins states that '*The moat has a very long and complicated history of over seven hundred years – the scale of things that we are finding is reflective of that complicated story.'* The moat lies like a sleeping dragon of old, curling majestically around the Tower complex now its heart is being torn asunder by modernity and the mechanical digger; its blood, artefacts, piled aside out of context for the pleasure of rummaging and the ever-decreasing timescale marches on. With reference to the eminent archaeologists and presenters such as Robinson and Aston (2002, p. 152), who inform us *'once out of the ground an artefact is out of context'*, and Roskams (2001, p. 223), who mentions metal detectors as an aid to finds recovery and using metal detectors as a *'spoil heap artefact rescue tool'*. Both these two publications are now more than twenty years old, but little has changed with regard to attitude and practice, as the article quite clearly shows. Machines were unable to excavate some areas due to service cables and pipes, so archaeologists mostly dug by hand, leaving large lumps of clay soil to be deposited upon spoil heaps. Jason Sandy mentioned that *'it was very difficult to metal detect the many big lumps that they were excavating'*, and a telling picture shows Nick Stevens atop of a very large heap at least two metres in height tackling those very clods (Sandy, June 2022, Fig. 6, p. 61). During the metal-detecting exercise, the detectorists, while working on the machine-created spoil heaps, recovered bottles, clay pipes and ceramics, including a spout of an old teapot. On one of the larger spoil heaps, numerous coins were rescued (see Sandy, June 2022, Figure 16, p. 64), but again the detectable range of depth would leave roughly 60 percent of soil undetectable before once again the spoil is redeposited. The issue of the Treasure Hunting magazine (Sandy, August 2022 p. 41–47) included the third and final day of Moat Larking for the Mudlarkers as they tackled the monumental spoil heaps, and metal-detector users Tim Miller, Nick Stevens and Jason Sandy, author of the article in the magazine, are faced with spoil from the machine-dug trenches (Sandy, August 2022 Figs. 3, 4, p. 42) . The trio were accompanied by Stuart Wyatt, London PAS, FLO with the task of recording any finds. Apparently in their absence, most of the old spoil had been covered with fresh topsoil, leaving very few areas that required the use of a metal detector, and one of these was a large fresh spoil-heap composed of overburden containing sherds of ceramics, bottles, clay pipes, bones and the odd metal find. With such a small workforce, even the visiting Alfred Hawkins from Historic Royal Palaces assisted by breaking down the clods of heavy clay (Sandy, 2022, August p. 42, fig. 3). There were numerous finds of bone, ceramics, glass (mainly of the bottle variety) and the odd clay pipe along with an occasional metal find. Nice to see that the detectorists had the benefit of an official PAS employee, Stuart Wyatt FLO for London, who was responsible for logging finds and bagging accordingly, which no doubt contained finds contexts, numbers, and site references. There are interesting connotations involving the many hours that were saved by not having to XYZ the vast collection of small finds; XYZ is an archaeological methodology discussed in a later chapter, but briefly means latitude, longitude and altitude, which gives the artefact a 3D position within the landscape or excavation and a procedure that is null and void once the find is removed from the position of discovery. What I did find a little puzzling was the fact that these artefacts reached the spoil at all; indeed, what had the archaeologists recorded, as it would appear that these few intrepid explorers had been tasked with searching a couple of lorry loads of overburden almost as a public relations exercise. A few choice words from Alfred Hawkins during an after-dig interview are informative: '*During the construction phase of Superbloom we excavated over 1,000 square metres of spoil within the moat*', and enlightened the readers to the fact that '*Due to the scale and timeframe of the project, this spoil could not be assessed 'archaeologically' but fortunately, the mudlarks gave us a way to find and retain artefacts that would not have been possible otherwise*' (Sandy, 2022, p. 46–47). What has not been qualified is the entry '*excavated 1,000 square metres of spoil*' and whether that refers to cubic metres of excavated soil creating a spoil heap covering 1,000 square metres, or 1,000 square metres of spoil was then subject to excavation; either way, most of the excavation was in fact carried out by mechanical diggers.

'Tower of London Moat Superbloom' was a project that, on paper, offered a programme of alliance between archaeologists and metal detectorists, but after reading the reported articles it appears that the exercise fell short of expectations and was, in analysis, more than a little disappointing and an opportunity missed by all parties involved. With regard to the metal detectorists, there was one mention identifying that one of the two involved in the detection process, on day one, possessed a metal detector; that was Stevens, with Sandy, long-time Thames Mudlarker and classed as a 'detectorist', using a detector supplied *gratis* (on loan) by a major supplier, which could be interpreted as a piece of good marketing, giving the impression that Sandy did not own a metal-detecting machine. That would give us an FLO and two persons using detectors with differing expertise. On the second of the three visits, the metal detectorists were joined by James Wyatt, who works in the Tower of London, and Tim Miller, who is the Chair of the Society of Thames Mudlarks. By the third and final day, the contingent using metal detectors consisted of Miller, Sandy, and Stevens (Thames Mudlarkers), and Wyatt the PAS FLO, who was responsible for the recording of 'small finds' found by the small team from the Thames Mudlarkers.

On the archaeological front, there were concerns that the excavations were mainly conducted by machine in such an archaeologically sensitive location as the Tower of London, which is a Scheduled Monument as well as a United Nations Educational, Scientific and Cultural Organization [UNESCO] World Heritage Site. This exercise showed that the machine-excavated soils contained a multitude of non-metallic artefacts and the comments by the Assistant Curator of Historic Buildings for the Tower of London, Alfred Hawkins, were indicative of limited resources to match apparent timescales: *'Due to the scale and timeframe of the project, this spoil could not be assessed archaeologically'* (Hawkins in Sandy 2022, p. 47). He adds: *'The use of metal detectorists to examine spoil can be an incredibly effective way to retain artefacts that would have otherwise been missed.'* Why archaeologists did not remove all artefacts that were predominantly non-metallic is a matter for the world of archaeology and we can only presume that both time and money came into the equation, but it was quite obvious from the amount of material in the large spoil heaps that only a small proportion of this high-profile and sensitive Scheduled Monument was excavated by hand. This project, at one of Britain's most prestigious and historic sites, can only highlight that after the many years since detectorists assisted by searching only spoil, the practice is still, unfortunately, at the fore and in this case, detectorists were even used to search and remove non-metallic artefacts, for whatever reason. So, does archaeology, as a whole and/or commercial archaeology, now expect this practice to continue or do they wish archaeologists to recover *in situ* finds before deposition somewhere upon a forgotten spoil heap, or indeed has finance begun to dictate the extent of both archaeological and metal-detectorist involvement? The latter, at this moment in time, is unfortunately available as volunteers so often would not figure into financial outlays; something that I personally deplore and are now hopefully classed as essential and therefore warrant appropriate reimbursement for their specialist expertise.

Concerning the use of metal detectors during the archaeological process and which section would a skilled operator come from: Would the equipment come from a field archaeologist or from a member of the geophysics team, and who would actually operate the machine? One would think that equipment that requires fine tuning, a battery, a display, an array of switches (metal detectors) would require personnel conversant with electronic equipment, as would magnetic gradiometers, fluxgate gradiometers, resistance meters, and ground penetrating radar, which are all in the armoury of practising geophysicists, but unfortunately a metal detector, which in itself is an example of a high-tech electronic equipment, appears to be pre-labelled as being possessed with some sort of anathema. Not that any of the geophysicists did not have the equipment; the search was thorough but not exhaustive and the conclusion is that it is a rare phenomenon indeed. The majority of the archaeology units, which have had the pleasure of dealing with individual metal detectorists or usually members of local detecting clubs, do so on a voluntary basis, which gets the WSI boxes ticked and is most definitely cost-effective. I have come across the odd professional field archaeologist who admitted possession of an early detector and who did, on occasion, use it as a search tool inside trial trenches. This brings to mind my latest experience working alongside professional archaeologists as a metal detectorist and witnessing recovery techniques of previously located and flagged metal-detected small finds. With reference to the art of artefact removal, there appeared to be the use of a rather unorthodox recovery technique when dealing with a top-soil layer. The different techniques of artefact extraction employed by both metal detectorists and archaeologists will be discussed in full in a later chapter.

As a mediator who is offering a balanced argument, there is no departing from the fact that there are some members of the archaeological and heritage sectors who will never agree to acknowledge the benefits of metal detectorists as an essential resource to aid learning and knowledge of our historical past. Some stalwarts of the now bygone years still possess the authoritarian qualities that past antiquarians and archaeologists enjoyed, but times they are a-changing; in fact, they have already changed. There are new sciences, new techniques, new equipment ,which cannot really be ignored but should be embraced with eagerness and a willingness to learn and the knowledge that you can persuade people to change. The fact is that there will always be someone who is discontented with almost any subject, procedure, or rule, but if the majority acknowledge change, so be it, and in reality, acceptance is often not a change at all but more of an addition to the norm. Remember the fervour created with the birth of 'Talkies' at the end of the era of silent movies, or even the novelty of electricity? Who was it who said the wheel wouldn't catch on?

In the early years, archaeologists appear to have acted with near impunity on mainly research programmes until regulation and common sense were introduced to counteract the enormous threat to archaeological and historical remains from the building and construction industry. There was the birth of commercial enterprise in the early 1990s following the introduction of open tendering, and the birth of legislative guidelines with regard to the, in most cases compulsory, use of an archaeologist in the construction planning processes and development of Government Planning Guidelines [PPG]. These initial guidelines were, as described by Heaton (2011), *'brutally simple and poorly explained*' as commercial archaeological companies as well as individual entrepreneurs multiplied at a tremendous pace, exploiting new horizons and opportunities in the wake of these new guidelines. This meant the involvement of archaeologists, who in the past were mostly employed regionary, but now these new commercial building projects were springing all over the country and as a consequence contracts were available to bid by outside-of-region archaeologists. It soon became apparent that the initial guidelines were outdated and the guidelines morphed accordingly from PPGs to, in 2010, Planning Policy Statement 5 [PPS5], and in 2012 the government of the day published Planning Practice Guidance with an all-encompassing National Planning Policy Framework [NPPF], updated 2016, 2018, 2019 and 2021. It makes one wonder what guidelines and regulations archaeologists and antiquarians were following for hundreds of years at home and abroad when literally shiploads of cultural artefacts found their way to our shores, worldwide. Archaeology felt the impact of the government instructions that were directed at the construction industry for the purpose of putting in place a procedure that would make the developer responsible for the expense and implementation of any archaeological investigations required to satisfy the legislation presented by these Planning Policy Guidelines. With constant monitoring, the NPPF is updated as appropriate and is still functioning. This merely highlights the commitment of the relevant government departments to safeguarding our heritage during construction development by including archaeological involvement, but with obvious financial constraints archaeologists are not governed by their ethics but by targets and this does not normally lead to an acceptable archaeological outcome. Archaeology is quickly becoming, or indeed may already be, a developer-led occupation, with regard to a field archaeologist, no longer controlled by regional or county archaeologist but archaeological businesses, leaving the classic example of antiquarian, adventurer, and scholar confined to the rostrum of academia, the trowel but a memory and a keepsake of the good old days; times they are a-changing. It could be suggested that there is a limit to the involvement of a full complement of appropriate skill sets, including the involvement of metal detectorists, and even then, unfortunately, limited to spoil heaps or test areas, both of which are far from acceptable. At this moment in time, full use of the skills of both detectorists and archaeologists is not catered for, as time and finance are finite resources.

As discussed, there are archaeological institutions that do accept the need to use the skills of the metal detectorists and some, it would appear, only as a token gesture of appeasement to planning applications and WSIs, which refer to involvement of metal detectorists, as we have seen on many occasions, such as when the detectorists are only used to search spoil heaps. Even then only because it is written into a construction unit's WSI and the archaeological units, in a way, feel obligated to comply, with in some cases a token attendance predominantly involving spoil heaps. In this case the extremely sensitive equipment and skills of the detectorists are being used almost exclusively in a voluntary situation with apparent reluctance, otherwise a detectorist would be paid accordingly and used seriously, as all ground should be detected before and during excavation. I, as a freelance archaeologist and detectorist, have practised full detection procedures for well over thirty years; this procedure is discussed in full in a later chapter. So, a more detailed WSI may well acknowledge the capabilities and benefits of conducting a stratified searching technique, which could also increase knowledge of the sites under investigation and excavation. Another especially crucial point is that the majority of detectorists are exploited in so much that they are mostly used on a voluntary basis, or at best some expenses may be paid. I have encountered the all too familiar retort that we can get one any time, they are two a penny. Time Team did pay expenses, a daily rate and a decent meal thrown in, so they were moving with the times, but detectorists were not very often seen in camera shot. A Dickensian attitude similar in format of the saying, children should be seen and not heard, but in the case of a detectorist a little modification is required as detectorists should be used but neither seen nor heard, almost thought of as a second-class citizen, used and abused.

The acknowledgement of the involvement of metal detectorists does appear to be stifled somewhat, especially in print as we see again and again. Is the archaeological profession still unable to accept this activity even when the information and knowledge obtained often forms the backbone of their subject? Often, I can be seen dressed in my finest Anglo-Saxon garb complete with shield, sword, spear, helm and scramasax, and nearby one of my now favourite publications, a 1,078-page study concerning that particular period in our history. One contributor, Sonja Marzinzik, who in Chapter 52 explores *Anglo-Saxon Archaeology and the Public* in Hamerow, Hinton and Crawford (2011, pp. 1029–32) under the subtitle *Entertainment and Leisure*. It covers, among others, the subject of re-enactment; now what has all that got to do with this study you may ask. Metal detecting is not included as a leisure activity, but what is included is a programme of learning activities designed and developed by namely PAS Explorers, especially for children, and teaches archaeological methods. There is also a mention that the PAS has access to adults who wish to learn about good practice with regard to metal detecting. Strangely, I thought, metal detecting would have been more appropriately placed under leisure but is covered under the subtitle of '*Government Initiatives and Legislation*' (Marzinzik (2011, pp. 1033–34)), along with multiple references to the public when the term metal detectorist would have been nearer to the truth, as again entries to the PAS database by metal detectorists taken from PAS records is near 96 percent and still an indication that a concerted evert is being made to not cement a link between metal detectorists and archaeologist, but to create ownership of metal detecting by archaeological academia. Nonetheless, acknowledgement of a group comprising more than 30,000 individuals from all creeds, beliefs, educational levels, and walks of life, the majority of whom are dedicated and competent individuals who are saving, on a daily basis, this country's heritage. Somewhat of a double-edged sword is swung by John Pearce and Sally Worrell (2015, p. 20), who begin, unfortunately, with the all too familiar phrase when referring to the PAS database and finds by '*members of the public*' and quite rightly point out that during 2014 alone, more than 100,000 finds were recorded. A page later, Pearce and Worrell (2015, p. 21) question the legitimacy of metal detecting and concerns that the hobby has led to '*substantial loss of information*' owing to a '*lack of recording finds*'. Rather a strange comment, as Worrell is national finds advisor for the PAS and published many articles covering the subject of Roman artefacts recorded on the PAS database, and Pearce has written and co-authored many publications including 50 Roman Finds from the Portable Antiquities Scheme (John Pearce and Sally Worrell, (2020)). Just to convey that they are not alone in the practice of producing publications introducing the finds made by metal detectorists, another dedicated archaeologist and long-time FLO, Angie Bolton (2017), authored 50 Finds from Warwickshire, Objects from the Portable Antiquities Scheme, and the list of publications depending on the PAS and detectorists is long indeed. So here we have an excellent example of archaeologists totally dedicated to obtaining a livelihood from the study and publication of heritage and cultural artefacts rescued from topsoil and plough soils 96.39 percent by metal detectorists and 0.03 percent by archaeologists and 1.29 percent by, as described by archaeology academia, a group of the populous called members of the public. The very same who gave the impression in this article that if metal detecting was deemed illegal, there would be a certain contentment, but Pearce and Worrell (2015, p. 26) do kindly include a reference to a programme of metal detecting that revealed a high density of Roman occupation; all very good, but their reference to Brindle (2014), who informs us that this was *in an area where extensive fieldwork was unlikely to be undertaken*. This not only discounts the arguments against metal detecting by Pearce and Worrell (2015) but also highlights the glaring fact that the few words by Brindle (2014) could easily refer to the locations of the vast majority of metal-detectorist activities that take place in the far reaches of rural tranquillity. On a number of occasions, the word 'exploit' was used in reference to metal-detecting finds, but not in a manner that would be indicative of metal detectorists exploiting our cultural heritage, but on the contrary. Pearce and Worrell (2015) state an eagerness to 'exploit' the metal finds recorded by metal detectorists on the PAS databases for archaeological research and material used in their own publications alongside hundreds of other archaeologists. Now that, I agree, is exploitation by archaeologists, with a conclusion that could be conceived, in fact, as a substantial gain of information. I did attempt to provide statistics for the number of books, journals and articles that would not otherwise be available if it were not for the efforts of metal detectorists and their reported finds, but the task proved to be, if not impossible, then improbable for a sole researcher when my figures ran into tens of thousands. This in turn raised yet another extremely important avenue of legitimate argument and the fact that those many thousands of published research papers, reference books, pending theses and dissertations involving historical and cultural artefacts recovered by metal detectorists and recorded on the PAS: Who has benefited from the efforts of metal detectorists, financially or otherwise, and have these gains been ploughed back into the hobby by the beneficiaries of the efforts of metal detectorists? Or have we been missing the reports of backing, gifts, and support for the metal-detecting community? PAS does acknowledge that among others, the database was used in 422 research projects, 15 large research projects and no less than 87 PhDs. The problem is that there are hundreds of thousands of finds from archaeological sites, both commercial and otherwise, that do not record artefacts on the PAS databases, and as we have seen in Figure 4 (this publication), only 0.03 percent are listed as reported by archaeologists, and that figure is not broken down into categories that state whether the finds were found by amateur, professional, educational establishment, academia or commercial archaeologists. There are of course thousands of volumes covering excavations over many years, but research of artefacts is confined to the accessibility of said volumes, which unfortunately are spread far and wide and the good majority are not even available and out of print. An example is from my own small library, a large volume by Michael Fulford and Jane Timby (2000) covering excavations of Late Iron Age and Roman Silchester, which has not been recorded on the PAS databases; because of this, statistics for many categories and types of artefacts, not just metallic finds, are surely more than a little unreliable because archaeologists are not recording finds on one of the largest small finds databases in the country, *id est* PAS. This one volume by Fulford and Timby (2000) amounts to more than 600 pages, mostly covering thousands of artefacts that include metal artefacts (Fulford and Timby (2000, pp. 322–79)), describing page after page of Iron Age and Roman brooches; this is just one of many thousands of printed works that have not been taken into consideration in the statistical analysis of not just Pearce and Worrell (2015), but many others who have predominantly relied on PAS databases. But the alternative would involve an almost impossible feat of research; research that in itself would span thousands of publications and even more archaeological, commercial, or otherwise, reports that are out of reach of not only the public but also archaeologists and private researchers alike. A paper presented at the annual Theoretical Roman Archaeological Conference [TRAC] held in Amsterdam, by archaeologist Tom Brindle (2009), offered an insight into the archaeologist's point of view when referring to metal detectorists portraying a version of the assumed thoughts of professional archaeologists in reference to metal detectorists. The very first word of the title of the paper is a term that, for many years, has been used almost with a derogatory emphasis. That word is 'amateur': *Amateur Metal Detector Finds and Romano British Settlement*. 'Metal detectorist', etc. would have been a little more accurate and a lot less antagonistic. What could be easily mentioned is that the title refers to possibly a home-made metal detector and not the operative of such; the same would be if someone wrote about a trowel or spade instead of an archaeologist. On the PAS databases the term metal detector is used but not to indicate a group membership, *id est* metal detectorists, but refers to the actual method of finds discovery, hence the PAS does not use the term 'amateur'. 'Amateur' has been discussed previously and one does not need a degree to be given a title of a professional, as skill, knowledge, operational ability and going about business in a professional manner and the membership of a governing body are suffice. That subject has been discussed earlier, but Brindle (2009) has taken, with seemingly deliberate forethought, to both use of the term and avoided even a reference to a detectorist, although Brindle (2009) mentions detector or detecting forty-seven times and the word detectorist appears but once with a telling breakdown that is worthy of a mention, just as a clarification of a possible concerted attempt to deny the existence of live and active detectorists by persistent references to an inanimate object. An object that obviously possesses cognitive behavioural tendencies and a piece of equipment that enjoys the ability to be, not exactly hermaphroditic, in so much that it can be both amateur and non-amateur at whim; see Brindle (2009, pp. 53–72) and Figure 7 below. This reminds me of the many times when occupation crept into light conversation and when archaeologist is mentioned, the retort of 'Ah, a fossil hunter', which is quite understandable if someone is not a practitioner of a certain occupation or hobby. A good example being, a metal detector is a technical machine, the operator is called a metal detectorist, or we will be reading about amateur stirrup user, amateur jockey, amateur trowel user, amateur archaeologist, amateur anvil user, amateur blacksmith. The best instance that I frequently give to the thousands of archaeologists that insist on describing metal detectorists as amateurs is that, if the archaeologist is a motorist and drives any sort of a vehicle, the driver, even after forty years behind the wheel, could be classed presumably as an experienced driver, but they are still classed as an amateur motorist, unless of course the archaeologist in question or anyone else for that matter holds an official Driver Qualification Card [DQC].

Amateur, used as a negative term of status for Metal Detectorists

Epithet	Terminology used in text	No. of entries
Amateur	Metal Detector User	2
Amateur	Metal Detector	1
Amateur	Metal Detector Data	7
Amateur	Metal Detector Finds	6
None stated	Metal Detector User	10
None stated	Metal Detector	2
None stated	Metal Detector Data	2
None stated	Metal Detector Finds	8
None stated	Metal Detecting Data	1
None stated	Metal Detecting	8
None stated	Metal Detectorist	1

Figure 7. Used by Brindle (2009, pp. 53–72) of amateur and none-amateur inference as a descriptive for a metal detectorist

So, with a presumption that calling non-professional vehicle drivers 'amateurs' would not go down lightly, I suggest a little thought is required before labelling someone as an amateur. On occasion, there appears to be a noticeable bemusement by the once hallowed profession, archaeology, governed by an apparent elitist attitude to their own importance, a profession that has and is diversifying with a realisation that their structure is geared towards and often dictated by the construction and development industries. Gone are the days of the respected pioneers who have filled the museums of the world with now reclaimable, cultural belongings; gone are the days of the Carters, Pitt-Rivers and a long list of the 'old school' antiquarians, archaeologists and Indiana Jones's, whose exploits were welcomed possibly by the academics and persons of higher social positions than the average current-day metal detectorists. After unsuccessful attempts (Suzie Thomas (2009)) to discredit, ban or rule what is now a thriving portal between artefact rescue and increased knowledge (see also pages 104–06), this publication, which has been and still is the result of the work of experienced metal detectorists, and a recovery method resulting in artefact rescue and increased knowledge; knowledge that has been and is freely accepted by the world of archaeology. The last vestiges attempting to secure and govern a hobby as a means of either growth, stability or importance, which has led to, I am not afraid to point out, glaring signs of a concerted effort to encompass and therefore control, govern and take the credit for millions of new artefacts recovered by metal detectorists. This appears to emanate from an influential nucleus with tendrils attached to both academia and the media, managing a determined effort to reach what appears to be a long-time goal, a goal that may well backfire and harm an honoured institution. A mention of one of the many academic achievements that would not have been possible without metal detectors, their operators and the apparent unmentionable metal detectorists and their finds. The study that springs to mind is again by John Naylor (2007), who, with a background in archaeology, carried out post-doctoral research between 2004 and 2007 with the Viking and Anglo-Saxon landscape and economy project alongside Professor Julian Richards, by analysing landscape through metal-detecting finds. Small finds recorded on PAS databases by an archaeologist amounted to 0.03 percent of the total, so why the constant reference to *archaeological* objects again? Why not use doctrine-neutral Historic Artefacts, Small Finds, Heritage Finds or even Detector Finds? Finds are what they are and nothing to do with archaeology, unless recovered during an archaeological process, and metal detectorists are not archaeologists, nor wish to be. Only archaeological academia, commercial archaeology, research archaeology and community archaeology do not wish to record their finds with the PAS and only they can explain why. One wonders where their finds are, where are their descriptions and databases; not all in museum storage as there has been an extreme shortage of storage space for many a year. That missing information would undoubtedly, if available, alter a number of research studies and the knowledge to the public as a whole. All the 1.5 million detectorist finds on the PAS are freely available to archaeological academia, and numerous books and resulting royalties have been from the outcome of the labours of the humble metal detectorist. This in turn suggests, does it not, that the publications that have relied on the data obtained only from the PAS and/or UKDFD databases without the information of finds from hundreds of thousands of commercial, academic, and research-based archaeological excavations, are at the very least misleading and incomplete from an overall holistic point of view. Maybe archaeology as a whole does not wish, for whatever reason, to use the services and skills of not only metal detectorists but also the actual metal detector, as a tool, because maybe it cannot match the stupendous efforts of the metal-detecting fraternity. Or is it that the PAS as a voluntary service, which happens to be backed by an archaeology-based establishment, is not geared, nor has been from the outset, towards the not compulsory entries; so where o' where are all the archaeologists' small finds, which would form part of the knowledge and information of our heritage and culture? One glaring question is who from the world of archaeology decided not to use the excellent recording system of the PAS? One can only hope that the answer is not that metal-detectorist finds of treasure, national importance and historical interest perhaps outnumber those of the archaeological fraternity. If that is the case, it is worth pointing out that this is not a competition and the outcome would in no way be an embarrassment, but it may well be the case if information is not freely available to the populous of the land. There must be a mountainous pile of reports, both pending and written, denied to the scrutinising and eager eyes of the public, metal detectorists and their peer archaeologists. There are of course plenty of excellent and monumental reports from dedicated archaeological trusts and larger societies, such as the 600-page report of the excavations of the Roman Forum-Basilica, Silchester, 1977, 1980–86 by Michael Fulford and Jane Timby (2000). Significantly, these Silchester excavations were financially backed by Hampshire County Council along with funding from several other institutions, including support by English Heritage for publication and 'generous' support from the Roman Research Trust. The multiple volumes emanating from excavations in Colchester between the early 1970s and late 1980s, each volume referring to a different finds category, including Report 2, which specifically covered the admirably illustrated small finds (Nina Crummy, 1983). It must be a nightmare, or has been in the past, for members of the archaeological community who attempt or have attempted to study particular artefacts by assimilating archaeological research excavation reports from across the UK, let alone attempting a thesis with the subject being small finds from commercial archaeological excavations. So, thank goodness for the databases of the PAS, which in itself is constructed predominantly from metal-detectorist voluntarily records finds. As Robbins (2014, in Lewis 2016, 131) confirms with a short comment: '*Invariably finders in most cases…detectorists.*' It is truly encouraging that knowledge gained by hundreds of thousands of portable antiquities located and saved from the ravages of agricultural activity, constant weather variations and corrosion (natural and manufactured) by the stupendous efforts of metal detectorists has been an open pathway for study by others.

1.7 CBA Archaeological Reports 2007, 2008, 2010, 2012, 2013 and 2019

To ascertain not only if archaeology (as a whole) is using the resource of metal detectorists and to what extent but also if the use of a metal detectorist was respectfully acknowledged in reports, I delved into the archives of concise reports submitted by archaeologists from various regions of the Council for British Archaeology, and not only give examples of said reports but in some cases, unfortunately almost like Sherlock Holmes, read between the lines. I studied some 886 reports covering the Council for British Archaeology volumes 50, 51 and 52 of West Midlands Archaeology [WMA] (Sheena Payne-Lunn (2007, 2008 and 2010)) and more than 1,100 reports from CBA volumes 42, 43 and 49 of South Midlands Archaeology [SMA] (Barry Horne (2012, 2013) and Nick Crank (2019)), with the intent of identifying and recording both metal-detectorist usage and obvious missed opportunities for metal-detector use within the archaeological reports. The entries themselves are not full reports but roundups of archaeological activity within the catchment counties of the West Midlands, which are listed as: Herefordshire, Shropshire, Staffordshire, Warwickshire, West Midlands, and Worcestershire. WMA request a six-figure national grid reference, but the majority of the reports were submitted with a more detailed eight-figure grid reference. The SMA publication covers a different geographical location and offers archaeological reports from the counties of: Bedfordshire, Buckinghamshire, Northamptonshire, and Oxfordshire, but unlike WMA the SMA does not stipulate nor request the size of grid reference but merely offers an example that gives an eight-figure national grid reference. The majority of references in both SMA volumes 2012 and 2013 record eight-figures, while a few have cautiously given six and the minority have generously supplied ten.

Of course, not all the archaeological activity would even benefit from a detectorist's involvement, such as investigation of pre-metal manufacturing cultures or building recording and building assessment assignments. From a total of near 2,000 reports by contributors, only thirteen admitted to the fact of involving the use of metal detectors either by archaeologist or dedicated metal detectorists during any part of an assessment either pre- or post-excavation. The term 'admitted' has been used because a handful did use, to my knowledge, metal-detectorist assistance but with no acknowledgement, and two or three more contributors possibly did use metal detectors only by the sheer amount of metal finds that came forth by excavation. On other sites, considering that topsoil would have been removed by most, before archaeologists would have even bent their knees, and with some excavations showing large numbers of metal finds being recovered, presumably, by the trowel, a metal detectorist should have been called in, as a matter of principle, to assist in recovery; it leaves one wondering what the topsoil and resulting spoil held *in situ* never to be recorded.

There are, among these reports, a great diversity of periods, site sizes, and archaeological methodologies, which in turn are governed in part by excavation objectives, all of which must be given due consideration. With the knowledge that there may or may not have been limited timescales or financial restraints in place, which none of the reports provide information of, I can only supply information gleaned from the articles and enlighten the reader to some possible thought-provoking scenarios. There are mentions, possibly from desktop assessments, that on or near particular sites, that, in the past, a metal artefact had been found by a detectorist, the information invariably would come from researching the PAS databases, which gives in turn a welcome clue to what may or may not be an expectation of artefact occurrence during any archaeological interventions.

There are several types of archaeological categories and terms used in the process of reporting that, when used in combination with information of the investigation type, highlight any possible need for the assistance of a metal detectorist, the non-disclosure of the use of a metal detector, or apparent inappropriate use of said equipment. Very useful during the assessment of the CBA Archaeological Reports [1.7]; the main categories are listed below.

Building assessment, is used to provide a more detailed and up-to-date history and condition of any building or complex.

Building recording, this takes place when a building is to undergo either alterations or to be demolished, and the recording procedure is often accomplished before any planning application is applied for. The Historic

England's Guide to Good Recording Practice, prepared by Rebecca Lane (2016), thoroughly explains these procedures and the relevant four levels of the recording process; the number of levels that can be accomplished depends on the level of detail required and can exceed the information required in level four, so this process offers a certain amount of fluidity.

Desk-based archaeology, research into what is actually known about a site before any proposed alterations or additions and their threat to any existing archaeology without the involvement of fieldwork.

Desk-based assessments, provide information of any previously known archaeological evidence for activity, which usually involves an investigation of information in the vicinity.

Evaluation trenching, usually used to quickly evaluate larger sites to ascertain the level of archaeology and plan more detailed excavation if required. These trenches are dug by machine and only on rare occasions by hand, and cover a predetermined percentage and can cover up to 5 percent of the total site.

Geophysical survey, this gives a quick and efficient record of underlying archaeological features and structures from which any invasive excavations can be planned with a degree of precision. To note, there have been discussions, back-stage as it were, to place metal detectorists in this category if archaeology does succeed with an ambitious programme of control and command; corralling metal detecting and detectorists into their hold.

Historic building appraisal, provides archaeological, architectural, and historical influence that as a whole would provide information to identify anything that could limit any planning proposals in respect of any alteration or reuse.

Metal detecting survey, on archaeological research-led investigations this method of artefact detection delivers quick results from large and small areas alike before and after topsoil removal, and also during excavation, to highlight metallic finds spots and before the artefacts reach spoil heap status. Methodology has over the years changed from searching spoil heaps to full and detailed investigative techniques; discussed in a later chapter.

On commercial sites metal detecting usually mimics the trial-trenching procedure by searching a number of predetermined areas that are set out as gridded transepts, which mirrors the sometimes hit-and-miss approach of trial trenching. A more logical approach would be to conduct a full topsoil-detecting survey. On research and commercial sites, I usually cover a minimum of four acres per day, encompassing a full survey inclusive of finds recovery and bagging; methodology of this process is discussed later, then the small finds are, on an archaeological site, transferred to the finds department for finds recording and research.

Strip-map-sample, a method of excavation favoured when a site covers a large area and is considered by some archaeological contractors to be the most cost-effective procedure. Stripping is the removal of topsoil, usually by a mechanical digger in conjunction, hopefully, with an archaeologist performing a watching brief, and any archaeological features or remains are then subjected to the mapping processes by being photographed, drawn, and described. In some cases, other layers are removed by machine to reach the levels of suspected archaeology.

Topographic survey, this involves recording details of the 'lay of the land' and any natural features including contours, water courses and trees, along with any manufactured features such as ditches, mounds, structures of any sort including boundary structures.

Watching briefs, are carried out by an archaeologist when work of a non-archaeological nature is carried out with the intent to monitor and record any archaeology that comes to light and recommend more detailed archaeological investigation if and when required. Although the odd find may be spotted during this process, primarily the objective of a watching brief is to identify archaeological features and recommend appropriate action.

Some of the larger sites under investigation include a possible hillfort near the small village of Hope-Under-Dinmore in the county of Herefordshire, which took place in 2009. The site, covering forty-two acres, was subjected to a geophysical survey followed by insertion of a number of trenches, but no artefacts were found to date the possible hillfort and its status was left as uncertain (Dorling, P., Pryor, FM., Ray, K. (2010, pp. 9–10)). This could have been a case of missed opportunity, especially when maybe the information required was datable evidence and there was no provision to include any metal-detection surveys.

An educational-led excavation near Ludlow, Shropshire, organised by two school governors with the help of a local landowner for the benefit of 9–11 year old children under the guidance of a professional archaeologist and an area FLO. Surveys were carried out by a geophysics team and a comprehensive survey by local metal detectorists (Buckard, J. (2010, pp. 20–22)). The results from the detector survey answered the main research question, which concerned the name of the field, '*Horsehides Field*', as quite a large assortment of harness and cart fittings became known along with a varied spread of horse and ox shoes; the earliest dated to the thirteenth century. All of this would not have been recovered without the valued help of the team of metal detectorists.

An archaeological evaluation in Nuneaton, Warwickshire before development involved nine excavation trenches, which resulted in evidence of Roman activity by way of a gully and ceramic sherds (Richards, G. (2010, pp. 53–54)) but no mention of either metal finds or using a metal detector, even on the spoil heaps from the nine trenches dug during archaeological investigation.

On a large site of the former Peugeot factory at Ryton-On-Dunsmore, the practice of strip, map and search was implemented, which uncovered one area containing evidence of an Iron-Age settlement and enclosures, complete with round house, and in another area Roman pottery from the third to the fourth century (Mason, P. (2010, pp. 57–58)). Unfortunately, there is no mention of any metal artefacts found, nor an explanation of why metal detectors were not used on a development site that clearly accommodated notable remains, all of which were crying out for a detector survey.

A similar site, in historic content, was found during preparation for road construction works near the Longbridge bypass, Sherbourne in Warwickshire. The excavations conducted by Cotswold Archaeology (2010, pp. 58–59) revealed evidence of late Iron-Age and Roman occupation, including two Roman inhumations identified as third to fourth century and a possible double-ditched enclosure. The M40 junction 15 construction site covered 27ha of farmland with the knowledge that Late Iron-Age and Roman were in evidence, but there is no mention of any involvement of metal detectorists as an aid to date or identify cultural activity.

Works before a housing development on a site adjacent to a Romano-British settlement at Leintwardine, Herefordshire involved excavating six trenches covering 116 square metres. According to the report (Arnold (2008, p. 18)), it is likely that significant archaeology survives on this site but artefactual dating evidence was lacking. This is an excellent example where we see that no artefacts suitable for dating are available when a metal detectorist could have offered a viable solution.

An evaluation of a large site, which may contain evidence of a section of one of the main Roman roads, known as Icknield Street in Perry Barr, Birmingham, incorporating a total of seven 50m trenches. Expectations of locating historic remains labelled this excavation as possessing high archaeological potential and a number of ditches were located, but as Burrows (2008, pp. 104–05) states unfortunately could not be dated. Another possible missed opportunity by not employing the use of a metal detectorists to maybe locate something dateable.

A desktop assessment with a walk-over survey was planned for a pre-development proposal near Little Comberton, Worcestershire. A number of cropmarks were noted along with a possible double-ditched Roman enclosure, and the planned walk-over survey produced, as pointed out by Napthan, M. (2008, pp. 128–29), no artefacts. Interesting that the term artefact was used in the context of an archaeological walk-over exercise as manufactured objects such as tools, jewellery and sculptures would be more commonly associated within the category of artefact and are the mainstay of museums and showcases. An archaeologically conducted walk-over would be more of a search and record exercise involving anomalies in the landscape, humps, bumps, hollows, and platforms, so in this case no anomalies of significance were noted. However, there may or may not have been artefacts underfoot waiting to be discovered by other means.

A metal-detector survey covering land for construction of a new road junction near Warwick, Warwickshire, resulted in six finds of the seventeenth to nineteenth century being recorded (Gethin, B. (2008, p. 81)). Although the results were far from outstanding in the world of artefacts, it conveys the use of all resources available to reach a satisfactory outcome, enabling the construction works to continue with confidence.

An archaeological project in conjunction with a housing development in Rose Hill, Worcestershire required a metal-detector survey before any groundworks and was followed by a planned watching brief; over a period between 2007 and 2008 there were a number of occasions where, as suggested by Napthan, M. (2008, p. 144), perhaps the content appears to be more informative rather than in quantity.

Before a building construction project near Little Kineton, Warwickshire, with the possibility that it may be within the boundaries of the 1644 English civil war battle. So, as Gethin, B. (2007, p. 78) explains, this project warranted a metal-detecting survey, which recovered twenty-four artefacts dating between the seventeenth and twentieth centuries but recovered only a musket ball, which could possibly be related to the battle site.

A similar exercise of metal detecting was conducted before the construction of a new road junction on Banbury Road, Warwick, Warwickshire with a positive outcome by recovering sixteen metal artefacts dating from the seventeenth to nineteenth centuries. The detector survey was, according to Gethin, B. (2010, p. 61), duly followed by topsoil stripping, but no mention of further metal detecting either post-stripping or even detection carried out upon the obviously forthcoming large amounts of spoil.

An archaeological evaluation before a housing construction project revealed '*significant*' archaeological remains covering multi-periods with numerous pits, ditches of which, according to Mann, A. and Vaughan, T (2008, pp. 9–11), the majority remain, at present, undated. They go on to add that there is a lack of pottery and cultural remains. This I have included as a prime example of the importance of employing metal-detecting machines as standard practice as an essential tool that should, quite rightly, be a part of the archaeological arsenal of available equipment and maybe answer a few questions, which would in turn embellish any report.

There are still a number of Roman villa complexes that benefit from a revisit or two and one of these was Yewden Villa near Hambleden, Buckinghamshire. During 2008 and 2011, Chiltern Archaeology examined the surrounding area by a number of different approaches such as geophysics, field-walking, and metal detecting, all of which enhanced the existing knowledge of the villa complex. The benefits of entertaining diverse methods are a wider range and type of information gleaned by their use. Among other things (Eyers, J, (2012, pp. 13–14)) it initiated a reassessment of finds from previous years.

The evaluation near Fleet Marston, Buckinghamshire by Oxford Archaeology, where excavation techniques were coupled with two phases of controlled metal-detecting surveys. As Watkeys, D. (2012, p. 21) elucidates, dateable finds added greatly to the site knowledge with the recovery of metal artefacts covering later Romano-British, Saxon, and Medieval periods, which complemented the excavation ceramic finds. The results are a credit to the use of any methodology and technological innovation, by archaeologists, historians and developers that may answer questions posed.

An archaeological evaluation as a prelude to construction in Sandy, Bedfordshire during three consecutive days in 2010 and four consecutive days in 2011. Hogg, I. and Edwards, C. (2012, p. 3) suggest that the evaluation apparently lived up to its name when natural sand was found in all trenches. Why this is mentioned in this study is that the evaluation comprised nineteen archaeological trenches, all machine excavated, and not one mention of any topsoil search, topsoil management or even spoil heap searching, especially when a possible Iron Age ditch along with three Roman-period burials and further ditches were recorded within some trenches. These excavations continued in 2012 when Edwards, C. (2013, p. 12) mentions the discovery of further evidence of Iron-Age and Roman occupation, including a possible kiln and a nearby extended Roman cemetery with a total of twenty-nine burials recorded. I can only conclude that maybe in foresight the use of a metal-detector survey, pre- and post-excavation, during the previous years could have been of benefit to the knowledge database.

Planned open area excavation of 1.8ha before a pending housing development near Burton Latimer, Northamptonshire by Albion Archaeology showed evidence of human activity from a small selection of Bronze Age flints, but, according to Luke, M. and Phillips, M. (2012, pp. 23–25), the main focus centred around a substantial Romano-British settlement that showed a timespan from the late first to fourth centuries, which also possessed a later Roman cemetery. The main point to raise with this excavation is the rather huge amount of metal finds including bracelets, brooches, rings, various tools, key, knife, nails, weights and apparently near 200 coins. This amount of metal finds does point towards the use of metal detectors, but there is no record in this report at all and again it is hard to believe that the finds were all recovered by the trowel alone. So convinced was I that there may be either a lack of acknowledgement in the involvement of a detectorist or, if that was not the case, with that many finds being uncovered metal detectorists should have been involved at the earliest opportunity. So, either way there were questions to answer. I did manage to locate a copy of Albion Archaeology Monograph No. 4 (Luke, M. and Barker, J. 2019), which went to print some eight years later than the comprehensive report by Luke, M. and Phillips,

M. (2012), and only then do we find clear evidence of the employment of a metal detectorist, under one of the artefact reports, 'Coins', by Peter Green (2019, p. 67). It was the introduction by Cardiff University numismatist Peter Green (2019) that shed more than a beam of light on the suspected situation: '*The excavations produced 191 Roman coins and a single 16th-century copper Jetton. The assemblage is large for a Romano-British rural settlement and the level of recovery, particularly of the small copper-alloy coins typical of the later Roman period, was **undoubtedly enhanced by the presence of an experienced metal-detectorist** on site for much of the fieldwork*'. One would think that after more than forty years of metal detecting alongside archaeologists as unpaid spoil heap lackies, it is about time archaeologist/archaeology comes 'out of the closet' and admits to using the skill banks of this environmentally friendly group of artisans and their magic wands. Why this important inclusion was omitted from the initial report is a question that can only be answered by the archaeologists or maybe their employers, and one can only hope that the experienced, as stated, metal detectorist was employed as a consultant or at the very least a technician.

One of the largest archaeological evaluations found within the five CBA volumes of excavation reports was carried out by Oxford Archaeology East, near Kettering, Northamptonshire when 253 trenches were inserted across 205ha of land. An initial geophysical survey was used as a guide for trench location and the evaluation pinpointed eight areas of Late Iron-Age and Early Roman activity. The substantial amounts of ceramic finds, amounting to 1,354 Roman sherds and 449 later Iron-Age sherds, would suggest an expectation that in or on the favoured eight trenches and their spoil (let alone the other 245 machine-dug trenches and their associated spoil) a little more in the way of cultural evidence if there had been a modern metal detector in the hands of an experienced metal detectorist on hand. There is no mention of metal detectorist use even on the enormous amount of spoil; the only metal finds included in the report were a pre-Conquest copper-alloy brooch and an early Anglo-Saxon iron bell (Gilmour, N. (2013, p. 46)). It is hard to believe and can only conclude that metal detector use was not part of the remit and an opportunity missed by not employing such specialised equipment as an aid to recover cultural activity from both such a large area, targeted trenches, and spoil. But after reading the full archaeological report covering 106 pages (Gilmour, N. (2012)), it becomes both enlightening and informative in so much that in Methodology 2.2 Gilmour's (2012, p. 10) entry (see italics

From research, it is shown that 80 percent of metal finds are recovered from topsoil (see figures 5 and 6). It is of interest that the only stratigraphy from which a metal artefact was recovered was that of subsoil (Gilmour (2013, p. 46)) and not a single mention of any sort of metal-detecting survey of the usually artefactually richer topsoil; but perhaps the final report, which is not available, will be enlightening. There is a realisation that most of the above questions may be left unanswered after a gap of ten years, but it does highlight certain ambiguities.

One of the projects carried out by Northampton Archaeology during 2012 was an excavation on a known late Iron Age transitional Romano-British settlement before development. The excavation found both ample evidence of ceramics and querns, enclosures, 2m-deep ditches, along with possible medieval evidence, but Burke, J. and Walker, C. (2013, p. 37) offer no evidence of the methodology used. No mention of topsoil management, machine or otherwise, nor a metal-detector survey, which on a known site that encompassed both pre- and post-Conquest periods one would have thought essential.

Unfortunately, this was included with no polemical intention, but merely as an example of many reports in the study of CBA regional archaeological reports that are completely lacking any description of methodology, equipment or qualified personnel employed. With the realisation that these are, in the main, an indication of works carried out by 'whom' and 'where', but would and most likely have left both archaeologists and interested parties alike lacking in what was actually involved, or not, and indeed why.

A large Roman settlement in North Oxfordshire that has for many years been part of a community excavation formed by a small group of amateur archaeologists submitted a more detailed annual report than the mostly rudimentary excavation notes. This was more of an interim report rather than an informative description of archaeological technique methodology and purpose, but the article did relay a certain dedication and achievement. We are left with no information of topsoil removal or initial geophysical surveys or any other pre-excavation surveys and assessments of any kind. Let alone why there was no mention of the involvement of metal detectorists or metal detectors as an archaeological aid to activities of amateur archaeologists. It can only be a supposition after Shawyer, E. (2013, p. 59) states: *'there has been a large amount of pottery found across the entire site, along with over 1,000 coins, as well as all the usual metal and bone* below) does admit to the use of a metal detector, but interestingly does not mention a metal detectorist nor type of metal detector used. '*Methodology: 2.2.4 Spoil, exposed surfaces and features were scanned with a metal detector. All metal detected and hand-collected finds were retained for inspection, other than those which were obviously modern*'. The metal finds report (Gilmour, N. (2012, pp. 79–80)) lists two artefacts of note: a late Iron-Age brooch and an Anglo-Saxon period bell; other finds listed are a fragment of Iron-Age sheet metal and evidence of metal working, a couple of later period nails and part of a plough blade, possibly post-medieval. We know that the use of a metal detector was not forthcoming in the CBA (2013) report. I find it inconceivable that in 253 trenches, of which all but one was 50m in length by 2m width, that only six metal finds were recovered and no finds were recorded from topsoil where at least 80 percent of metal-detecting finds are normally located. The spoil heaps themselves must have been in excess of 10,000 cubic metres (with a conservative estimate of 0.5m depth), not counting a topsoil area that must have covered at least 25,000 square metres. So, the questions raised, not by me, but by common sense are:

a) Was the topsoil of all the trenches, or indeed, any trench metal detected before removal of topsoil by the machines?
b) Were the only trenches to be metal detected the eight found to contain archaeology, which was then deemed worth further attention?
c) Were any areas untouched by trenches metal detected to act as a comparison?
d) Was the metal detector operated by an independent metal detectorist or by an employed field archaeologist?
e) What type of metal detector was used?

The associated Catalogue of metal finds by Nina Crummy (2012) does enlighten us with the fact that a Colchester-type Brooch was recovered by a metal detector in the subsoil of Trench 161. Ideally, it would take direct contact with contractors and archaeological units to answer the above questions and involve numerous phone calls and/or emails, and it is not my initial intention to interrogate report contributors but to highlight problematic methodologies and certain recording practices. Either way, there appears to be an extremely large gap in the number of metal finds recovered that could be expected by conducting a full metal-detecting survey.

household artefacts'. The amount of metal artefacts recovered suggests that here, again, have we encountered evidence of non-documented co-operation with metal detectorists, or indeed are the amateur archaeologists making use of the appropriate equipment themselves? It is conceivable that metal detectors were used but not recorded because of possible backlashes from the world of archaeology, which possibly would then call these amateur archaeologists by another title, maybe amateur detectorists, which in turn may fuel the fires of any anti-detectorist supporters. But back on the site it would appear to also be a travesty for archaeology and the archaeologist if this site was not subjected to extensive metal-detecting surveys.

Wessex Archaeology provided one of the last entries in the South Midlands Archaeology and CBA South Midlands Group reports 2013 and evidence for, in any way or form, with either the use, or not, of employment of metal detecting and detectorists. Two evaluation areas were involved, both conducted on behalf of a local county council and involved machine excavation of Area East, which included part of a Deserted Medieval Village [DMV] being fifty-five machine-cut trenches before proposed construction works, and Area West consisted of thirty-two trenches. The trenches were placed, according to Williams, M. and Brennan, N. (2013, pp. 81–82), from the results of both a desk-based exercise and geophysical survey conducted the previous year. To the east, twenty-five trenches exhibited archaeological remains with five of those trenches producing dateable evidence. The thirty-two trenches to the west produced evidence of archaeological remains of various postholes, gullies, pits, and ditches in fifteen trenches, but no datable evidence was found. All excellent methodology, but not a single mention of a metal detectorist on-site even to search the spoil of a total eighty-seven trenches, or even those forty trenches that contained archaeological evidence, or even in the fifteen trenches to the west from which no datable evidence was located. Even when the geophysics supplied evidence that there were remains present, a controlled detector survey before the topsoil was machined away may have provided vital evidence by way of a cultural background as the desktop evaluation had identified the DMV and geophysics recorded signs of habitation and excavation evidence of Neolithic, Bronze-Age, Roman, Medieval, and later periods. The reason this turned into a possible case of ignoring the benefits of metal-detector involvement or maybe the use of a metal detector was not written into any planning application consent. In any case, this study is concerned with highlighting the amount of involvement of metal detectorists working in co-operation with archaeological contractors, county archaeologists, local authorities, and planners. The reason such a minute percentage of metal detectorists are employed in the world of archaeology is a matter solely in the hands of those who work by or govern archaeological principles and practices.

These reports are just a small portion of CBA regional publications involving condensed archaeological reports covering five years from 2007, and as a comparison I have included in this research another 380-plus reports from Crank, N. (ed.) (2019). This is meant to show any progress in the documentary evidence, during an average gap of ten years, of a more congenial acceptance towards the use and acknowledgement of metal detectors and metal detectorists and the obvious documented benefits of a workable workplace ethic.

An interesting evaluation by trial trenching on land near Potton Road, Sandy, Bedfordshire on land suspected of containing evidence of both Iron-Age and Roman occupation. The point that is raised here stems from the information supplied by Leslie, I. and Luke, M. (2019, p. 24), which imparts that three Iron-Age coins were recovered and that apart from numerous ceramic finds, a number of dateable metal objects as well as a total of more than forty coins were recovered. This does suggest that a metal detectorist was used during excavation, but the information is lacking about not only detectorist use but also whether the artefacts came from detected topsoil before excavation or during excavation by trowel or from metal-detected spoil heaps.

Next is an evaluation, before a programme of housing development, involving thirty-one trial trenches near Hanslope, Buckinghamshire, the results of which led to a substantial open-area excavation. A number of mid-to-late Iron-Age features including two roundhouses as well as evidence of medieval land management, and the report by Ingham, D. and Williams, A. (2019, p. 48) includes a photograph of the large area machine-stripped excavation. The points here are that there is a mention in the report of using a metal detector, whether by a bona fide metal detectorist or a field archaeologist is not stated, but several metal artefacts along with a number of silver coins from the Medieval period were recovered from the subsoil by the use of a metal detector. We could presume therefore that the topsoil was, unfortunately, not searched by the detectorist pre-machine stripping, which would also have generated exceptionally large spoil heaps in the process. It was refreshing to see in print a reference to metal detector used on an archaeological site. Of note is that the mention of a metal detector was found in the very last sentence of the report and one wonders if the words metal detector would have been forthcoming if some of the finds did not warrant recording under the Treasure Act.

One of the few excavations to mention the use of metal detectors involved a geophysical evaluation that followed four 50m trenches. The artefactual dating evidence was, as Michaels, T. (2019, p. 74) informs us, limited and along with ceramics there were coins from the Roman period along with some copper alloy artefacts recovered by metal detecting. The latter artefacts were apparently from the subsoil, but alas there is again no indication of where the other datable artefacts were located, *id est* pre-excavation of topsoil, in trenches, and if so were stratified or simply but unfortunately out of context on spoil heaps.

This short report followed the clearance of, as Jones, C. (2019, p. 82) informs us, an area of land that was prepared for development by stripping soils down to natural. It can only be surmised but expected that machines were used for this purpose, but archaeology was located and no dating evidence was recorded, and there is no record of any excavation, so again we can only assume that this exercise was not an excavation but a watching brief, and just maybe a sweep by a metal detector of the exposed ditch and furrows may have given an indication of a date.

One of few service trenches in the reports happened to be across a sensitive area of land within a fifteenth-century Registered Battlefield in Northamptonshire. The observation and investigation recorded by Fisher, I. (2019, p. 83) did not locate any archaeological features, but a much-needed and most likely required metal-detecting survey did recover later metal artefacts from the sixteenth and seventeenth centuries.

Another evaluation on or near a battle site was given the full works with a programme of geophysical survey, fieldwalking, metal detecting and a planned strip, map, and sample excavation, all of which were carried out on agricultural land south of Edgcote, Northamptonshire. The metal-detecting survey was, according to Attfield, B. and Davies, A. (2019, p. 87), performed across ground that may have contained battlefield evidence; the topsoil and surface finds were of later medieval periods and not associated with the earlier battle. Although this evaluation constituted nine open trenches revealing mainly Iron-Age occupation and more than 3,500 square metres of machine stripping, there was no further mention in this report of metal detector use.

Worth a mention is a short, but telling, report by Leon Hunt (2019, p. 92) from exploratory excavations at Mickle Well Park, all of which located no archaeological remains and that no artefacts were recovered from the spoil heaps. Here I believe is another evaluation exercise that probably used metal detectorists, who searched spoil heaps, as one does not usually, as an archaeologist, go searching spoils heaps as artefacts should not reach those heaps and a spoil-heap is out of context and a discard area.

An excavation in readiness for construction in Thame, Oxfordshire identified areas of medieval activity. Pierre-Damien Manisse (2019, p. 137) points out that thirteenth- to sixteenth-century ceramic evidence was identified. A rather interesting mention followed, informing the reader that the coins and metal finds gave a wider date range, *'though most were recovered from the topsoil'* (Manisse, 2019). To recover metal items from topsoil is indicative of an active use of a metal detector, but again there is no mention in the report of such.

A development-led evaluation by the local council in Chalgrove, Oxfordshire was conducted with prior knowledge of Iron-Age, Roman occupation in the vicinity as well as a strong chance of evidence from a Civil War battle nearby. In the report Stone, D. (2019, pp. 107–8) states that a metal-detector survey of the trenches did not locate any evidence associated with the battle. In this instance I would have expected the same results as any or most of the evidence would have still been *in situ* in the topsoil and not in a trench, but then again Stone (2019, p. 108) does not give an indication of how deep the trench was. I can only suggest that the vital top layers (turf, topsoil or plough soil) had been removed in readiness for archaeologists to excavate or it would not have been called a trench.

An extremely large evaluation for Rail Central (2018) surmounting 293 hectares near Milton Malsor, Northamptonshire, involving an eye-watering 733 trenches, mostly 1.8m x 50m, must have generated mountainous amounts of spoil. The results of the evaluation according to Barton, T. (2019, pp. 71–72) identified fifteen sites of archaeological interest covering a variety of periods composed, in the main, of: two medieval, two Iron Age, five Roman sites and a further five Roman sites classed as apparent, likely, appears and two possible. There was no mention of either topsoil management or searching by a metal detectorist, but as we have read, other reports that only mention anything to do with metal detecting in another report are not always easily available. In this case research recovered a copy of the WSI, in which there were a number of interesting pieces of relevant information to this study (Rail Central 2018, pp. 1–14). The first bullet point of the WSI Research Objectives (Rail Central 2018, p. 5) was to investigate the evidence for, among others, pre-Roman, Roman, Saxon, and medieval. Makes one wonder if a dedicated metal detectorist could have solved the 30 percent possible and maybes of the Roman era, *id est* Sites 4, 6, 9, 13, and 14 (Rail Central, 2018, pp. 4–5). Under the title Construction Phase Embedded Mitigation Method Statement (Rail Central 2018, p. 6), we see that Strip, Map and Sample excavation is called for, with all topsoil and overburden being removed by machine, all under supervision of an archaeologist. Technically, 'overburden' when used in an archaeological sense is anything between the surface and the object of interest, so the removal of overburden is an open licence to disregard *in situ* small finds and archaeology that does not concern the subject of that particular search. With the knowledge that the vast majority of dateable finds are in the topsoil and overburden can be a fluid measurement, meaning that this practice is not conducive to the recovery of 'small finds' but excellent at highlighting archaeological features. Under 'Excavation and Recording Strategy' (Rail Central (2018, p. 7)), we find an elusive mention of a metal detector, which was scheduled for use only on either archaeological features before excavation or the spoil heaps that should be routinely scanned as a means to recover (out of context) small finds. There is no mention of the use of a metal detector as an aid to conduct a full survey as significant small finds are found on a daily basis nowhere near archaeological features. It would be a wonderous gift if any archaeologist can honestly determine that there are no small finds in the 90 percent of the site that was not subjected to excavation and the huge areas stripped by the mechanical digger. Now the expected reply that would instantly be on the lips of the developer is probably 'that would cost the earth', so is there a price on our historical heritage that beyond which is unacceptable? It would appear so. Out of interest, if the whole site was surveyed by a metal-detectorist team before the archaeologists arrived and the digging machines started up and an estimate of the cost was forthcoming: this large site of roughly 700 acres at five acres per detectorist per day and a team of five detectorists would take 28 days at a financial outlay of £250 per detectorist each day; a total of £7,000 would be the lowest figure, but a mere drop in the ocean for that particular project: to save our heritage and gain a vast amount of knowledge, respect, and backing for the enterprise.

Comments are not confined to the thirty-two examples singled out to highlight points in question, but an overall discussion would be of benefit to all concerned. The 2,000 individual reports submitted to the various CBA regions involved in this study cover all levels of archaeology, from small amateur groups, community societies, educational research excavations to commercial enterprises large or small, and are varied in style, project, and content. All 2,000 reports were read in full, with the intention of monitoring and documenting the involvement of metal detectorists in archaeological investigations and if there were any indications that both involvement of metal detectorists and procedures had changed over time.

Having no preconceptions, one of the most notable and recurring themes was that on excavations that published the fact that either 'no datable evidence found' or 'no dateable artefacts recovered', especially when one of the main tasks of an excavation is to date the features and stratigraphy, the use of a metal detectorist may have solved the problem. On that point, it was noted that, out of 2,000 archaeological reports, a total of thirteen admitted to either using metal detectors or metal detectorists, which can be broken down a little further: seven reports used metal detectorists for detecting surveys, two used a detectorist in general and the remaining admitted to using a metal detector on-site. The three that admitted to using a 'detector' did not stipulate whether the machine was used by an employed field archaeologist or again a volunteer dedicated metal detectorist. Not one of the thirteen reports mentioned if the detectorists were volunteers or indeed received remuneration of any sort as the majority of the thirteen were commercial sites. This is of course not a question but a point in question, as along with others I have experienced both; small and large development sites that do use metal detectorists quite often come under the advantageous title of 'community involvement', which does look good on paper and goes down well with planning committees. The reports gave an overall impression that both the non-use of metal detectorists and in some cases non-publication of the act of metal detecting had taken place and there appears to be still an issue with admission of either using or employing the use of a skilled detectorist, as if it were a deadly sin or an unmentionable disease. There are a number of others that mentioned things such as nothing was recovered from the spoil or finds were recovered in the topsoil, and just by the type and description of metal finds in the reports they are all indicators of the use of metal detectors and/or metal detectorists. Reading between the lines, one can draw conclusions, such as archaeologists may be either inflicted with 'peer fear' or even a dread of being labelled an archaeological outcast and suffer a backlash of an expected loss in revenue and status if an organisation is seen to employ metal detectorists.

One of the fundamental questions here is how archaeology and archaeologists can, as a whole, request metal detectorists to become a little more diligent with detail in recording and sharing information regarding their finds and techniques of recovery when archaeological institutions, contractors and archaeologically functioning groups fail significantly to do so themselves? That statement is of course backed by the many thousands of reports that are freely accessible to the general public via CBA publications. Metal detectorists have themselves been under threat for decades, notably by constant attempts to either, in the extreme, ban the hobby, pastime or sport altogether, or even more radical and call it an archaeological process, therefore govern the use of a detector and dictate their use and govern activities all in the name of archaeology. Professional field archaeologists are these days mainly employed in the commercial sector, working hand in hand on construction and development programmes, whereas amateur archaeologists work in the main on community-led sites. Often behind the scenes, specialist archaeologists handle a myriad of doctrines involving a bucketful of ologies, sciences and research, and should be commended for their dedication, foresight, and expertise. Many of the aforementioned have benefitted from another, much larger group of dedicated personnel, metal detectorists, who tirelessly rescue our cultural artefacts, adding to our heritage knowledge on a daily basis before those green and pleasant lands, along with the information they hold, are lost for good. Previously I have presented concise information based on solid facts such as 96.39 percent of finds reported to the PAS are by metal detectorists and 0.03 percent by archaeologists. The figures from CBA taken from 2,000 regional archaeological reports show that just 0.65 percent admitted to using either metal detectorists as specialists in their own right or a metal detector as an essential piece of equipment, and to confirm these figures are compiled from information supplied by official archaeological publications.

1.8 The murky world of antiquities collecting and its consequences and repatriation

There are many publications that deal with the trade of ancient antiquities, mostly through international auction sites, and I will highlight the concerns and repercussions for professional archaeologists and archaeological establishments An informative Chapter 5 of a joint effort by Tony Robinson and Mick Aston (2002, pp. 148 – 53), primarily aimed at the archaeology beginner or volunteer, delves into the world of artefact exploitation fuelled by financial investment companies, collectors and museums, whether the artefacts are rare works of art worth tens of millions or a mosaic, tomb contents, treasures from the seas and oceans, or the vaults and exhibits of museums *acquired* from decades of archaeological contributions from abroad. The practice is unfortunately widespread (worldwide) and deep-rooted, and has been the norm for many centuries and decades before any metal detector was invented. This did not only happen in places such as Egypt, Cyprus, Peru, and other artefact-rich countries such as Turkey and the UK did not escape. We need only look at the demise of the magnificent Frampton Mosaic uncovered in 1794 and later sketched by Samuel Lysons (1763–1819), a well-known archaeologist and engraver. Unfortunately, it was apparently stolen or as local tradition (Perring (2003)) destroyed by soldiers on their way to Plymouth mid-nineteenth century – why or how is not stated – or by what were called 'souvenir hunters' now; a couple of hundred years hence, I do wonder where those very portions of the Frampton Mosaic are today. To answer the reference to metal detectorists selling artefacts on the open market, I can only presume that Robinson and Aston (2002) meant 'illegally selling artefacts', and as stated previously we cannot condone any illegal activity by any party. Illegally obtained artefacts, including works of art bought and sold by museums, auction houses, the internet, dealers, or private investors, run into millions, if not billions, of pounds sterling. What is quite clear is that tens of thousands of artefacts from these establishments and institutions have been recovered by the ongoing repatriation programmes; even artefacts excavated by archaeologists taken from their rightful owners (countries) ending up as part of this vast and lucrative trade. Very few, if any, of these artefacts in museums are the result of illegal metal detecting in the UK; not to insinuate that there are no 'illicit' metal-detected artefacts out there, because at times an artefact pops up on certain websites, but they would account for an extremely small percentage. No, this does not make it right, but a balanced argument is offered. When this study warranted research into stolen, looted, and misappropriated artefacts, it appears to be clear that illicit metal detectorists' finds are as rare as hen's teeth and offer a miniscule percentage, as the main culprits appear to be museums, art dealers, looters, state-sanctioned looters, auction houses, unscrupulous officials, and archaeologists. The outcome of research on the subject of questionable acquisition and movement of marketed antiquities would indeed fill a number of volumes and is best left with a minimum of examples with the knowledge that informative information is easily available and the reader is welcome to delve into the scruples, consciences and ethics of institutions, collectors, and dealers worldwide. Addressing the question concerning looting of archaeological sites, Grant, Gorin and Fleming (2008, p. 343) informs the reader that the problem is mostly funded by western collectors and involves the removal and export of artefacts and artwork '*on an industrial scale*' and that it is a growing problem, but does not mention the involvement of metal detectorists in connection with these particularly lucrative, mostly unethical and illicit activities. In the UK there is still an undeniable recurring problem with nighthawkers, which appears to be lessening as time goes by, and Grant, Gorin and Fleming (2008, p. 359) add, '*However most detectorists are not members of criminal gangs*', nor for that matter participate in individual illicit activities, but as with other crimes there will unfortunately be thieves and vagabonds out there. Interesting is the entry under a section covering *Geophysical Survey* (Grant, Gorin and Fleming (2008, p. 8)) that metal detecting was listed under 'Other Methods', but in the latest edition (Grant, Gorin and Fleming (2015, p. 28)) it is again listed but now under the new interpretation of 'Other Non-invasive Methods'. That statement is a little confusing in so much that, yes, a metal detector is indeed totally non-invasive, but the said equipment is used in unison with the operator, who is certainly invasive, while other geophysical equipment is not used to locate and rescue small finds. It is a bit like categorising a spade or trowel as non-invasive archaeological equipment, but it is the expected use of these tools in the hands of a skilled operator that turns the equipment magically into invasive tools of the trade.

There are countries worldwide whose citizens and governments are not just requesting, but demanding that their cultural artefacts and art be returned; most of the items in question were either looted or inappropriately sold and exported abroad. A high proportion of these items are to be found in museums and others in private collections; some have simply disappeared off the radar as it were. An example are the concerted efforts by the citizens of Nepal, as documented by Gibbon (2022), who want their cultural artefacts returned from major museums and art galleries from around the globe and have even constructed a database of objects that have somehow found their way out of Nepal, not all looted but most sold via questionable processes; some of the objects in question have already been returned and others are in the process of being so. There are a number of articles that give a valued professional opinion and an insight into the oft questionable world of antiquities salerooms, such as the well-documented reports on the subject by Dr Alice Stevenson (2014, 16). These two publications by no means stand alone and the objective here is merely to highlight both the licit and illicit sales opportunities, mostly through the auction houses, and the obvious consequences for the archaeological profession. Sales that have seen the transfer of millions of artefacts, the vast majority by way of archaeologists or the archaeological processes. This does not in any way forgive the illicit sales of artefacts recovered by nighthawkers using metal detectors, but a response to the frequent concerns from some archaeologists who would of course be very interested in the findings of Stevenson (2014–16) and a realisation that in the widespread multimillion-dollar trade of artefacts from antiquity, apart from paintings and art, the vast majority of items are emanating from archaeological processes. This gives an overall impression that highlights an apparent natural trait of the human race: avarice and a need to possess things of beauty, curio, and value. It is of interest that Pitt Rivers appears to have held views of that ilk and that archaeology was but an extension of anthropology, but added a methodical approach to recording all types of artefacts, not just the highly prized items of culturally significant attraction. Published online by Stevenson (2016), the work is both informative and enlightening, giving a recognition that this is not a recent phenomenon because for many years various countries have been requesting the return of artefacts that are of cultural significance but are now housed in museums and private collections throughout the world. Artefacts that were removed, collected, excavated, bought, looted, and plundered furtively by grave robbers, archaeologists, tourists, and invading armies, most with a disregard for cultural heritage of the conquered nations. Keepers and collectors of these mostly cultural artefacts are now under extreme pressure by various bodies all with the same goal: to return the objects of cultural heritage to their homelands. There have been instances of conflict even when requests have been agreed, and the final repatriation has encountered conflicting rights and certain domestic laws. Sarah Irving (2013), in a study concerning the restitution of artefacts, points out the difficulties involved regarding the repatriation of four valuable drawings plundered in 1939, three of which were sold to the British Museum [BM] by auctioneers Sotheby's in 1946, and the fourth was bequeathed to the BM in a will, but apparently the BM is governed by section 5 of the British Museum Act (1963) so repatriation is, for now, not available. Again in the UK, an article by Martin Bailey (2021) in the Art Newspaper informs us that the Victoria and Albert Museum [V&A] were obliged in 2021 to return an ancient, more than 4,000-year-old gold ewer to Turkey after it was revealed to have been looted, most likely in the 1980s. The gold ewer was housed and on display in the Gilbert Collection apparently with no supporting export licence, and experts have recently linked it to the illicit antiquities trade. Benin bronzes looted from Abomey Palace by French forces in 1892 have now been returned from France to Nigeria (Porterfield (2021)), some in the Quai Branly Museum Paris, and more than 3,000 of these Benin cultural artefacts can be found in more than thirty other museums worldwide. Others already repatriated, such as the museums of Glasgow, have agreed to return their looted antiquities. Examples of the looted and smuggled artefacts in almost all the museums would fill many volumes and would no doubt cement the recognition that metal detectorists are being treated as the proverbial 'whipping boy'. Concerning objects looted from the palaces of Benin, a number of museums, which includes the British Museum, have formed the 'Benin Dialogue Group'; full details are given by the British Museum (2022). The information available about the Benin Bronzes, of which the British Museum have more than 700 examples, most given as donations from private collections (British Museum (2022)), is that nearly all are the proceeds of looting by British forces and are the subject of repatriation discussions, but one wonders how even a single Benin Bronze will be given back owing to the criteria of the British Museum Act 1963 Section 5; see below. The criteria for repatriation cannot be reached and if a Benin Bronze was repatriated it would also open the doors for repatriation of the Elgin Marbles. These large collections of looted cultural objects are, for a number of museums, a thorn in the proverbial as repatriation issues gather momentum. Another example are the looted spoils in the aftermath of the Battle of Magadala, Ethiopia when in 1868 looted treasures, which took 15 elephants and hundreds of mules, were taken to auction; hundreds of these cultural objects can still be viewed at the V&A London. As Miranda Moore (2020) recounted, Ethiopia has requested their return. The outcome, so far, is that the V&A have agreed to return some of, not all, the artefacts, but only as a loan, and even then only if the Ethiopian government withdraw any claim to ownership; in reply, Ethiopia did decline that offer (Moore (2020)) so the V&A has executed a classic *fait accompli* and in doing so forced somewhat of a stalemate. One of the main causes I believe is the fact that archaeologists have spent many centuries brandishing a free hand both at home and abroad when they unquestionably raped the cultural heritage of whole countries and we as a nation are still paying the price now governments and institutions of the world are with cap-in-hand as it were, and are giving back hundreds of thousands of artefacts. One Benin Bronze that is being returned is the Jesus College example of a bronze cockerel named Okukor (Farrell, C. and Isman, S. 2021). The Parthenon Marbles, or the Elgin Marbles as they are commonly known, is as good an example as we can get, just because it is one of the best-known Greek cultural artefacts known in the UK, and an update from a correspondent in Athens (Graig Simpson (2022, October)) informs us that British MPs have recently flown to Greece for in-depth talks. Of note, the building from which the marbles were removed is the infamous Parthenon, which was one of the first Greek structures to use *Phi* during construction, most likely used two millennia earlier as suggested by Hancock (1995, pp. 336–337)) during construction of the Kings Chamber in Egypt's Great Pyramid. The situation is not as simple as just handing over these 2,500-year-old monumental sculptures because according to Kate Chernitsky (2022, March), the British Museum has its own set of laws that, unless the artefact meets the pre-set principles, which otherwise forbid the return of any artefact, and the Elgin Marbles did not meet the criteria in any of the three categories that would lead to the release of artefacts from the British Museum. The reader could be more than a little bemused by the list of the three criteria, of which only one is required, and all three appear to be set in stone (pardon the pun):

British Museum Act 1963, Section 5 (updated 1 September 1992) refers:

5. *Disposal of Objects.*
(1) *'The Trustees of the British Museum may sell, exchange, give away or otherwise dispose of any object vested in them and comprised in their collection if-*
    (a) the object is a duplicate of another such object, or
    (b) the object appears to the Trustees to have been made not [sic] earlier than the year 1850, and substantially consists of printed matter of which a copy made by photography or a process akin to photography is still held by the Trustees, or
    (c) in the opinion of the Trustees the object is unfit to be retained in the collections of the Museum and can be disposed of without detriment to the interests of students: Provided that where an object has become vested in the Trustees by virtue of a gift or bequest the powers conferred by the subsection shall not be exercisable as respects that object in a manner inconsistent with any condition attached to the gift or bequest.
(2) *The Trustees may destroy or otherwise dispose of any object vested in them and comprised in their collections if satisfied that it has become useless for the purposes of the Museum by reason of damage, physical deterioration by destructive organisms.'*

So, it would appear that back in 1963 someone had a bright idea to provide protection for every artefact in the British museum older than 170 years and as a result to become imprisoned within the museum unless it can fit into one of the three criteria. Given that it is a museum, the vast majority of objects are indeed over that age and even if the object, at one time acquired from the proceeds of looting and theft along with a complete lack of providence and exported from countries without a licence, there is apparently no way that they can be removed: a shrewd piece of legislation that is apparently legally binding. In North America particularly there are repatriation laws that also concentrate on the protection and repatriation of Indigenous inhabitants' artefacts and remains with the North American Graves Protection and Repatriation Act. [NAGPRA] 1990). The US have also taken very seriously the growing repatriation campaigns of ever-increasing intensity that have shaken the world of antiquity collectors including museums around the globe. One particular example is highlighted by Matthews (2021), whose account of the recent surrender of £53 million worth of antiquities by a US billionaire collector who for many years dealt in the questionable acquisition of artefacts from numerous countries, and it would take many volumes to elucidate upon the extent of this inherent problem. It can only be a matter of conjecture when the heritage and culture of any of near a million cultural artefacts that were taken into care by Russian forces when Crimea was invaded in 2014 and now Ukraine, where even the remains of an eighteenth-century prince were spirited away. This invaded country is, unfortunately, at the mercy of the invaders *Victori spolia*, no matter what agreements or international laws are in place. Such as, but definitely not limited to, the loss of an untold number of artefacts and works of art (Franey (2022)). The trials and tribulations of Ukraine were brought to light by a correspondent at Radio Free Europe Radio Frequency [RFERL] Scollon (2021), who informs us that during the invasion of Crimea, Russia placed all the museums under their form of administration and excavated, with earnest, and laid claim to untold golden relics of the Scythian past. This procedure appears to have been followed during the current activities in Ukraine (Gibbon (2022)) as cultural buildings, museums and other institutions are earmarked for possible extinction. One wonders how long it takes before heritage and cultural objects of invaded countries appear on auction lists and internet sites and archaeologists are being recruited to assist in the process; not only unfortunate but also saddening indeed. How many institutions and individuals would be in the queue to obtain them? If the past is any guide, there could be a rather long queue. The article underlines a sordid culture surrounding auction houses and museums, emphasised in an article discussing the ethical dilemma of the trade in artefacts and art (Tharoor (2015)). The connection between trade and the words looting, illicit, illegal and export are unnervingly linked with a market that is worth £100 million a year, and money talks when many listen. Having the daunting realisation that after taking a mere fleeting glimpse into this subject it would fill many volumes, and my intention was to balance the misdemeanours of the tiny percentage of thieves and vagabonds of the metal-detecting fraternity, as a comparison to the devious exploits of the Indiana Joneses, looters, dealers and collectors in the world of the art and culture and the underground networks that are deeply rooted with tendrils reaching most countries around the world.

In the past, archaeologists had no competition, apart from graverobbers and looters, and were the only finders and custodians of heritage and cultural 'small finds', but now they, archaeologists, are playing second fiddle to the metal detectorist with regard to the legal recovery of metal artefacts and in particular the knowledge gained; this must be a bitter pill to swallow and perhaps an obligation has been, and still is for some, a little hard to acknowledge. Archaeology is today predominantly financed, oriented towards and reliant on construction and commercial enterprises who, by legislation, govern the archaeologist's actions and procedures. This in turn has, in part, fuelled the world of archaeology's need, as a profession for someone else to govern, perhaps, to prove their worthiness and that they still have some power over something, and that something could well be 30,000 metal detectorists, but that is only a whimsey; so an alliance and a willingness to understand that detectorists are not competitors and nothing more than contributors to historical knowledge would be better than a conflict and undoubtedly a way forward in this ever-changing modern environment.

Chapter 2

Metal Detecting, In the Beginning

2.1 Metal detecting and detectorists

It may come as a bit of a surprise to readers that the birth or idea of the instrument that could detect metal emanated about 140 years ago after scientists explored the countless possibilities that the discovery of electricity had unleashed. Back in 1269 AD knowledge of loadstones was well known and one Petrus Peregrinus (Britannica 2022) used the stones to align metal to the poles, but the use of loadstones goes well back further in time. No doubt the use of magnetism dates further back than 600 BC when the first documented evidence is found emanating from the Greek philosopher, mathematician, and scientist Thales of Miletus 626–623–548–545 BC (Patricia O'Grady, 2002); although a mystery to early travellers as to the reality of why it worked, they were put to good use, especially among seafarers. A number of factors have contributed to the development of countless machines over the last 400 years, machines that relied upon the many discoveries and inventions emanating from scholars of diverse and varied subjects and backgrounds. The machines in this section are metal detectors, so our focus is on their development and manufacture involving the main components and sciences, and an abridged timeline of some of those learned pioneers of their day. This gives us a fairly narrow field concerning coils, transmitters, receivers, amplifiers, electricity, magnetic currents, an amalgam of eureka moments and several sparks of wisdom. The following, very brief, descriptions are a representative example, with the knowledge that not all the people involved are mentioned and those that are, are primarily to form a timeline of the scientific research culminating with the modern metal detector.

William Gilbert (1544–1603), a physician from the court of Queen Elizabeth I, penned *De Magnete, Magneticisque Corporibus, et de Magno Magnete Tellure,* (1600 AD) during research into the properties of electromagnetic fields, and that publication lay the groundwork for many years to come. Gilbert, who died two years after Queen Elizabeth I, also takes credit for the term electricity (BBC, 2014). In the process, Gilbert developed an instrument called a versorium, which responded to electromagnetic fields; it specifically was the first instrument that could detect the presence of a static electrical charge (National High Magnetic Field Laboratory, 2022), which was not exactly a metal detector but a link in the chain of the development of such.

John Michell (1724–93) made great inroads in experimenting with magnets and introduced a cheap method in the production process. In 1750, Michell published a short book entitled *A Treatise of Artificial Magnets*, which concentrated on the repulsion and attraction of magnets and magnetic fields, and discovered that if you doubled the distance between two magnets the attraction diminished by a factor of four (Famous scientists.org 2018). Michell was one of the first to suggest the theorem of there being black holes; not of course suggesting that a metal detectorist would ever come across such a thing (an empty hole maybe). These works by Michell at Cambridge, Queens College, like those before and after him, all played their part in constructing a solid path leading towards the machines of today.

Hans Christian Orsted (1777–1851), who gained a PhD while studying at University of Copenhagen, notable for an 1820 lecture during which, apparently by accident, a compass needle moved slightly when placed under a live wire. Further investigation by Orsted substantiated that the magnetic field around the live wire was circular; this in turn gave a solid foundation to the later combined works by Faraday and Orsted in developing the galvanometer, and even back then we can see that these scientists were making great leaps in electromagnetic science and the Coil Galvanometer (Orsted, Jelved, Jackson and Wilson, 1998). A galvanometer is a device that measures or detects small electrical currents (Collins English Dictionary, 2014, p. 795) identified by movement of a needle; with appropriate modification it can be converted into an ammeter to measure the currents in the order of an ampere or millimeter or in the range of milliamperes or microammeter to measure microampere current. They have been used as a primary contraption to calculate small quantities of electric current. André-Marie Ampere (1775–1836) and according to Shank, J. B. (2022) named it aptly electromagnetism, giving mathematical expression to Orsted's discovery, named the device after the Italian researcher Luigi Galvani (1737–98), who in 1791 laid down the concept of what would be the galvanoscope as Dibner (2022) suggests in an informative biography.

Henry Cavendish (1731–1810), also a student at Cambridge but at Peterhouse College, followed in part the same footsteps as Michell with regard to using a modified version of Michell's famous equipment associated with the measurement of the weight of the world, as George Wilson (2010) outlines in a selection of Cavendish's papers. Not exactly a subject for archaeologists or metal detectorists, but merely an indication of progression of science as well as highlighting the benefits of communication between persons and institutions reaching towards the same goals. Cavendish investigated the laws governing electrical attraction and repulson and the properties of a variety of materials and their ability to conduct electrical current using some of Michell's apparatus with some modifications. Cavendish was in 1760 duly elected for Royal Society Fellowship (Royal Society, 2022) and most of the scientific papers have been reprinted by Frederick Seitz (2005).

Carl Friedrich Gauss (1777–1855), head of the Geomagnetic Observatory in Göttingen, and Mastin (2020) unfolds the story of a giant in the field of mathematics who made great inroads in the field of magnetism, which had excellent responses from a number of fellow scientists and the basis of many an experiment, leading to the magnetometer, which could be used as a metal detector. These days, miniature versions are used widely in a multitude of devices including mobile phones. Described as a genius, a Titan of science and the most romantic of epitaphs, 'The Prince of Mathematics' (Tent 2006).

Michael Faraday (1791–1867), after becoming an assistant to Sir Humphrey Davy in 1812, went on to invent the first electric motor in 1821 (Welford, 2021), and by 1831 Faraday is able to show that currents could cause interactions between circuits. It was not long at all until he explained his ideas of changing magnetic flux. He devised the 'Faraday cage', a 12-foot cube covered in wire, as a means to investigate electric charge. In the 1840s Faraday shifted interest with intent to discover the nature of magnetism, beginning with the question of why it appeared that only iron and nickel possessed this property (L. Pearce Williams 1965). He sought to prove that it was a property of all matter, known as diamagnetism. As a result of his experiments, Faraday laid the foundations for the field theory of electromagnetism, in that he described the concept of lines of magnetic force.

James Clerk Maxwell (1831–79) Studying at Edinburgh and Cambridge Universities, Maxwell's idea was that each graduate should go straight into a piece of research after a short course of training in measurement. It is hard to comprehend those graduates, most of whom were highly successful mathematics fellows, that they would actually require training unless they were not previously taught or had experience of scientific measurements. An early publication by Smith-Rose (1948) gives an excellent account of the life and times of Maxwell and experiments designed by Maxwell to train his graduates in these, to us, automatic techniques. One of Maxwell's favourites was the 'Kew Magnetometer', a large device abundantly covered in scales, things requiring delicate adjustment, and with a swinging magnet to time. Everyone was 'invited' to measure the earth's field with this device, which played an extremely long-lived role in Cambridge Physics, being still in use half a century later (Moralee, 2022).

William Mitchinson Hicks (1850–1934) was one of the first students to attend the newly opened Cavendish Laboratory at Cambridge in 1873 and later professor at Sheffield. After his battles with the 'Kew Magnetometer', he constructed an electrometer using a newly published design (Hicks (1890)), then embarking on what was presumably the first research project done in the Cavendish Laboratory. Hicks attempted to measure the velocity of the electromagnetic waves that had been predicted in Maxwell's studies of the previous year. Hicks independently invented the *'toroidal function'* (Hicks, 1881, pp. 609–52), which in part helped with other discoveries and continued studies that contributed to the advancement of technologies that accounted towards the production of a myriad of devices from both our past and our modern world. For those who wish to learn more of the exciting and fascinating world of *'toroidal functions'*, it's not as boring as it sounds.

William Thompson (Lord Kelvin) (1827–1907) invented the concept, in 1850, of magnetic permeability and susceptibility (Gray, 1908); the latter is a word that should be familiar to most archaeologists and detectorists alike. Although William Thompson was best known for inventing the Kelvin temperature scale, that was but one of his near seventy patented inventions over his lengthy career. A number of inventions did concern instruments for measuring electricity and magnetism, as Matthew Trainer (2004) points out that Lord Kelvin invented the Mirror Galvanometer; an essential component used in cable signalling. It was in 1866 that Lord Kelvin oversaw the laying of the first transatlantic cable. Lord Kelvin was a significant help to many colleagues and would have been an influential contact of James Maxwell and Michael Faraday.

Alexander Graham Bell (1847–1922) Best remembered for the invention of the telephone, although there is a long running claim that repudiates that fact, which may be, but there can be no denying that Bell was quick off the mark and first to obtain the patent No. 174,465. Another milestone event concerning Bell occurred after an assassination attempt on US President James Abram Garfield (1831–81). A disgruntled voter in the guise of Charles Guiteau (1841–82) fired two shots at the president, one of which struck the spine. As the President lay wounded for three months in the Whitehouse (History.com, Eds. 2009) with the doctors unable to locate any signs of the bullet, Alexander Graham Bell, hearing of the problem, designed a metal detector (most likely the first to be used for medical diagnostics) to detect and locate the offending bullet, but to no avail (Rosen, 2016). The metal detector apparently worked well but the bed had a metal mesh that interfered with the machine, causing static. Unfortunately, President Garfield died two months later from infection and Guiteau was duly executed in 1882. In a report by Bell to the American Association for the Advancement of Science [AAAS] 1882, Bell gave an explanation as to why there were difficulties in locating any bullets as nobody realised that the bed on which Garfield lay dying had a metal frame that could be causing problems with this experimental machine put together hurriedly by Bell and colleague Sumner Tainter (AAAS, 2021). That machine was in fact the first working metal detector, although the scientific principles were known about but not yet fully developed.

Gerhard Fischer (1899–1988) From a background in electronics and development in aircraft radio direction finders in the 1920s, during which Fischer, or Fisher as he was also known, identified that metal objects caused errors in the equipment, leading to the invention of a small portable device that could pick up the signals of metal (Fisher Labs, 2021). In the early 1930s, Fisher Research Labs were commissioned by the United States Navy [USN] to install Fisher's directional finder devices in the airship *USS Macon*, and coupled with the rise in popularity of the portable Metallascope, the company was able to move to new premises (Fisher Labs, 2021). The ability to manufacture this portable metal detector was due to the development programme by Fisher who, according to the sole UK distributor of Fisher detectors, Joan Allen Metal Detectors, was granted the first patent for the portable version, leading to a successful outcome, and by 1931 was selling these portable machines to the public. Fisher at this point was destined to become the world's oldest metal-detector business, beginning the work of Fisher in a garage where, along with a handful of employees, they produced radio directional finder equipment for the aviation industry and almost as a sideline the portable detector named as a Metallascope or M-Scope, forming Fisher Research Labs (Joan Allen, 2021). The name of this detector was shortened using its nickname to the now legendary M-Scope, providing a benchmark for things to come. By the late 1930s, the popularity was growing fast, prompting a move to larger premises still in California when in 1939 Fisher Labs led the way in the development of Geiger counters and radio communication systems. Fisher continued to develop an inimitable electronic range of products and retired in 1967, but the company continued to flourish when in 2006 it was acquired by First Texas Holdings Corporation, finally moving to Texas where it continues to develop a complete range of products, including metal detectors and equipment, under the Fisher name (Fisher Research Labs 2021).

The use of these portable detectors was more than popular with prospectors, but it was also, as it turned out, an essential and lifesaving piece of equipment that during the Second World War [WWII] a new use for them was welcomed. The original designs of the portable metal detector were subjected to modifications by Lieutenant J. S. K. Kosacki, a Polish officer, to take on the task of mine detection, and used by sappers during the North African campaign 1942, which is on display in the National Army Museum [NAM] (1999-07-14-1). This machine was called an M1 Electronic Mine Detector, weighing in at a back-breaking 30lb or 13.6kg but quite adequate for the job in hand. The NAM collection of WWII photographs includes those taken by Major Wilfred Herbert James Military Cross, during training exercises, somewhere in Egypt 1943, with what appears to be the same type of equipment with, maybe, further modifications: a slightly longer and narrower arm. Usually, a mine team would consist of six personnel composed of a detectorist and an assistant, a taper to mark out, a controller and two reserves. During the final phases of WWII, the German army were using a Pioneer metal detector to locate mines during the Battle of the Bulge in the Ardennes Region near the Belgian Luxembourg borders between 16 December 1944 and 25 January 1945; an example of this machine was shown by Crompton (2022). Although a primitive machine, compared to a modern detector, it was a lifesaver in its day and a rarity, and Crompton (2022), a buyer and seller of old military vehicles and equipment, purchased it for €3,000. The technological advances post-WWII enabled machines, which were forever being updated and modified, to develop into and geared towards machines with the purpose of saving literally thousands of lives by recovering unexploded mines laid in their millions during the First and Second World Wars and other conflicts; a practice that continues today in countries across the globe. Both mine detectors and metal detectors improved considerably with models developed primarily for not only the military but also as security devices. As with all mechanical devices they are governed by invention, practicality, necessity design, scientific feasibility, and results. To the military, metal detectors were an immense help during the Iraq and Afghanistan campaigns from 2001–11 as an aid to detect improvised explosive devices [IEDs]; notable is the Handheld Driftway Detector (NAM (2013–11–32–1)), which was designed as a very portable piece of equipment to locate ordnance hidden within walls and other inaccessible, to other types of mine detectors, nooks and crannies. The Driftway detector has the appearance of a ski pole or even a walking stick, but once again it was designed with function in mind as an instrument that has been responsible for many a life saved and the exclusion of countless injuries. A number of distinct types emerged in these latter years of the most recent conflicts, such as the Handheld Horn Detector incorporating a telescopic shaft used to search both ground and walls, which replaced a similar machine, the Vallon Detector. The updated version contained light emitting diode [LED] bar graph displays coupled with audio or vibration responses (NAM (2013–11–30–1)), giving an extra advantage in detecting IEDs, which contain low or little metallic components.

Charles Garrett (1932–2015) Another pioneer of metal-detector development and manufacture displays the full history on an up-to-date comprehensive website (Garrett (2022)). From an early age Garrett had a history of electrical engineering and led a navy electrical department during the Korean War before graduating with a Bachelor of Science [BSc] in electrical engineering. Garrett worked in a number of establishments with teams that designed and developed various equipment associated with space exploration and aircraft technology, which included electronic radar scanning templates and controls and seismograph circuitry, during which time he had to rent commercial metal detectors but found those available unsatisfactory. So, with a solid background working with circuitry and high-level instrumentation, Charles L. Garrett in 1963 retreated to his garage with the aim of designing and building better ground search metal detectors and set up as a business in 1964; the first machine to be marketed was the

Duel Searchcoil Hunter, competing with thirty-five other manufacturers. Realising early on that Garrett as a company had to offer something special to beat the opposition and development was at the fore, in 1968 Garrett became the first to eliminate oscillator and searchcoil drift; that was the turning point, and by 1971 Garrett had moved into new larger premises and produced their first low-cost metal detector with 'The Mini Hunter'. Over the next few years Garrett continued with research and development, which in a world of constantly changing advancements in technological progression was a top priority and still is. We have to thank Garrett and his dedicated team for being able to use adjustable very low frequency [VLF] ground mineral cancellation discriminating instruments. Another breakthrough in the marketing department came when in 1978 we saw a significant increase in the price of gold, which in turn caused a knock-on effect as Garrett sales increased and requests from overseas gathered pace. Within a few years Garrett had become the largest metal-detector manufacturers and had established a network of more than 1,800 distributors worldwide. After being granted the first US patent covering the use of microprocessors in metal detectors, Garrett went on to develop walkthrough and pocket probe metal detectors, which became the norm for large gatherings, starting with the prestigious 1984 Olympic Games and security products to many airports as well as the World Cup venues of the Federation International Football Association [FIFA]. The sad loss of a great man in 2015 and an honourable person who spent literally a lifetime striving for perfection in whatever he was involved with, Charles Garrett leaves a lasting legacy with Garrett metal detectors. Today, Garrett is still a well-respected name and still a well-respected innovative company.

There are of course numerous other manufactures out there that all deserve a mention, but this would need another study. So, for the purposes of this publication, those selected were to show how, in the early years, individuals with an idea and motivation evolved through the years, resulting in marketing their products that have been not only life-changing but also living in the knowledge that their particular machines have given either security or pleasure to millions of people worldwide. The list below showing a representation of metal-detector manufacturers is formidable and to extend information including their histories would not be applicable to this publication, so the listing is more of an example of the many manufacturers with a realisation that between them there are near 200 different metal detectors. The random list giving the reader a glimpse of the said detectors: Aqua Scan Metal Detectors, Bounty Hunter Metal Detectors, J. W. Fishers Metal Detectors, Lorenz Metal Detectors, Garrett Metal Detectors, GPL Metal Detectors, Minelab Metal Detectors, Nokta/Makro Metal Detectors, OKM Metal Detectors, Pirate Metal Detectors, Titan Metal Detectors, Pulse Star 11 Metal Detectors. Quest Metal Detectors, Tesoro Metal Detectors, Treasure Commander Metal Detectors, Whites Metal Detectors and XP Metal Detectors, to name but a few. Two of the longest-serving suppliers of metal detectors, accessories, coupled with excellent customer service and purveyors of information and advice, are Regton's and Crawfords, who both owe their beginnings to an interest in the hobby and an enthusiasm to succeed, and who, between them, boast more than 100 years of experience building both product lines and a reputation to be proud of.

Regton Ltd: The material evidence concerning the historical information of what has turned out to be an adventurous and successful business venture, culminating in Regton Ltd, was kindly sent to the author with good will by Nigel Ingram (2022). More than fifty years ago back in the 1970s, Derek Ingram established 'Treasure Hunting Specialists', having started detecting with very crude home-brewed detectors and eventually using professionally manufactured units made by Whites, Garrett and Candle International, better known as C-Scope; Regton still possess some of the early machines in their private collection. It was in the mid-1970s that Derek's son, Nigel Ingram, started detecting using Garrett Groundhogs, Fieldmaster, C-Scope and Savo (made under license from White's), and a couple of years later in the late 1970s saw Nigel using Garrett Deepseeker models such as Arado. During the 1970s, Derek ventured over to the US entering a few competitions and flying the flag, as it were, and staying with Charles Garrett and family. Derek also invented a handle-shaped design that is now commonly used by most detector manufacturers; this was his design and patent. In more recent years, XP borrowed that design and took it to the next level by incorporating a collapsible middle stem into the handle; that impressed Derek no end and XP patented that particular design. Derek Ingram closed 'Treasure Hunting Specialists' to concentrate on his other business activity connected to the manufacture of tin cans; this information is quickly followed by an apt two-word quote from his son, Nigel: 'Ironic, eh'. A realisation it could be a subtle hint that a tin can, or part thereof, is the bane of many a detectorist. Nigel at the end of the 1970s was working as a technician in an industrial research laboratory, strangely enough using metal detectors to detect non-ferrous ties in reinforced concrete panels, but, as with President Garfield's bed springs, the concrete panels contained reinforcement bars and Nigel found the solution by using small four-inch x three-quarters of an inch [100mm x 19mm] coils. It was while working at the lab that Nigel also started making detectorist spades and trowels for Whites to sell under his new company, 'Regton'. Operating part-time and evenings plus attending the odd rally, it took a further year and a half to before the company became a Limited enterprise and Nigel eventually left the laboratory to start Regton full time, making coil-covers for C-Scopes, Whites, Arado, Garrett, Fieldmaster and Viking. The tools were also selling to other detecting businesses and Regton were also buying used detectors, and came across a new brand called Tesoro, which were new-fangled motion detectors that were not particularly noted for deep signals but easy to use, well made and found small thin targets easily, all of which impressed Nigel. It was in the 1980s that Nigel was to follow in his father's footsteps and visited the US, entering events on the east coast and meetimg some of the Garrett personnel who had met his father years earlier. Nigel was surprised when during one of these events he was invited to Texas to visit the Garrett factory, an offer he could not refuse. The outcome of that visit was that Nigel returned to Britain as the new Garrett distributor for the UK and Ireland and admitted that he did not see that coming, but recalled that it was probably not a coincidence that Garrett personnel had attended one of the Newbury [UK] rallies, attended by Regton Ltd the year before, as they could have been on a scouting exercise. During the 1990s, Regton Ltd grew. Nigel's sister Lesley and shortly to follow brother Marcus joined the workforce, and coupled with new showrooms Regton Ltd was now a truly family-run business with an intention of creating the best detecting outlet this side of the Atlantic. Selling everything associated with the 'sort', which must have impressed both purchasers and suppliers alike because in the early twenty-first century Regton Ltd was approached by XP in France to take on their then little-known detectors. By 2002, Regton Ltd had, at the last count, thirteen employees and attend, on average, four or five rallies each year where they recreate, as Nigel calls it, *'their shop away from home'*, and in doing so support the many charities involved with detecting groups around the UK. The company, Regton Ltd, as a whole, are proud to be not only Garrett and XP distributors but also work with other brands such as Nokta

Makro, C-Scope and Viking, bringing the best manufacturers' products to their customers.

Crawfords Metal Detectors: Another determined pioneer, enthusiast, entrepreneur, and owner, Craig Allison, who persevered, out of necessity, showing that the survival instinct was strong and focused, and an excellent example of dreams coming true; but hard work plays a role. The main information concerning the history of Crawfords and story so far was conveyed by Allison (2022) via personal communication. Craig Allison, who had his first experience of metal detecting as a child when he and his brother both received a C-Scope TR400, which they happily played with and recovered a few coins and other bits and pieces, but nothing of note. As inquisitive children they broke into the machine to see how it worked and what it was made of, and that was the end of metal detecting for a number of years. However, that experience must have sown the seeds and when Craig purchased his own house, which happened to be in a historic village, getting out into the countryside seemed the obvious thing to do. So, with a C-Scope CS770D, Craig became so hooked that he soon moved on to a Tesoro Toltec 100 and then onto a Whites XLT. By now, Craig was in his mid-twenties and from the age of 16 had worked for the family horticultural engineering business, Crawfords lawn mowers, and as a small business he was required to be very hands-on with all aspects and particularly enjoyed the sales and customer service aspects. There was a problem, though, because of the huge competition from large DIY chain stores, etc. selling competitively priced lawnmowers as no one ever wants to buy a lawnmower, but when someone does, the cheaper the better. This meant wages were low and Craig reached a point where he could no longer afford to work there, but hit upon the idea of starting a side business. *Voilà*, Crawford Metal Detectors was born. Craig's father let him use a corner of the of the showroom and built a counter and display area. It was then a case of talking to manufacturers and importers to stock the little shop, and he found them all extremely helpful and encouraging and it was an exciting time. Interestingly, following a feature that he had read in Treasure Hunter magazine about the Minelab Sovereign, Minelab became the first brand to adorn the display wall, which was soon followed by all the other popular brands of the time. Craig took out small adverts in the appropriate magazines, Treasure Hunter and Searcher, resulting in a steady growth of business. Right from the start, and to this day, there has always been an emphasis on customer service, and an inner belief that this was and still is one of the keys to Crawfords' success story. A business also needs a bit of luck, and a couple of fortunate breaks came Crawfords' way, which helped financially in those early days; number one being a chance meeting with a local manufacturer of material products such as carry bags for sports equipment, etc. Craig quickly saw the potential for the industry and while they were sceptical at first, the business soon had a range of control box covers for popular detectors and various-sized carry bags, etc. Break number two was a friend with an electronics company that built custom headsets for rally cars and with a little adaptation, they were the perfect metal-detector accessory. This procedure was very labour intensive and Craig spent many hours out of normal working hours, but the outcome was that they were very popular and the headsets alone helped to establish Crawfords. By 1998, Craig was looking for new premises. Crawfords Metal Detectors was now Craig's full-time livelihood and new premises were found in an ex-butcher shop and excited all the villagers, who had no idea what was on offer, but the shop served well as most of the business was by mail-order and now with an established marketplace it flourished. Two years later continued growth meant that again there was a need to relocate, both to accommodate the need for extra storage and employ more staff. Over the next decade Crawfords was indeed a household name, albeit within the metal-detecting industry. It was in 2012 that Crawfords' big break appeared when they were approached by Minelab with an offer they could not realistically refuse, giving the option of supplying other dealers in the UK with Minelab products and therefore a chance to build up a dealer network. Their business partnership with Minelab accelerated rapidly after Minelab released their new Equinox series incorporating its new multi-IQ technological innovations. Crawfords today is the result of laying concrete business foundations and the determination and business acumen. Crawfords is now proud to have two stores, along with an impressive warehouse and an ample selection of accessories (Crawfords, 2022). Craig Allison informed me that there are some brilliant things in the pipeline, and although looking forward to the future never forgets the humble beginnings of the few metal detectors hanging on the wall next to the lawnmowers in the 'shed'.

XP Metal Detectors: One of the later manufacturers to come into the metal-detector marketplace was Alain Loubet when along with his brother bought metal detectors, but it was not until sixteen years later in 1997 when Alain decided to improve what was available at the time. A year later during

1998, XP Metal Detectors was born (Loubet, A. cited in Sabisch, A. 2018, p. 6). Since then, according to Leonardo Ciocca (2013), there have been some notable advances with the XP Gold Max and a couple of years down the line the development of wireless headphones. The latter innovation was welcomed with open arms by thousands of detectorists, which had for many years been eagerly wished for. I experienced all too often episodes of entanglement in leads of a pair of headphones, the spectacles flying onto a muddy field, and on one occasion when descending into an ancient hollow way the headphone coil decided to entangle itself around a large bramble, causing me to slip down the proverbial slippery slope, resulting in what I thought was an attack by a demented lion as part of me was clawed mercilessly as I landed into a blackthorn bush; I never did find the lens from my glasses. So, thank you XP for the development of wireless headphones. XP was a latecomer to the metal-detecting scene and the technological advance of XP is indicative of a handpicked team of researchers, which again showed when another prototype reached the market in the form of the XP Deus, which was released in the US and later in the UK, and a detector described as a Porsche of metal detectors and lightweight as well. There will always be a Holy Grail that we strive to find and at the time it was thought that the XP Deus as a detector was it; well, it may have been then but there will always be another.

2.2 Metal detecting and media representation

A newly presented TV programme from Channel 4 and aired on More4 Freeview Channel eighteen at nine pm gives an insight into the world of the metal detectorist, but geared towards the more fortunate who have rescued valuable artefacts classed as treasure. Episode One of *Great British History Hunters*, ably presented and narrated by Emma Slack (2022), brought together ordinary metal detectorists who had been fortunate enough to find something that could not only be classed as a treasure find but also as a notable treasure find. The most notable was the Sun Pendant found by Bob, which was a magnificent Bronze-Age adornment made of 15 percent silver and 80 percent gold, and its sheer state of preservation and artistry made this small artefact stand upon a pedestal when it comes to detector finds. This Sun Pendant was later bought by the British Museum after a bout of hectic bidding for a hammer price of £250,000 and from there this historic artefact was loaned to the Shropshire-based Shrewsbury Museum. Episode Two, aired on 4 May 2022 and again narrated by Emma Slack (2022), follows each of the detectorists in the programme who were singled out for their good fortune in discovering a rare find of treasure and, in most cases, it would be considered a once-in-a-lifetime experience. One statement that gave a rather misleading impression at the beginning of the programme was that every week *'tribes of amateur archaeologists set off to discover archaeology'* Slack (2022). This could be yet another possible attempt to inform and convince the public that metal detecting is a remit of archaeology and archaeologists. Detectorists are neither archaeologists, amateur or otherwise, nor do they wish to be, and nor do they set out to discover archaeology; they [detectorists] are metal detectorists and set out, primarily, to rescue and record historic and heritage artefacts, socialise and enjoy the countryside without the confines, pressures and timescales associated with a commercial work ethic. The programme does give a true to life representation of a well-run local club of metal detectorists appropriately named 'Soil Searchers' in Hampshire, UK and one of hundreds of clubs up and down the country, and the programme focused on Andy, who had spent many years enjoying the hobby, and on this day he was accompanied by his 10-year-old son, Patrick. It was Patrick who uncovered a ribbon of Bronze-Age gold, possibly part of a hair adornment, which was duly recorded with the PAS. The four episodes do concentrate on what are called passionate metal detectorists, which would cover the vast majority of practitioners, but these are the detectorists who, while carrying out their chosen pastime, recovered and saved a significant piece of history from destruction; after all, in the realms of archaeology how many archaeologists find what could be deemed as treasure and become household names such as Howard Carter or Basil Brown? During the last episode, the highlight appears to have been a report on the Chew Valley Hoard (2019, CA, 356) recovered by two detectorists taking part in a detecting rally, and interestingly an opening comment by one of the discoverers was *'it's like fishing, you never know what is going to emerge'*; a truer statement would be hard to come by and having participated in both of these activities, one can only agree. The concentrated hoard turned out to contain 2,528 silver pennies centred around the Norman invasion of 1066 AD containing coins from both the final years of the Saxon rulers ending with Harrold II and the first years of the victor William the Conqueror 1066–86, including unidentified types, mints and offering access to previously unknown historical information. This hoard must have had the medieval numismatists at the British Museum in a state of utter euphoria as well as the group of detectorists, as the initial estimated value was a staggering three to five million pounds; but this is definitely a case of knowledge gained is worth more than the actual monetary value. Although this was by far the most valuable find discussed in the four programs, it does not take away the enthusiasm and dedication of the many thousands of metal detectorists who venture outdoors braving all weathers with a thought that one day it may be me. The series did promote the activity of metal detecting and was in fact a great ambassador for metal detecting as a whole package, encompassing enjoyment, of a healthy, almost therapeutic hobby, coupled with an adrenaline-producing expectation of discovering some long-lost noteworthy artefact. The seemingly never-ending work by the PAS is also brought to light, but what did not make sense was the constant use of metaphors suggesting that the programs were about amateur archaeologists, which was more than a little misleading to the viewing public. A small mention that metal detectorists account for approximately 96 percent of finds handed into the British Museum PAS [see figs 1–4 above] and that the amateur and professional archaeologists' combined contributions are near 0.03 percent would have enlightened the public in an honest and presentable way. A follow-up theme-base series in four episodes was aired weekly on TV Channel 5 between 26 August and 16 September 2022, employing a group of metal detectorists to search a large field with the finds examined on-site by Andrew Agate, one of forty FLOs employed by the PAS under the watchful eye of archaeologist Raksha Dave. The presenters were Michaela Strachan and Dan Walker (2022), and the opening sequence showing many detectorists at work and the narrative from Dan noticeably did not mention metal detectorist but introduced the detectorists as '*history hunters*' (Digging for Treasure S1, Ep1, 2022); but by the close of the programme Dan did use the term detectorist. Even Raksha appears to avoid the metal-detectorist term when introducing Andrew, the PAS representative, as '*people's first port of call*'. It is heartening that the usual term of members of the public was not used but, in this instance, it would be nearer the truth if the term metal detectorists had been forthcoming and would have been more appropriate and acceptable. People is not, nor has been, a category within the British Museum PAS databases (PAS, 2022) and this programme was predominantly about metal detectorists in live action. There was more than a little exuberance and exhilaration displayed as one of the presenters attempted to hype the audience by badgering the FLO for a quick valuation of a gold coin recovered by a detectorist, but Andrew the FLO was quick to point out, quite rightly, that it was not the monetary value of an artefact but the historical and cultural knowledge gained that mattered. Unfortunately, it is probably one of the media's aim to excite an audience and frequent applause for artefact finders was a little over the top and rather embarrassing, when a simple heartfelt thank you for the metal detectorists and the PAS representative would have been suffice. Episode two of Digging for Treasure (2 September 2022) saw a more apt introduction that involved *'fantastic detectorists'* and *'archaeological experts'*; one can live in hope that in the next episode there may be expert detectorists and fantastic archaeologists, or perhaps this was a reminder that any experts in the programme are those within the realms of archaeology. There is little doubt that all the archaeologists were expert in their chosen fields, but equally there were undoubtedly expert metal detectorists who could easily and quite rightly be described as such. During this episode, a very good example of detecting trash or rubbish was shown and that would be absolutely an occurrence that every metal detectorist would encounter every time they detect and would have been enlightening to the viewing public if a mention that, on an average all-metal search, well over 95 percent of finds would fall into the trash and rubbish category. Of course, some fields are more productive than others, but that small piece of information would have been greatly informative and, again, nearer the truth. Even better when, in the end-of-episode summary, the total finds recovered solely by metal detectorists in the field in Scotland was given as sixty and these are what are called recordable finds, and a mention that the metal detectorists would have rescued many hundreds of pieces of metal trash or even the exact number of unrecorded artefacts would have raised an eyebrow or two. There is a mention by eminent archaeologist Raksha Dave that *'all finds were recovered from plough soil, which is unstratified'*, a word used freely in geology meaning not a solid stratified layer of rock or other material, but in archaeology a term used with indifference. Unstratified in archaeology is often interpreted as of little consequence along with the word overburden, both of which are often labels given to something that can be and, most likely is, subjected to removal by machine and in most cases is considered by archaeologists to be nothing more than a barrier leading to 'proper archaeology'. Having for many years treated plough soils as a layer and therefore of archaeological significance, I find it strange that this has not, in the now changing face of archaeology, been fully appreciated. So, the point here is if it is insignificant in the eye of an archaeologist, why is an archaeologist so concerned with metal detectorists saving artefacts that inhabit plough and topsoil? The conclusion I came to many years hence transpired from the definition of the word unstratified, *'not in distinct layers'* (Collins, 2014 p. 2168), and is an antonym of stratified, meaning *'to form or be formed in layers'* (Collins, 2014 p. 1946), and to complete a trio, stratigraphy, which is defined as *'a vertical section through the earth showing relative positions of the human artefacts'* (Collins, 2014 p. 1946). Another name used for plough soil is ploughzone, which was subjected to an in-depth study by archaeologist Anni Byard (2013) in connection with metal detectorists and that does highlight the detectorists' main source of detected artefacts. The description of different types of soil by the Potash Development Association (2016) in connection with field mapping of over-compacted soil layers is enlightening in so much that they are named as layers such as arable layers and plough layers. Now there's a quandary as we have plough soils and presumably topsoil, which are identified as layers, and layers in true archaeological terminology offer stratification in its truest form. Unless the layer above subsoil is not a layer; so is an archaeologist suggesting that the top layer of a field is subsoil? I think not. The third episode of Digging for Treasure (2022) included archaeologists and FLO Helen Geake alongside some members of a local Norfolk metal-detecting group from King's Lynn, which showed a slight deviation from the format of the previous two episodes as there seemed to be a rather concerted effort to encompass the metal-detecting community into the realm of archaeologists by showing a Neolithic axe head found some miles from the field in King's Lynn that detectorists in this episode were searching, and the finds tent where the archaeological experts were situated. Why this was mentioned in association with metal detectorists was a little bewildering, then sherds of a Roman ceramic pot found by a detectorist, not evidentially found during the program, were shown, shortly to be followed by a stone Roman cameo that was also not found in the field in which metal detectorists were working and was again stated to have been found miles away. Then co-presenter Michaela Strachan, lovingly cossetting a small part of a quern stone, stated that it was found by a metal detectorist, and the next item shown was a small piece of cube of tesserae. There is no mention of why these items were presented to the viewing public and actually mentioned as being found by detectorists, who must have been using some magic equipment that detects stone, ceramics, and Neolithic axe heads. So, we can only presume that someone somewhere must have asked if any detectorist had in the past picked up any items that were non-metallic, but why and for what purpose was this concentrated on by the programme presenters? One can only imagine that viewers were asking the same question and a sense of possible ulterior motives prevailed, especially after a rather peculiar statement from resident archaeologist Raksha Dave (2022) when she stated quite categorically *'that metal detectorists find surface finds and do not actually dig under the surface'*. A little misleading, if the statement was in association with the collective presentation of non-metallic finds, which one can only presume was meant to be the case, but why, unless the motive was due to a hidden agenda, categorise metal detectorists as field-walkers and therefore perhaps another attempt to categorise metal detectorists as archaeologists. More confusing was another statement, this time from the very learned, respected, and experienced archaeologist Helen Geake, when explaining the difference between archaeologists and metal detectorists, stating that *'archaeologists dig holes to locate settlements and graves and metal detectorists dig holes to recover lost items'*. So what has happened to the deliberately buried artefacts and multiple hoards, as these artefacts are not losses and metal detectorists have rescued them by the thousands? The final program, Episode Four of Digging for Treasure (September 2022), was full of the now usual hype building of applause and cheers as the programme headed to the banks of the Thames in the heart of London and the amateur archaeologists, aptly named Mudlarkers, scour the tidal riverbanks with Professor Michael Lewis, head of the PAS, in the honorary finds chair. Another rather unfortunate remark by co-presenter Michaela may cause many a bemused smile from the viewing public after introducing the mudlarking procedure as *'metal detecting without a metal detector'* because mudlarking is an eyes-only exercise used to recover artefacts from the mud and shingle and detritus of many thousands of years of a tidal river's jetsam. Sounds like an enjoyable pastime, but nothing at all to do with metal detecting and apparently, according to Robinson and Aston (2002, p.152), of *'no interest whatsoever of the archaeological profession as all finds would be unstratified and out of context and therefore useless'*. It was somewhat of a surprise after the initial programs were broadcast with the appearance of expert archaeologists following the adventures of metal-detecting groups with the intent of uncovering treasures, live, on television. The early episodes were interesting, but one thing a metal detectorist is not capable of is finding treasure to order and this became apparent when artefacts from outside the search areas were brought to the finds tent; artefacts that were found miles away in years gone by. By the fourth episode two hoards from Gloucester were displayed and the largest hoard of coins ever found in the UK was shown, which did not follow the script of the original programme format but made good, exciting television, although the hoards were well-advertised in all media formats; the latter hoard was found more than ten years ago on the Channel Islands of Jersey and at the time, made worldwide news (Morrison, 2013) So, did the programme as a whole run out of steam with a realisation that TV cameras could follow the efforts of detectorists for many, many years before a group uncovers another treasure? In the last programme even fossil hunters were recruited as part of the act of uncovering an assorted array of fossilised plants and creatures, but if the title of the programme Digging for Treasure was to be lived up to, the collecting of fossils is not, nor has been classed as, archaeology, and is in fact palaeontology and did nothing to alleviate the confusion. Or, do we now call fossil hunters amateur and/or professional 'Treasure Seekers' as the title of this series purports, or as previously suggested the cameras did not witness any finds of treasure recovered live, but the series did highlight that finding treasure is indeed a very rare occurrence in the world of a metal detectorist; just like fishing for a record carp or an elusive thirty-pound salmon, and how many anglers out there are just enjoying their hobby and is every single one of them to be classed as an amateur?

2.3 Of contexts, stratigraphy and finds

To address the worries and exasperations of the archaeologist concerning contexts and stratigraphy, the largest contexts by far from which metal detectorists rescue artefacts are plough [cultivated] and top-soils [pasture], and as stated previously in Chapter 1.6 above, which explained that the general practice of the archaeologist before excavation, either by machine or manual methods, was to remove said plough and topsoil before beginning archaeological investigations proper, as suggested by Addyman and Brodie (2002, p. 180). The removal of soils by machine for the archaeologist is in most cases governed by cost-effectiveness, workforce strength and time, all of which are usually a priority of a commercial enterprise. The consequence of this procedure is that artefacts in those contexts classed as plough and topsoil are lost, unrecorded and no longer in their contexts of deposition. Addressing the concerns of metal detectorists who can only stand back with the knowledge that they cannot rescue those artefacts from almost certain destruction, detectorists could recover most artefacts before what could be classed as the wanton rape of the land by the action of machines and the working practices of archaeologists. It is well known that a usual practice by commercial enterprises who have WSIs that include metal-detectorist involvement is to allocate the detectorist to search spoil heaps from which, depending on the size, roughly 10 percent of an average spoil heap can be searched as there is a limit to the depth a metal detector signal can reach. Pre-excavation searches, if carried out at all, are usually limited to test strips and a full search is an extremely rare activity. A metal detectorist is or should be aware that they can recover artefacts up to the depth of plough and topsoil and not interfere with the next layer down, classed as subsoil, so as far as stratigraphy is concerned a metal detectorist only needs to know that as soon as the soil changes colour and density the search boundary has been reached. If a detectorist is required to work alongside professional archaeologists on-site, whether commercial or private excavation, then it became an essential prerequisite that the detectorist has proven extensive knowledge of the archaeological processes and techniques, possibly as a starting point a certificate of archaeology; then the detectorist would possibly be welcomed as a specialist and paid accordingly. If the detectorist is only used for scanning spoil heaps or trial strips of a field pre-excavation, these are in the main, unfortunately, covered by volunteer metal detectorists with little or no gratuity. Finds, their recording and disposal in the detectorist community has been the subject of many an argument over the years; the situation is far from ideal but is improving year on year. A good proportion of detectorists carry out their hobby as individuals detecting their own permissions and therefore the recording of finds cannot be monitored by any outside organisation and based on trust. A little better for clubs and rallies, but both of these are again subject to the commitment, enthusiasm, and willingness to record all of their finds: notable finds on the PAS and all finds on the detectorist's personal database. There could be an opportunity for more precise instructions/guidelines as to what, where, why, how, and where recording and record keeping should take place. Different categories of finds require more details than others and types are not quite endless but can become a daunting but necessary task to record all finds, trash, as all modern trash or rubbish is tomorrow's history that a detectorist throws away. There are moral issues at stake that accompany the sport/hobby of metal detecting, which requires that certain procedures are followed not only to show that historic and heritage information is documented and accessible but also handled in a professional manner. That is the very least detectorists could do, and the correct collection of information would indeed be indicative of an avid interest in the historical information and the knowledge saved and the information sent to a central point similar to the PAS but only dealing with the documented evidence. This documentary information could be handled by any suitable metal-detecting representative organisation, where the benefits of research could lead to numerous publications that do not fill the coffers of non-metal-detecting personnel. In contrast, commercial archaeologists destroy the levels that produce detectorists' finds and archaeologists selectively record artefacts using sampling methodology and in most cases the documented information is not freely available, if at all, and disposal methods of all finds is not well documented, if at all, but more important finds may filter through to museums if of interest. On archaeological sites, both large and small, as little as 10 percent of find types are kept, either as reference collections or the singular as significant examples of a particular artefact type, but for some unknown reason archaeologist finds are not normally recorded on the British Museum PAS databases, which currently show entries totalling 0.03 percent from archaeologists.

The initial statement by Pearce and Worrell (2015 p. 21) concerning the subject of non-recording when referring to small finds does not indicate the type of finds in question as the generalisation could refer to the millions of pieces of rubbish found on a regular basis during metal-detecting surveys, ranging from rusty nails, fragments of tin cans, bottle tops, green waste, crisp packets and the annoying pieces of foil from popular chocolate bars; all these items are 'finds' *per se* but fall neatly into a category labelled as trash, which can account for anything from 90 to 99 percent of finds from a day's outing.

If the archaeological hierarchy requires – a little strong one thinks, suggests – that detectorists should record the trash, put it in writing, and if they, the archaeologists, both amateur and professional, practise what is preached, I doubt if any archaeological site, commercial or research based, would ever get past the plough soil or topsoil, with the resulting numbering, identification, preservation, cataloguing, staff hours and storage all presenting more than a

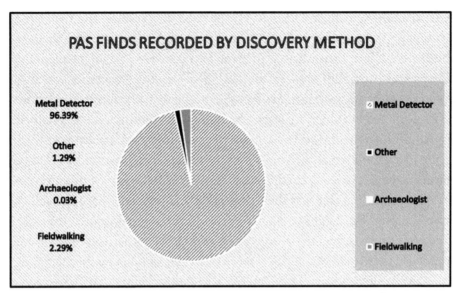

Figure. 8. PAS finds recorded, recovery methods at a glance. (*Spackman, P. 2022*)

little food for thought. Unless of course the archaeologists remove the soil and dump it on some exceptionally large spoil heap, which would be the exact same soil that metal detectorists search, and is, or should be, a cause of concern, thought, discussion and explanation. The question that looms large regarding the recording of finds is that detectorists search contexts that archaeologists discount and remove wholesale, and the detectorists save artefacts from that level, identify, and responsibly record said finds, as required. So, should not the argument be directed at the archaeologists who destroy the level? Detectorists are limited to detect and with it the finds *in-situ*; unfortunately, a practice that has continued unabated for many a decade. The recommendations of Oxford Archaeology in the 2006 Nighthawking Survey go a long way to reinforce the remarks above concerning the removal of top and plough soils: *'the treatment of topsoil during commercial needs reviewing, at present it is typically machined away as overburden without any systematic examination for artefacts'* (Historic England (2009)). That survey was conducted more than seventeen years ago and those recommendations have literally fallen upon stoney ground and the gap is still a-gaping, in fact more of a crevasse concerning the employment of metal detectorists, particularly during the pre-construction processes; the reasons for this are wide and various, not just concerning the local authority planning departments, but also the construction companies, WSIs or archaeological contractors.

Even then metal detectorists may only be used to accommodate the all too customary practice of limiting detectorists to exploration of spoil heaps to confirm that detectorists had been involved, usually to placate the planning departments, and WSI requests for local involvement agreements, and in so doing ticking an appropriate box. Another of the resulting recommendations of Oxford Archaeology's survey (2006), again highlighted by Historic England (2009) and directed solely at archaeology and archaeologists, is, to the metal detectorist, rather obvious: soil management, or should that be mismanagement in regard to finds that are just machined away; this problem emanates from the fact that the metal-detecting fraternity have the ability, time, skill, and the means to extract historic artefacts that would otherwise, on a regular basis, become a lost entity upon yet another spoil heap. One wonders if there is indeed an appearance of an almost jealous aspect radiating from archaeology academia, or could it be a guilty feeling that archaeology does not admit to wanton destruction, by machine, of the top layers? It was encouraging that the survey was conducted by a well-respected and more than capable archaeological institution, but in reality the survey that was probably well overdue merely highlighted a practice that was, unfortunately, not only knowingly ignored but also chastised metal detectorists, who for decades have rescued finds from topsoil. In retort, would it not be proper to accuse the commercial developers and archaeological contractors of unethical practices by not treating all top layers of artefact-bearing soil with respect, meaning a full metal-detecting survey.

As far as detectorists are concerned, small finds fall roughly into five categories: trash, unrecognisable, recognisable, non-valuable, recordable, usually of some value or of national or local historic interest, and treasure, according to the current Treasure Act. The latter two categories would require find-spot grid references and being reported to an FLO within fourteen days. All finds should be shown to the landowner, who is the rightful owner of any artefacts that are recovered from their land unless there is an agreement in place to the contrary, unless the artefact falls into the last category. A recordable find should be voluntarily recorded on the PAS database by way of their website or via the area FLO. This procedure should either be or become general practice for all metal detectorists, but in the past one of the major drawbacks, especially for the novice, is categorising the artefact within a high degree of certainty; these days the internet and the many finds databases freely available are at times a blessing, even for the experienced practitioner, as there will be a mystery finds that look important and once useful that require further investigation. Over the years, most detectorists accumulate reference books that cover both common and rarer finds and a good philosophy is that, if someone has spent time and effort compiling information of all the find types and publishing their sometimes monumental efforts and your find 'type' is in any publication, it is worthy of recording. Even if your find is identical to another found among the thousands of well-presented pages of reference books or a database, it should be recorded in readiness for the efforts of the next researcher as every artefact adds to the knowledge base of past cultures, their movements, skills, and our historic heritage as a whole. One thing that is imperative for good practice is the addition of at least a six-figure grid reference for the artefact. The non-reference of eight- and ten-figure references is in line with the ideas and wishes of Historic England, English Heritage, DEFRA, DCMS, CBA, NCMD, FID and CIFA, who are all in agreement that our heritage needs to be protected, so the limitation of exact locations is a benefit for all. Ten-figure references could be a temptation to the unscrupulous, and exact find spots are most often limited by the freedom of choice of landowners and finders, who are both stakeholders with subjective input, often with the contribution of outside bodies and reference to previous unwanted visitations of thieves; hence the lesser six- or eight-figure references that are normally supplied. Just remember: there are 1.44 million rescued artefacts on the PAS databases for all to see, study, and research, not to mention the thousands of works by archaeologists, numismatics, and historians literally on the backs of the finds recorded by metal detectorists incorporating the knowledge gained or gleaned from the effort of the dedicated detectorist practitioners. All artefacts recovered from the earth where they lay, not only slowly decaying from natural erosion, chemical attack, and bulldozers but also to not attempt a rescue mission is in my opinion nothing less than a sin. The very practitioners who are repeatedly called amateurs, a moniker that is rarely used, if at all, by 35,000 detectorists themselves, of which a good percentage are very skilled in the setting and operation of often detailed programmes on ever-increasing technologically challenging equipment. Skilled in the operation and detection of metal objects, methods of removal, basic conservation, identification of an almost endless list of artefact varieties and classes, storage, their place in the historic timeline and their values. Another consequence of intentionally being called an amateur is that the term is often used in a derogatory sense, almost as a class system, when in fact someone with twenty, thirty, forty or more years practising and mastering a skill is in no way an amateur. There are no degrees in metal detecting, so are all 35,000 detectorists amateurs? Obviously some are, but I have come across a number of detectorists who work as and are paid to detect. Are they still called amateurs, or should the descriptive be artisan, practitioner, specialist or, in some instances, professional? On many occasions I have been in the company of fifty or sixty detectorists, among whom are lawyers, doctors, professors, electricians, pilots and even qualified archaeologists, to name but a few, and roughly 70 percent would be a professional in the own field [pardon the pun]; the other 30 percent would think twice before calling them amateurs; all of them would be called amateurs and that would include the professional archaeologist who was metal detecting. On a visit to an archaeological contractor on-site and witnessing an archaeologist using the 'site metal detector', the technique of operation would have been called amateurish, but there lies a problem: would the operating archaeologist be an amateur metal detectorist or a professional archaeologist? Think carefully on your answer because if you pick the latter, you will be picking the profession of the operator and not the skill level required to discount the epithet of amateur detectorist, and if that were the case surely the aforementioned professional lawyers, doctors and professors would take their titles as professional metal detectorists. So, the suggestion, in a publication by senior archaeologist Professor Suzie Thomas (2009, p. 1 that '*the unequal academic and social positions between a professional archaeologist and a metal detectorist are the cause of discontent*' is somewhat condescending and one wonders just what the eminent archaeologist is trying to convey to the reader. Surely they [archaeologists] are not insinuating that this is a class thing, and can only describe that comment with modern vocabulary as a little 'crass', but I did not realise that archaeology or archaeologist was a class and show my own ignorance by thinking that archaeology was a profession and always had been; although there is a mention of King John in 1201 AD searching the Roman settlement of *Corstopitum* to replenish the royal coffers (Hodgson (2015, p. 45)). The comments by Thomas (2009) continue with '*Metal detector users are at the very best a major nuisance*', and the next remark is, reluctantly, included here as an example of what a possibly small group of influential archaeologists believe, with reference to metal detectorists: '*at worst a group that fosters and propagates the illicit trade for its own financial gain*' Thomas (2009). Those quite antagonistic, almost venomous comments are someone's point of view, which could easily have turned into a tirade of reciprocal disrespect, especially with the remark of *'propagating the illicit trade of antiquities'*. I am afraid that that trade is fuelled by the wealthier, better educated, and more intelligent, and we can only presume, by the comments of Thomas (2009), most likely a few steps above the social class of a metal detectorist, or as Thomas (2009) doggedly calls *'metal detector users'*. The last comment we will deal with, which again refers to the operational practices of metal detectorists, as Thomas (2009, p. 1) states *'whose antics destroy the primary context of artefacts'*. That last remark is hard to believe as the layers that a metal detectorist works are plough and topsoil, which by their very nature are, unless I am mistaken, not classed as primary layers and where more than 95 percent of detectorists' finds are rescued from so well away from where primary archaeological contexts are usually found. However, plough soils [arable] can reach one metre or more in depth, especially on the headland where ploughs are manoeuvred and deposit extra soil from the blades as they are turned, which can be a substantial amount when the technique of deep ploughing is involved; a practice that is rarely employed these days. The standard recommended practice and one that is advised is that metal detectorists do not venture below plough and topsoil levels and in so doing stop at the first sign of subsoils, which act as an *event-horizon*, but unlike a blackhole where everything that goes in never comes out, a detectorist's spade should not go into any layers below the recommended search depth and treat subsoils as the forbidden fruit. There are of course noticeable exceptions, usually on unploughed pasture where, on extremely rare occasions, a hoard may have lain undisturbed since deposition, which by its very nature and purpose are mainly deposited either as an offering or as a means of storage with a plan of retrieving at a later date; hence, both could be near the surface and in a primary context, and therefore a detectorist calls in an archaeologist via contact with the local FLO to excavate said hoard. Sometimes a shallow grave is located with metal artefacts *in-situ*, which would also be a primary context and if located by a metal detectorist, in normal practice either contact the coroner, the county archaeologist or an FLO; the latter is usually the easiest to contact. All meaning that there are very rare occasions when the primary context is near the surface and inevitably within a detectable depth. A brief but perhaps essential explanation of the terms used in reference to context nomenclatures is below, simply to clarify any ambiguities and act as a reply to accusations that metal detectorists destroy primary contexts. It also enlightens the reader to the categories generally used when describing the three main contexts when referring to contextual identification.

Primary (first) context: this is the precise spot where a find was left by the last user.

Secondary (second) context: the position of a find that has been either partially or wholly disturbed from its original resting spot.

Tertiary (third) context: the artefact is separated from the place of its original use, such as spoil heaps, machine- and manually stripped soils, and of course the detectorists rescuing layers of plough and topsoil.

A simplified section from one slide of a PowerPoint presentation (Spackman (2012)) showing a Roman third-century wall 60cm below the surface and under a 30cm-thick layer of plough soil (Spackman (Figure 9, 2023)) on a site where a fifth-century migration period Anglo-Saxon low status burial was discovered 65cm below the surface.

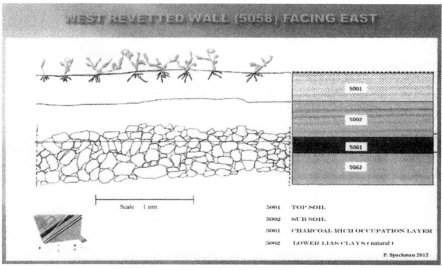

Figure 9. Section showing basic stratification and depth. (*Spackman, P. 2012*)

The burial itself was in a shallow grave scraped into the Roman-period stony courtyard. An indication that even an archaeologist had to remove literally tons of soil before any primary context was encountered; obviously, this is only one site, but having worked on many a site over the years, a conclusion is that it is far more likely for an archaeologist to encounter primary contexts containing artefacts. So, for a detectorist, who is not in the employ of an archaeological unit working on private permissions, they would consider uncovering primary contexts as very rare indeed. I will add at this point that on the site of the Anglo-Saxon burial excavation was stopped immediately as the skull came to light and reported to the county archaeologist, and the site metal detectorist was called over with the result that the detectorist plotted signals of metal objects one each side of the shoulder and informed the rest of the interested archaeologists that this was likely to be Anglo-Saxon and the gender female. This was later confirmed by excavation as the signals turned out to be a matching pair of small, long brooches of the migration period. Yes, I have encountered archaeology near the surface in the form of Roman mosaics that had been ripped to pieces by the plough and a large area with thousands of tesserae spread over the ground unrecognisable as to content, a mosaic that had survived a few centimetres under pasture for 1,600 years before the field was cultivated and now it is gone. One more demeaning inclusion by Thomas (2009, p. 1) is the entry of a single word 'antics', which if used in a different context would not raise an eyebrow, but when used as it was it could be construed as an intentional slur and rather derogatory with intent. The dictionary definitions of 'antics' are: Antics --- absurd or grotesque acts, Collins English Dictionary (2014, p. 84); Antics --- stunts, tricks, horseplay, rogueries, Merriam-Webster Dictionary (2022). The whole language of Thomas (2009) is quite obviously anti-detectorist and although that is the professor's opinion, the derogatory content is in my opinion rather uncalled for, especially from such an academic of note and someone of, as stated earlier, *a higher social position*' Thomas (2009). There is no need on my part to counter the multiple adverse comments of Suzie Thomas, Professor of Heritage Studies, University of Antwerp, and instead just let the reader arrive at their own conclusions. What is offered is a reply to address the initial remark by Thomas (2009, p. 1), *'unequal academic and social positions'*, by giving an example of an archaeologist. A university Don, who possesses a combined high academic and social position, which on paper appears to fit perfectly into the elite category of Thomas's, which is the *cause of discontent* (Thomas, 2009), and that is an article concerning said Don: '*in 2015 a university Don pocketed near £240,000 of lottery grants for bogus archaeological programs*' Evans (2015). Another example covered again by a national newspaper when a professional archaeologist, according to Nolan (2013), employed by MOLAS stole three vases during excavations in Somerset during 2008. Nolan (2013) continues that four years later the professional archaeologist attempted to sell the three vases on eBay in 2012; just to compound the situation the culprit had a criminal history, because in 2001 the same professional archaeologist had been jailed for a similar offence (Nolan, 2013). As stated previously, it is not the intention of this publication to vilify the greedy and the unfortunate, and there are many more articles that could be used for the benefit of those who believe that the higher educated and professionally trained are somewhat exempt from some or all of the deadly sins. There are sins of the rich and educated that match those of the poor and needy, so I will not mention that the outcome of achievements in that department could theoretically rely upon being higher educated or possess a level of social standing than any other class below. Recently a hoard of Roman denarii was recovered, in the county of Rutland UK, by two detectorists who duly handed the finds to the PAS, as required by the Treasure Act (1996); the hoard of silver and coins were then locked safely up in a museum, but according to an article in Mail Online (2022) the hoard has since disappeared from the museum stores and as Kuepper (2022) enlightens, along with other artefacts of value since being handed over for safekeeping. There are ongoing investigations by both the police and museum staff and it would be a little presumptuous, for the benefit of both the readers and Professor Thomas, to conclude that the staff are possibly from *higher academic and social positions* (Thomas, 2009) with clear insinuations suggesting that archaeologists possess the nabobisms of the modern era, and the lowly law-abiding metal detectorists, who followed to the letter the directives of the Treasure Act (1996) as well as the PAS Code of Practice (2017), are they still [the metal detectorists] thought of as the serfs and nuisances of society? Above are a mere sprinkle of crimes from the higher educated and apparently a few rungs higher on the social ladder, and one can only wait with bated breath along with: PAS, police, detectorists, Professor Thomas, the media *et al*.

What I must do now, to honour my original aim of an equal unbiased opinion, is present two cases of crimes orchestrated by thieves using metal-detecting equipment. The first is from a report from Amos (2022) covering a successful operation leading to the capture and charging of four heritage thieves on an ancient monument site in Suffolk and that made the headlines when they were charged with a contravention of Section 42 of the Ancient Monuments and Archaeological Areas Act, and also criminal damage and going equipped for theft [metal detectors] to carry out a crime. A spokesperson for Suffolk Constabulary's Rural, Wildlife and Heritage Policing Team added that '*we take heritage crime incredibly seriously, those responsible are stealing our heritage, our historical knowledge, once it is gone it is gone forever*' (Amos, 2022). This is an example of a handful of unscrupulous individuals adding fuel to campaigners who wish to ban the hobby of metal detecting. Although both the newspaper reporter and the police and the police report do not mention any involvement by metal detectorists, this incident threatens the very core standards of the metal-detectorist fraternity and the good work undertaken to bond an acceptance to the wider community. Those individuals involved will have no sympathy from either archaeologists, metal detectorists, or for that matter members of the public.

The latest report of nighthawkers illegally accessing a Protected Ancient Monument to steal heritage artefacts can be found in an article by Draper (2002), which informs the reader that the two persons involved were using metal detectors as a tool to locate any finds. The two perpetrators were caught and charged with contravening the Ancient Monument and Archaeological Areas Act (1979) and will appear at court in December 2022. To close this argument there should be a realisation that higher academic achievement and higher social standing does in no way guarantee morality, honesty, and professionalism. On the same theme I have worked alongside professional archaeologists who are without a degree in archaeology, or for that matter not even a member of the CIfA, so it is obvious that a qualification is not a prerequisite of receiving an accolade of being recognised as a professional or indeed the recipient of respect. One wonders how many professional archaeologists have an artefact adorning their mantelpieces studies and drawers and how many metal detectorists have rooms stored with all sorts of metal objects valuable or not; it matters not of size or value of the artefact, whether it be a patterned sherd of Samian pottery or an old buckle. All crimes of theft are not condoned by the author, but archaeologists do not, in normal circumstances, have any right to keep even a rusty nail; on the other hand, detectorists study, research, catalogue and store their legally rescued artefacts and as the years drift by build recognisable collections that are used for study and publication as reference catalogues or books. These are predominantly artefacts that would otherwise have been lost to either the elements or construction and 99 percent of the said finds would be or have been refused by museums and are of little interest to the landowners. Finds covering brooches, buttons, thimbles, coins and even ring-pulls can be found neatly presented in folders, drawers, and cupboards in homes of the most dedicated metal detectorist and hopefully the recordable items listed on the PAS database or similar. Likewise, an archaeological unit, institution or individual archaeologist would have their own collections, which are called reference collections, and depending on which branch of the profession is of interest, usually a specialist would curate a narrow artefact class, such as a ceramics expert who will house a pottery reference collection, or a coin specialist would care for a numismatic reference collection, and so on *infinitum*. Even within the two different finds collections mentioned, sub-specialists would have their reference collections by date or type, *id est* Roman pottery alone has many hundreds of types, styles, materials, and manufacturing sites. Coins have a staggering selection of different varieties, periods, metals, patterns, inscriptions, values, and mints, and all the above would possess specialists and sub-specialists. Over the years these collections become rather personal and not all housed in museums for public viewing, turning into a private collection with a sort of ownership by proxy, whereas metal detectorists are legally entitled to form collections from the rescued artefacts unwanted by either museums or the PAS.

2.4 Metal-detecting rallies and clubs

Modern-day metal-detecting rallies are in the main serious, well-run affairs offering the participants not only a chance to detect hundreds of acres over two or three days but also an opportunity to socialise, meeting new and old friends as well as exploring the many trade stands and outlets. Rallies used to be run typically as annual fundraising events for both local and national charities, which is still the case for most of the major players, and can be attended by upwards of 1,000 participants with full facilities provided and in the main held at weekends, predominantly after harvesting of crops, offering ideal or at the very least suitable conditions for the detectorist. The numbers and frequency of these events has steadily increased over the last thirty or more years and in the last five years have become more popular than ever and conducted in a more business- and commercially presented oriented way, presumably as a means of profit and not solely for a charitable cause. The smaller clubs have realised that there could be an opportunity to boost club funds and hold their own rallies with the hope that a one-off special manages to cover expenses, attract new members or perhaps new permissions. I have had the pleasure of attending at least one of these rallies every year for the last forty years, either as a detectorist or a marshal, and like many other enthusiasts it was somewhere new to detect and the camaraderie was always second to none. Meal breaks were treated as a chance to learn more about artefacts and equipment with new detectors and associated equipment reaching the market almost on a monthly basis; someone always had the latest model to explore. In the early years some holes were left unfilled and without pin-pointers; there were huge holes dug including disturbance of subsoils sometimes a metre in depth and the detector still giving a signal when the artefact was in fact still in the side of the hole. Holes left open were a nuisance and some permissions even lost as they were left unfilled due to nothing more than sheer laziness, but now that rallies are marshalled, holes have become a rarity due to not only marshals but also fellow detectorists, who will have a quiet word with any culprit; after all, a single non-conformist could threaten the loss of even long-time permissions. Another crucial factor concerning the digging of large holes is the advancement in the world of technological innovation when handheld pin-pointers come into force and machines also incorporated an accuracy of isolating a signal to within five centimetres or less, which allowed a small core of earth to be disturbed. Finds also went unrecorded and on one occasion, as a marshal, I witnessed the recovery of a half noble, the second gold coin of the day, but a couple of hours later on return to the FLO tent only one of them was recorded; then again, that was thirty years ago and the Treasure Act did not require anyone to voluntarily record single coins, and there was a certain amount of nervousness to the voluntary recording of artefacts in case they were taken from the finder and not returned, probably because of a lack of knowledge of correct procedures and there were also a lot more amateurs about in those early days. In the years since there have been some significant changes to the Act, with the latest changes to come into force until 30 July 2023 (NCMD, 2023). The rallies themselves have made significant changes in areas of health and safety, stewards, marshals, and facilities. A good example would be the Rodney Cook Memorial Rally (2022). I first attended in 2018 before it became an annual event, born from the untimely departure of a much-loved and respected detectorist, Rodney Cook. In 2018 the first rally to honour Rodney was organised by his son Gary Cook (2018) and some close friends to raise money for the Royal United Hospital [RUH] in Bath, which took care of his father. Further information can be found on the rally's own web pages and YouTube presentation. This rally has grown in a short time to become one of the largest gatherings in this country, incorporating all the usual trade stalls, entertainment, and facilities. Having raised well over £40,000 for The Forever Friends, RUH and also support and raise money for Cancer and Leukaemia in Childhood (CLIC, Sargent), this well-organised rally goes from strength to strength, creating an interactive forum for the sport of metal detecting and an avenue for charity as an epiphany of worthy causes.

Another of the larger rallies emerged during 2016, providing more than 1,000 acres of land, usually encompassing two or three days with entertainment and socialising. The venue for 2022, at the time of writing, has been given as the Cambridge/Suffolk border, accompanied by all the trimmings, and is organised by the aptly named Detectival. This event has, since its inauguration in 2016, enjoyed the presence of a number of FLOs from the PAS attending to record a multiplicity of finds, which are then entered on the PAS database for all to see. In the three years 2017 to 2019 running up to the break for COVID-19, Detectival recorded 1,127 small finds on the PAS database. A credit to both the organisers and the hard-working FLOs who attended the rallies, and of course the detectorists who found both time and dedication to recover the artefacts in the first place and take advantage of the free recording facility. Not all rallies involve searching for lost artefacts, but are geared towards locating and recovering finds that have been placed, salted, purposely on the land that the attendees are allowed to search. One of the largest of these types of rallies is the Garrett Memorial Hunt to be held in April 2023 near Canton, Texas in the US. The organisers have guaranteed that at least $80,000 worth of coins, relics, and prize tokens are there to be recovered by the searchers. This hunt will have unsalted land available for the enthusiastic out-and-out metal detectorist, but one would expect that the majority of participants will be hunters trying to locate the hidden prizes available. At most of the rallies held in the UK there are similar controlled treasure hunts when caches of coins are purposely hidden for paying participants to find, but here the majority of the detectorists at the event are there to search unsalted fields.

Although on a smaller scale, an enthusiastic stalwart detectorist, Peter Welch (2022), formed Weekend Wanderers Club in 1989. Apart from the major rallies it is one of the largest, if not the largest, bona fide metal-detecting clubs in the UK. It concentrates on the late summer and autumnal months and frequently holds, at the least, two meetings per week. Not with 400 or 500 and more participants, like the rallies, but the meetings are always well attended. The club as a whole actively encourages members to record finds on the PAS database and has over the years earned considerable respect and a reputation for promoting the standard PAS Code of Practice (2022). This is reflected in the sheer number of the reportable finds entered on the PAS system, which shows there have been more than 1,000 such finds rescued and duly recorded by club members, and even in 2015 there were more than 300 historic artefacts entered by Weekend Wanderers. As with a lot of clubs, holes unfilled were an unfortunately common occurrence, but over the years this phenomenon has been dealt with. On a recent visit during September (2022) to a Weekend Wanderers meeting, primarily to hand out artefact depth questionnaires, I walked some of the fields and not a single hole had been left unfilled. Any indication that that particular bad habit of ten or fifteen years ago was continuing by member detectorists was not evident, and the eradication appears to be the result of a combination of an increase in member dedication to the sport of metal detection and the continuing diligence of Peter Welch and marshals. There are many more clubs that take advantage of the popularity of a large, organised rally, of which a good percentage support a popular charity or local cause and a combination of both.

The Metal Detectives Group set up in 2021 by Mark and Karen specifically to help those who were interested in the hobby has given detectorists the chance to pursue their chosen hobby as a group. Mark and Karen had the foresight to realise that some detectorists were struggling to obtain land to search, and the various sites the couple had permission to search would give them somewhere to carry on with their hobby and benefit from an increased membership of kind, friendly and responsible detectorists. There is even a winter excursion by hardy members of the Metal Detectives Group, who hold an annual seasonal rally usually a couple of days before Christmas Day. The finds from this group are duly recorded with the PAS and are a credit to their ventures. The majority of larger clubs and organisations supply what is known as a community bin for discarded metal objects; best practice dictates that all metal objects are removed from the land including trash. Interestingly, when reading the Codes of Practice or Terms and Conditions of two of the larger detecting clubs, such as the Weekend Wanderers Detecting Club, its Club Rules (2022) stipulate that larger iron objects must not be left on the surface and that *'trash should never be placed back in the hole but taken with you'*. The Metal Detectives Group has one of the most comprehensive set of Terms and Conditions available among the metal-detecting fraternity, which is constructed of no less than thirty-eight bullet points, including *'remove all unwanted metal objects found and leave them at the dig-site headquarters for proper disposal'* (Metal Detectives Group, 2022)), and suggests that any large items are placed in the hedge. The latter suggestion may raise an eyebrow or two but it is not unknown for an odd scaffold pole, an extremely heavy ploughshare, chains and even metal sheets, all of which are better off the land, to be harboured by the hedgerow; making notes or taking a photograph to identify the location would be a great help to both rally organisers or the landowner.

There is a dilemma regarding the term rally or rallies, in so much that a decade ago there were concerns emanating from the worlds of archaeology and heritage, leading to attempts to ban the whole hobby/sport of metal detecting, if not specifically the rallies, when one of the main concerns was that of lost information involving contexts, stratigraphy, find spots, and even non-recording of finds themselves, and of course the illicit searching of scheduled monuments and archaeological sites. A quandary is with the actual definition of rally, and there are a number of dictionary explanations. A relevant entry is *'an assembly'* (Collins (1976, p. 808)), but that entry does not give any indication to the number of personnel required to form an assembly or rally. The later twelfth edition is the 2,305-page Collins English Dictionary, which gives an expanded choice for rally, [2] *'to organise supporters for a common cause or come together for a purpose'* [6]; *'a large gathering of people for a common for a common purpose'* (Collins, 2014, p. 1639). The importance of the latter definition is paramount to both the rank and file of individual metal detectorist and small clubs as the anti-detecting lobby have for many years concentrated their efforts on banning rallies; looking at the earlier definition of rally, a ban would also, by definition, have sneakily banned all metal detecting, by two or more persons, which in turn could be construed as an assembly. An example of a loose definition is that of an extremely small assembly of metal detectorists under the guidance of an archaeological unit, L-P Archaeology being called a rally in so much that the three-day event of detecting spoil heaps during the Tower of London Moat excavation (Treasure Hunter Magazine, 2022) was entered on the PAS databases by the FLO under the category of 'rallies' and called Tower of London Moat Metal Detecting of Spoil 2021–2022. We can only assume that there was some benefit to be had by calling this a rally as the PAS database in question was created by Stuart Wyatt on 20 December 2021, who stipulates that eight finds were recorded from this 'rally' over the three days' spoil heap searches. On day one, Jason Sandy, who settled in the UK from the US in 2017 and is a member of note of the Society of Thames Mudlarks, which, as the name implies, search the mud foreshores of the river Thames, loaned a metal detector from Crawfords Metal Detectors for use on the Tower Moat Project; colleague Nick Stevens used his own detector and friend Stuart Wyatt, who is an FLO from the PAS, accompanied to record any finds. The first day of the 'rally' saw two people using metal detectors. The second day we see again Stevens and Sandy with metal detectors, accompanied by Tim Miller, the new Chair of the Society of Thames Mudlarks; James Ilford, who works for the Tower of London; and of course the PAS FLO, Stuart Wyatt. We can only verify two persons using a metal detector, even from the several photographs containing personnel posing or using a detector among the thirteen pages of two articles in issues of the Treasure Hunter magazine (May and June 2022) and a possible third participant on the third visit. Why the term rally was used in the first place is a little confusing, unless the term was used solely to promote the importance of either L-P Archaeology or the illumination of the Society of Thames Mudlarks. The main point raised here is that this gathering of two or maybe three metal detector users was not only called a rally but also documented as a rally by archaeologist Wyatt (2022), and this may encourage the anti-detectorist lobby to quote that official entry on the British Museum PAS schemes database with the idea that they could ban every event with two or three metal detectorists attending, if a ban on rallies ever takes effect. This ban would, by its very nature, also cover all metal-detecting club outings and all private outings of two or more detectorists, all because the latter has been officially called a rally. This appears to be a grey area of definition of the term 'large' in reference to a group of people, and this alone could sway the balance upon which lies not only the livelihood of many businesses and their employees but also the legal sport or hobby of tens of thousands of metal detectorists. So, what does constitute large, one wonders, if the PAS-registered Tower of London Moat Rally with two, possibly three detectorists, the annual Detectival Rally, or the Rodney Cook Memorial Rally and many other large rallies all fall into the same category. Answers on a postcard please, I believe is the appropriate instruction.

Chapter 3

A Metal Detectorist's Guide, Designed for Archaeologists

3.1 A motive and an aim is an analysis of the mindset of a detectorist that will give, at the very least, an enlightening explanation as to why so many thousands of practitioners follow not only a dream but also a path of self-justification, leading to a sense of achievement and purpose as a metal detectorist. Outside of the woes and tribulations of modern living, any hobby has undoubtedly a twofold form of self-gratification (worth), exciting the emotions by a combination of escapism and enjoyment, causing one's endorphins to stimulate the mind and body alike; commonly known as a high or buzz. Metal detecting is but a single example of a pastime that requires a certain amount of physical effort and most often with no reward. The more physical effort involved, the greater the pleasure at the end of a session when even an old button looks like the crown jewels; so, but to a few, the vast majority of detectorists fall into the category of dedicated hobbyists. Knowledge within this category is shared on a regular basis and most can accurately identify the period, date, type, and metal of all the main artefact groups. Among these are dedicated collectors who are experts in one or more artefact types or periods, who are always willing to share their expertise and dazzle the recipient with detail learned over many years. As a result, and to the benefit of everyone, a myriad of publications covering artefacts of all periods that, without the hobby, academia and the wider audience would undoubtably be living in a dark age of artefact knowledge. There are forty-plus FLOs working for the PAS (2022) who offer similar skills, but these are easily matched by many thousands of metal detectorists who possess at least equal knowledge. There are always novices and learners within the hobby who would not know the difference between a penannular brooch and a shoe buckle or a sceat and an old jetton, but most are more than eager to learn. A very small group are the treasure seekers who concentrate, legally, as is their want, on areas noted for their museum-quality finds, including hoards, and consist of highly experienced detectorists who are renowned researchers. So basically, we have three tiers: novice, practitioner, and treasure seekers; the practitioner group contains a high percentage of experts who are conversant with the operation and functionality of a variety of equipment, knowledgeable in researching techniques, artefact types and post-extraction care and procedures. There is unfortunately another group who operate outside of the law that I will not class as metal detectorists but will call them criminals who happen to use specialised equipment, i.e. metal detectors, on land that they trespass upon (without permission), mostly protected sites of archaeological importance, with the sole intent of stealing artefacts of either historic, heritage or monetary value. It is just a fact of life that if there is anything of value someone, somewhere, will attempt to steal it; regrettably, this is expected but in no way condoned. In fact, I have failed to find any profession or occupation that has not suffered either internally or externally any form of criminal activity; again, it does not mean crime is acceptable but an expectation that some sort of preventive provision is in place.

3.2 Permission and research represent the backbone of a metal detectorist's portfolio as a week of research is worth every minute spent browsing through historical information and trolling through an almost endless source of online information, all for the purpose of a better chance to recover once lost artefacts. Choosing which to challenge first is a bit like trying to solve the 'chicken or the egg' enigma, and in the past both permission and research have been chosen as *prima facie* an indication that both have their benefits. Hours were spent, pleasurably, unravelling old maps and scouring hundreds of early aerial photographs searching for the tell-tale signs of previous settlements and ancient field systems, slowly crafting the detectorist into a person of great historical knowledge. On club digs or organised rallies there is no need to worry about permission as that should have been agreed beforehand and research before detecting would be the governing factor for the detectorist, as some of the rallies cover a thousand acres or more. Obtaining private permission to search land, arable or otherwise, can be a rather daunting task and fifty refusals before a permission is found would not be uncommon; a great deal of hard graft and networking is involved and the main reason clubs, larger rallies and other organisations are very popular with the rank and file of the detectorist community. A couple of downsides are that larger clubs and rallies are often not local and plenty of travel is involved, and membership is rather limited to the choice of available days, but all in all, the time and energy saved in obtaining permissions could probably outweigh any inconveniences. Not all detectorists are in favour of these larger business-oriented organisations who possess a substantial membership database and therefore a lot more influence, as it were, financially. Many times, I have heard of individuals who had, through hard work, obtained permissions and after spending many years enjoying the hobby lose their permission because the landowner has been approached and accepted a more lucrative offer. Such is the world of enterprise and in a rather unstable economic period, unfortunately a dog-eat-dog attitude surfaces as the victor. The rise and rise of rally management enterprises is one cause of concern for not only the individual detectorist with reference to permissions but also for smaller clubs, but an asset to others who cannot obtain permission, probably because of time constraints and work commitments and who actually relishes that someone else is doing all the 'leg work', so all they have to do is turn up, pay a fee, and enjoy the day. Over the last few years, as well as the usual annual charity rally, the present-day entrepreneurs are increasing each year and not just holding an annual event; they have moved on a pace and are holding two or more fee-charging rallies each week during the peak seasons. It is a case of moving with the times and gone are the days when a good bottle of brandy, given not as a bribe, but with gratitude, to celebrate a new permission won was enough to sustain the permission, followed by a similar annual gesture of appreciation.

3.3 The equipment used by a detectorist is varied and in the majority of cases chosen by personal preference due to either recommendations, advertisements or commonly an upgraded model of the one in use. Similar to the purchasing of a new vehicle with the choice of a banger, a head turner or usually something inbetween. The metal detector of course is necessary and can range from under £50 to more than £3,000, and the choice is often governed by economics, but as with all equipment, one should buy for purpose. I have witnessed a shared detector, dirty, caked in mud and batteries out of charge, which is just one good reason to either own your own or even better still have access to an experienced dedicated detectorist. Almost as bad is to purchase a top-of-the-range model (the head turner) without the experience in the use and operation of a metal detector, nor the technical knowledge. As an example, my own armoury consists of three detectors: a 40-year-old C-Scope, which is a bit of a workhorse and used on tough terrain. Although modern C-Scope machines are far more advanced in both design and technology, this machine is kept purely because the other detectors, which are superior in operation, technological innovations and sensitivity, are a little more delicate. A bit like using a Jaguar for a bit of all-terrain off-roading and is indeed a matter of horses for courses, as one could use the C-Scope on strong stubble. The second choice, Tesoro Cortes, is a model I use on less demanding stubble and has given me near twenty-five years of service and is still reliable. Finally, my latest acquisition, about five years ago, is the lightweight XP Deus, so I can physically manage a full day's detecting coupled with a greater choice of programs as well as excellence in the pin-pointing department. There are a few other high-end metal detectors that offer equal technological innovations, and again it is down to personal choice and in part financial outlay. The more expensive models come, in most cases, with better technological features incorporating advanced programs. Alongside the features and benefits of all the diverse types, sometimes the aesthetics play a part; again, like a motor vehicle with its sleek curves and innovative design, not functionality related, but the details are rather peer worthy. A good comparison concerning the subject of choice is a look at the smartphone, computer and search engine marketplace, where basically they all offer, more or less, the same service and it all boils down again to freedom of choice; like many other items we have purchased in the past, some will be put aside and others used until a more compatible item is found, or in some cases exchanged for something less technically demanding. What is recommended is a visit to one of the many outlets where metal-detecting supplies are available, the vast majority being manned by highly skilled personnel. At present, the most popular type of metal detector on the market are the VLF machines, which are extremely sensitive and use a dual coil system where one coil acts as a transmitter of an electric current, creating a magnetic field, and a second coil acts as a receiver, picking up any alteration caused by a metal object interfering with the field created by the transmitter. The resulting signal is then amplified and programmed to either a display or an audible response, or both simultaneously, at an amazing speed. Modern machines possess the technology to discriminate between the main components of metal that objects are constructed from and as a result are an essential on what are called trashy sites, which are sites containing a more than average deposition of not only ferrous (iron based) objects but also crisp packets or parts of, which the machine can be set to ignore. This is called discrimination, which eliminates signals that are not required, but its use should be with care because some early thinner coins can be missed by overzealous discriminator use, as well as items of gold if the discriminator is set a little too high. Most machines are accompanied by an instruction pamphlet and some have complete handbooks; one example is the publication by Andy Sabisch, which extends to 188 A4 pages A4. Sabisch (2018, pp. 58–66) does give an excellent guide to the art of discrimination, albeit geared towards a particular machine – the information refers to most VLF machines. The other choice is the pulse induction [PI] metal detectors. This technology, used predominantly in the security sectors, is becoming more popular in the world of the metal detectorist. The main advantage is found in searching highly mineralised areas because the PI system is unaffected by mineralisation, particularly in salt water, and the technology produces greater depth penetration, sending out around 100 pulses per second, but one huge disadvantage is the fact that PI, at present, does not differentiate between different metal types, so that a gold ring, a silver coin, a ring pull or a rusty nail will give identical signals, which means that every signal needs to be investigated. A pulse induction machine could be more expensive to purchase but is perfect for beach and saltwater exploration and sites of low trash. With the amount of trash recovered every trip, for the majority of users VLF is the first choice, but the detectorist must use a detector dictated by the makeup of ground being searched and have in reserve a PI machine, particularly if beaches are frequently visited or searching a well-detected field where trash and signals are a rare occurrence.

The two different types of operating systems mentioned above are not the only types of metal detector available but probably represent more than 90 percent of the metal-detecting market, of which VLF is by far the most popular. I am not offering a choice of either technology, which would, if possible, be chosen for the site in question, nor will I suggest a manufacturer, which would then represent a biased opinion. I can only advise that research before purchase would be most beneficial. There are retailers who will gladly answer any questions and concerns and there are also monthly magazines on the subject available from most appropriate outlets including supermarkets. Most of the popular detectors are programable and most exhibit pre-set programs that can be tweaked according to the search area's soil makeup. Personal choice should not be rushed into, and social media abounds with helpful metal-detector owners and instructions to alter programs, but most detectors are sold with operating instructions. One of the best opportunities to learn more would of course be from contact with your friendly local metal detectorist or club, who would be more than happy to show one and all how to use, and benefit from, a metal detector. Concerning both metal detectors and accessories, it is advisable to check on the waterproof capabilities of all operating parts including display screens, coils, and all other battery-operated equipment, although for most machines screen covers, etc. can be obtained as an extra. As a field archaeologist you are expected to work in all weathers, unless of course H & S or machine capabilities dictate otherwise, so again it is advisable to thoroughly investigate, by all means available, any questions about performance – and that goes for all specialised equipment.

Now you have a metal detector, there are a number of essential accessories that are part and parcel of a standard tool kit, just like a field archaeologist's equipment, which, if it is anything like my own, usually means a substantial dedicated tool box jammed full of personal equipment built up over many years, including: trowels various, tape measures, metal pegs, six-inch nails, string, plumb bobs, gloves, small saw, pruners, pencils, pens, pens waterproof, pencil sharpener, eraser, drawing board, spirit level, camera, notebook, Swiss penknife, and small finds bags to name but a few. This is entered here just to point out that one piece of equipment does not represent a 'tool kit' and an archaeologist would not walk on-site with just a trowel in their hand. On the other hand, a metal detectorist cannot be expected, because of the miles of distance usually covered even on a normal outing, to carry more than essential equipment accessories. Next in line and high on the list is a detectorist's spade, which has, over the decades, reduced in size because of both innovations in metal-detecting spade design and mainly because of the development in the area of detector technological improvements. The full-sized garden spade at 18cm or over resulted in the large square holes and piles of earth of forty or fifty years ago; normal procedure until my second detector, which gave me a more direct finds spot when I progressed to a small garden spade of just 14cm width, which resulted in a more acceptable sod of turf or plough soil. These days I use a bespoke short-handled spade with winged foot guides and a curved angled blade of just 9cm in width; so with my latest detector I can locate a find within a 4cm square and with the spade remove a circular plug with a diameter of 9cm, depending on the size of the artefact of course, and gone are the days of large holes and piles of earth; now the resulting plug, in ideal conditions, is replaced as a metal detectorist's invisible mend. Another digging tool and ideal for sandy and soft soil is the detectorist's trowel, which most often displays machined serrated edges and should not be confused with a standard archaeologist's trowel. The obvious variations in design between the two are due to the different methods of extraction used by a metal detectorist and an archaeologist; both methodologies are discussed in detail in a later paragraph.

Next is a pin-pointer, a small handheld device that goes by a number of names: pointer- probe, probe, pointer, as well as pin-pointer, and used to isolate artefacts located by a larger scanning detector, because quite often even in a small hole or plug of turf the artefact eludes your vision and touch as trying to locate a tiny mud-camouflaged find, which you know is there, is when a handy handheld pin-pointer comes to the rescue; a few tweets or vibrations as it comes in very close contact with a metal object and recovery ensues. Most times it turns out to be a tiny piece of lead, on occasion a Roman minim, or on a rare occasion a quarter stater or Anglo-Saxon sceat, or quite often a small splinter of a plough or remnants of a shredded drinks can or an annoying piece of silver paper from someone's discarded chocolate bar. So yes, a pin-pointer and the appropriate holster and you're almost looking and feeling like a professional metal detectorist; these very portable tools are wireless, so can be used as an example of a standalone machine. A piece of equipment that fills the gap between the small pin-pointer and the full-sized metal detector is a handheld device used primarily as an underwater detection tool, the aptly named Scuba Detector. The Scuba Detector can also be used as an excellent tool for the excavator because it can be carried in a tool bag and in areas of concentrated metal residue or concentrations of small finds. In fact, I have promoted that particular type of detector on-site for a number of years and used with advantageous results by volunteers, students, detectorists, and recognised archaeologists alike; not a detector for survey work and best, on *terra firma*, used as an aide to the trowel in so much as a scan, trowel – scan, trowel procedure. The updated versions of the Scuba Detector have now been remodelled, encompassing a combined pointer and scanner.

An essential, and on most club and archaeological digs compulsory, piece of much-needed electronic equipment is a set of compatible headphones, preferably of the wireless type; headphone use is voluntary in isolated areas, recommended when in company of others, compulsory on most club meetings

A Metal Detectorist's Guide, Designed for Archaeologists 151

and rally events, so the individual rules and regulations of all attended events must be read, digested and adhered to as a matter of course. Also because of past experiences involving flexible leads, glasses, and hats, which are stories to pass on over a meal and maybe a glass or two of vintage cider. One such experience involving headphone leads occurred during an investigation of an ancient four-metre-wide ditch, which formed one side of a field boundary. It was overgrown with blackthorn and bramble and on the steep descent one of the blackthorn branches hooked itself around the headphone lead, which not only caused my head to jerk back but in rebound ripped spectacles from my face and resulted in a slip and what one could describe as an act of levitation and entrapment by brambles. The outcome was an experience similar to visiting an acupuncturist who was also an amateur tattooist, and after scrambling out of the ditch realised that the lower undergrowth, for good measure, was well carpeted with mature nettles and a good pair of spectacles had been cunningly turned into a monocle; so take note: wireless accessories are now my personal choice. Headphones and their usage are recommended on almost all rallies, club meetings, and archaeological sites, unless H & S rules decree otherwise, as the resulting bleeps, pings, and often weird noises can be an unnecessary distraction to both humans and animals alike. Animal welfare must be taken into consideration as both audible and inaudible sounds that a human cannot hear can scare even the most docile equine, the family pet, and not to mention the unwanted advances of herds of the bovine kind; the latter tend to be very inquisitive anyway and their reaction to both high- and low-frequency signals can be a quite daunting experience, even for the hardened detectorist. Detecting in the vicinity of animals should be a last resort and normally avoided if possible; one animal that does seem less susceptible to metal detector use is the ovine variety, which tend to be a little more docile in temperament. As a rule, all animals with or without young should be avoided as a matter of course and even a field containing pregnant farm animals should be classed as out-of-bounds for all concerned for both human safety and animal welfare reasons.

Other accessories such as side bags containing finds bags, vital health and safety needs such as first aid necessities, insect repellent, suntan lotion, and these days instead of a compass a mobile phone with a variety of appropriate apps enabling grid references to be entered for the finds that require recording. On larger rallies a detectorist could find themselves many miles from their transport or camp, so the essentials must be carried including water bottles and nutriment. Of course, on a normal, more leisurely detecting outing certain areas would have been earmarked and perhaps a single small field, or part thereof, would only require a fraction of associated detecting paraphernalia as necessary accompaniments. A strong bag used solely for the retention of trash finds is a must; many years ago it was common practice to deposit the larger metal finds such as broken plough blades, pieces of pipework and unwanted broken tractor parts in the nearest hedge, the general accepted thought being that they would be less of a hazard out of the field, which meant less harm to either livestock on pasture or less likely to damage farming machines or contaminate crops, and universally aptly named '*hedge fodder*'. Nowadays a global positional system [GPS], either a dedicated handheld system or an appropriate app on the mobile phone, is becoming an essential part of the detectorist's toolbox, or even the use of the now popular what-three-words, which gives a good guide to a location.

3.4 Methodology on a non-archaeological site is not random and depends on a number of interconnected factors: the field itself, the number of times the field has been visited, the results of previous searches, weather conditions, the number of personnel taking part, and not least the time allocated to perform the search. This is best broken down into basic components, beginning with the first of a number of scenarios being a metal detectorist on a new oblong-shaped field. The methodology would begin offsite with a thorough, comprehensive, and well-practised research doctrine; the more time spent here is echoed by the number and quality of finds rescued from the ravages of not only nature but also from the products and practices of humanity. Researching old maps, reports and fieldnames gives substance to the hobby and adds research data to the cultural and historical landscapes. Now the detectorist is armed with preconceptions of identifiable evidence of land use and an indication of period, and on-site a visual search for any humps, bumps, and familiarisation, all of which gives the detectorist a feel for the lay of the land. Now is the time when a metal detectorist is 'at one' with the land and not there to strip the land of topsoil and destroy, but with an aim to rescue thousands of years of artefactual evidence with the knowledge that, to accomplish the task, a detectorist will also encounter hundreds of pieces of discarded and lost human detritus.

If the user is either a novice or a person who has purchased a new metal detector, it would be classed as good practice to fill a large plastic box with soil and place various types of metallic items at differing depths and then play about with various programs on the detector, especially the discriminator. Taking notes of the screen readings of each artefact type and the machine's response, both visual and audible, can lead to a more satisfying outcome when out in the field. The operator will soon learn what to dig and what to leave alone, but a cautionary note that there may be artefacts out there that will give iffy signals, so if you are unsure dig it and sometimes it may end in a pleasant surprise with the knowledge that thin artefacts on edge or small worn gold and silver coins are not always obvious and occasionally give weak signals. The more time that a detectorist spends getting to know the full working capabilities of their metal detector, the better, and the same goes for technique and obtaining a mastery over 'the swing', which is one of the most essential prerequisites of a first-class detectorist and is a skill that is both pleasant to watch and execute in operation. Looking at my own swing after forty years of practice, it is from left to right and at a constant height of 25mm above the ground with a swing width of 2.2 metres on a slow walk and two metres at a steady pace. There are detector users out there who, even after detecting for many years, use the dip-swing technique, which copies the cross-section of a rowing boat when the swing height at start and finish could be 25cm or more above the ground and the midpoint of the swing nearly touching the ground, meaning that that particular technique would at best efficiently cover only 50 percent of a swing.

The detectorist can now unpack the metal detector and follow a well-practised 'new field' procedure, which is a diagonal corner to corner X-shaped search pattern followed by quartering the field with an east-west, north-south with a + search pattern. The results of this initial search, on occasion, give a clear indication of what could be instore for any future visits, with the clear understanding that a negative result following the initial X and + search does not in any way mean that the whole field would be unproductive. On subsequent visits there would be a systematic search in manageable sections detecting both east-west and then north-south, eventually covering virtually every inch of the search area. Using this method, a single detectorist can cover, on average, four acres per day depending on the terrain and of course the number of hours spent detecting and the speed of the operative, which in my experience can vary substantially.

An entirely different search procedure would be adopted on club and rally events. The former are almost always single-day events and can consist of as little as four or five members; some of the larger clubs average more than fifty participants, and major rallies regularly attract well over 1,000 metal detectorists at events that are spread over two or three days. Club digs are in general held on long-time permissions incorporating fields that have been detected in the past, so generally any hotspots and dud fields have been identified and clubs tend to rotate access, with the result that many years may pass between searching the same fields, which allows arable fields to replenish potential artefacts just by the processes of general farming activities. Depending on how active and enthusiastic a club membership is, a new permission sometimes comes along, but these days it seems that in some areas the frequency of obtaining pastures new is a little longer than in the old days. A major difference involving both larger clubs and rallies is the plain fact that the major players have many times the membership and therefore a much larger purse to entice new permissions, sometimes to the detriment of original permission holders, but that is evolution and development in a hobby that is now more than two generations old and which has become a little more business oriented. Continuing the theme of search methodology, on these larger meetings everyone lines up on a start line in a variety of allocated fields until the whistle blows, then it's a free-for-all, reminiscent of a type of Californian gold rush or a land grab a couple of centuries ago. But over thousands of acres eager participants soon thin out and it is a case of survival of the fittest and the history of the land is often unknown until a few days before the off, so research has to be conducted at some pace if any advantage is to be had. All hobbyist activity is, to the dedicated, enjoyable, and metal detecting can either be a quite insular affair taking on a form of 'the loneliness of a long distant runner' or, as is in the majority of cases a truly social and educational experience involving the sharing of expertise and knowledge and incorporating a comradery only found in groups of like-minded individuals, but these active involvements are not at all compulsory and working as a team only happens during planned surveys. Most of the smaller clubs consist of detectorists who detect their own personal permissions and would only meet other members at either a monthly indoor meeting or a planned outdoor gathering.

3.5 Recovery, recording and care techniques for a metal detectorist is an area that requires a certain recognition by non-practitioners and with the appreciated recognition that an archaeologist is preprogramed with a horizontal plane work ethic when approaching the terra firma. The problem here is that the archaeologist is trained to not encroach on a lower layer until the layer above is scraped away, whether that is accomplished by machine, spade or trowel, and is therefore possibly unable to comprehend someone using a detectorist's trowel making an incision that is, on occasion, as little as 75mm in diameter. On commercial and archaeological research sites, an ample supply of flag markers and finds bags, Tyvek labels for larger finds with a supply of twine, a couple of permanent marker pens, a suitable pouch, and for the more important finds a small appropriately lined box. In a detectorist's reserve pouch will be deposited what is known as 'trash', or more commonly in metal-detectorist linguistics as '*hedge fodder*', which will include the vast majority of detected finds. As a metal detectorist who is recovering items from plough soil, which is 99.99 percent of the time, well away from any archaeological context whatsoever, there is little chance of disturbing archaeology, but when searching arable soils there are rare occasions when small finds are found in an archaeological context by a detectorist, on fields with shallow pasture topsoil under which could contain undisturbed archaeological contexts near the surface. On most archaeologist-controlled sites the actual recovery of finds is in the domain of an archaeologist, with the metal detectorist using their skill and equipment solely to locate any metal finds and then place a flag by the signal, which to me is a complete waste of resources, skill, and time. An archaeologist attempting to recover a metal find without the use of a detector, a pointer and using an inappropriate recovery technique is somewhat of a revelation and an obvious target for a training opportunity, and will be discussed in due course, because an archaeologist employs quite different recovery procedures to that of a metal detectorist. Although a metal detectorist searches by means of a smooth lateral movement using the metal-detector search tool, the detector does in no way disturb the plough or topsoil. A metal detectorist is focused on a non-destructive search methodology coupled with a tried-and-tested doctrine of vertical extraction by means of removal of small cores or plugs of soil, saves an artefact from further destruction, replaces the plug, records, and moves on. Nowadays it is a rarity, because of the isolation capabilities of the modern detector, for a detectorist to carry a full-sized spade as an implement of recovery. On occasion a detectorist will come across large pieces of metal such as a scaffold pole, a large ploughshare and even the odd gate when a spade is required; most if not all landowners will be pleased to see these larger items removed from their fields because of the probability of damage to either livestock or farm machinery if left *in-situ*. Of course, it goes without saying that in rare cases of hoards, burials, items classed as treasure under the Treasure Act (1996) and munitions, the appropriate person or authority would be notified as soon as possible. I recall an apt example of the two completely different techniques practised by a field archaeologist and a metal detectorist, resulting in a knowing realisation that the techniques are both correct but only within their own environment and work ethic. While undertaking a metal-detecting survey for a large construction company and following the strict instructions of no digging allowed by a metal detectorist, whose only remit was to locate finds and place marker flags as near as possible to the spot, with the understanding that an archaeologist would accompany and then later come along with navigation equipment such as GPS and/or the more accurate Global Navigation Satellite System [GNSS] and extract the finds; the latter is extremely accurate and predominantly used only by a member of a geophysics team. A couple of hundred flags later and the supervising archaeologist was joined by geophysics and began the task of recovering the finds by the use of an archaeologist's trowel and a spade, while I stood to one side after being told that the artefacts must be recovered by the correct process: that of recovery by an archaeologist and an archaeological process. The archaeologist removed the topsoil with a spade and began to scrape away with the trowel and ten minutes later the archaeologist declared that there were no finds by the marker flag. They were walking away when I checked the ground with a metal detector and located the find in the wad of turf and informed the archaeologist and the geophysics team that it was a small Late Medieval shoe buckle and received no thanks at all. So, the archaeologist's technique of trowelling was neither conducive or compatible with the fine art of recovering artefacts located by a metal detector and the regular detectorist's method of removing a plug of earth is the least damaging technique environmentally and the correct practice to use in the circumstances. A suggestion to the senior archaeologist that the metal detectorist recovers any detected artefacts and places them in finds bags numbered with depth recorded and placed next to a marker flag. The result would be the way forward and therefore saving both manpower and time, leaving the archaeologist to carry out other work and the geophysics team to efficiently log the finds. That is the reality of the power of debated dialogue when the methodology of one party does not accomplish the task,

A Metal Detectorist's Guide, Designed for Archaeologists 157

but to reach an amicable outcome both parties must be willing to present concepts with the aim of accepting the outcome without prejudice. In the first instance the archaeologist above paid no heed to the expertise of the metal detectorist, who could easily have left them to it and left the field. With a realisation that finds matter, and more than a show of stubbornness from the archaeological representative, the detectorists sought out the senior archaeologist and open discussion prevailed with the presentation of new instructions and a welcome handshake. Sometimes deep-set bigotry exists as a creeping slime, often unseen until its ugly head rises like the sway of a King Cobra, but over the years the level-headed are gradually disinfecting, as it were, the harmful aspect of an extremely narrow line of thought, not only in the world of academia but also in the workplace. It has been a slowly developing process not just because of a lack of communication, but also by the placement or attempted implementations of what could be called deliberate needless obstacles.

Having worked in conjunction with numerous historic and heritage societies who had the pleasure to conduct amateur archaeological excavations as research digs and new techniques were developed, which allowed diggers to trowel as an archaeologist should by scraping away in layers, honouring the stratigraphy. At the beginning of each session, the previous working area was metal detected and all signals marked by either small flags or preferably different-coloured golf pegs. The reader may sense the raising of eyebrows, but with this revolutionary, tried-and-tested methodology, using golf pegs was and still is a very productive aid to the recovery of historic artefacts; not quite 'a hole in one', more of 'one in a hole'. This procedure alleviated the number of historical artefacts that otherwise would have reached the spoil heap and therefore out of context. A metal detector has the capability of determining the metal content of artefacts and in doing so the golf pegs used as identifiers consisted of a number of colours, which were used so that the human excavator is aware that either a ferrous, bronze, or other metal artefact is within the path of their trowel and acted as a warning sign that extra care may be needed. The front cover of this publication shows a number of green pegs placed on the base of a Romano-British period cellar. When the final clean and sponge was conducted by one of the volunteer archaeologists, all ten hobnails located had become lodged between the pitched stone flooring and the *in-situ* Roman hobnails were duly recovered, recorded, and bagged. Metal detecting on 'live' archaeological sites, working side-by-side on an active excavation with archaeologists, amateur or not, leaves any pegged artefacts for archaeologists to uncover and any finds dealt with by normal archaeological processes. So, we can differentiate between the practice and procedures of metal detection as (a) pre-excavation survey work on pending construction sites, where the metal detectorists could locate, plot, recover and bag the flagged artefacts, and (b) live excavation conducted by the use of a trowel after the topsoil/subsoil removal when any detectorist-plotted artefacts are left entirely to manually excavating archaeologists and their particular recording methods. Finds care and recording for a metal detectorist is, apart from research, one of the most important aspects of the hobby, and can often become the most enjoyable part when the finds pouch is emptied at the end of a session when the mud and soil are carefully removed to reveal the secrets of forgotten bygone culture and history. Most times detectorist finds are nothing but rubbish, items that an archaeologist would discard without batting an eyelid, a small percentage would require due care and attention, and the odd one would be worthy of recording with the PAS.

The vast majority of metal detectorists are more than conversant with the aftercare and preservation of small finds and would present a recordable find with a certain amount of confidence as to the identification and date. It is a matter of courtesy that the find is shown to an FLO, although, generally, archaeologists will suggest that all preservation of artefacts be carried out by a qualified conservator; this would of course be the case involving finds that come under treasure, according to the Treasure Act (1996). With regard to the Treasure Act (1996), there is a much-needed update in process that will further add to the act, which on paper should be acceptable to all involved, once any teething problems have been ironed out. The new legislation is envisaged to be finalised with clarifications and come into force from 30 July 2023 (NCMD, 2023).

There are numerous publications that deal in depth with identification as well as a wealth of information freely available, on the internet, concerning the subjects of preservation and conservation of all types of artefacts. Publications specific to conservation are not common and often limited in information, such as the basic twenty-page guide produced on behalf of the PAS by Drakon Heritage (2022), aptly named 'Conservation advice for finders', which covers mainly non-metallic artefacts but does contain some useful links to both metal-detecting and academic institutions and organisations. One of the earlier books written specifically for metal detectorists was penned by professionals to deal with the subject of aftercare of artefacts. It was written by a British Museum Curator, an Antiquities Conservator and a Ceramic, Glass and Metals Conservator (Hobbs, R., Honeycombe, C. and Watkins, S. (2002)), and helpfully entitled Guide to Conservation for Metal Detectorists. This publication is a basic but comprehensive guide for the uninitiated conservator and would indeed be a very useful addition for anyone with an interest in conservation. A more technical approach to a subject that apparently eludes even the average archaeologist, as suggested by Samuel South (2004, p. viii) in the conservation manual, comprehensively presents more than just an insight by archaeologist Bradley Rodgers (2004). Written as a guide specifically for the archaeologist, Rodgers (2004) portrays an understanding that a field archaeologist would benefit by consulting the guide, which does offer essential information for metallic artefacts and all manner of artefactual types. The publication according to Rodgers (2004, p. 3) suggests that, primarily, the author is attempting to offer a bridge across a recognised gap between archaeology and conservation; whether this gap was intended does not concern the metal detectorist and it is the actual content that would be of great benefit to the more experienced and dedicated metal detectorist, the budding enthusiast and all those between.

One of the earliest dedicated manuals concerning the initial care and conservation of finds was and still is a must-have guide, aptly named 'First Aid for Finds', by David Watkinson and Virginia Neal (1998). This is a manual that even after twenty-five years is, at times, the first manual consulted. Although published for the archaeology sector, it would be of great benefit to the metal detectorist, with the aims of small finds handling, care, and in particular the identification of metal diseases.

Most often the metal detectorist will recover finds of little value, which may need a little help to recover from the ravages of time either by correct storage or careful and correct treatment. Another book that is, predominantly, dedicated to finds processing and storage but directed at both amateur and professional archaeologists is Norena Shopland's 'A Finds Manual' (2006). Possibly unwittingly, as are most publications concerning finds processing, it is now a welcome and helpful resource for metal detectorists. Of course, it almost goes without saying that one must be extremely careful when cleaning and treating finds, and an acknowledgement that the find, even when it is made of metal, is very susceptible to damage, as many a detectorist will admit. We have all heard the tales of coins soaked in various, almost alchemistic mixtures of experimental liquids and potions, and detectorists are renowned for possessing a favoured combination of oils. Major metal-detecting clubs have all sorts of helpful information available online covering care and treatment of finds, and one suggestion I always offer, akin to a stain removal advert or a skin treatment, is to first test it on something that is of little use. If in any doubt, even after consulting any of the manuals, it is recommended that contacting your local FLO for further advice may be of benefit, especially if the find is to be displayed.

3.6 Insurance and Representative Institutions: The sport/hobby of metal detecting has, over the years, been represented by a number of bodies, some of which have dropped by the wayside while others have developed and metamorphosed into respected institutions. The market leader today is the NCMD, founded in 1981 and one of the oldest groups to form. It soon became the forerunner spokesperson for the growing number of metal detectorists, and is still going strong even after a substantial split during 2021. The AMDS, founded in 2021 by a splinter group of discontented members of the NCMD, has designed what appears to be a well-constructed online site with forethought and expertise, coupled with membership consideration that offers free membership but charges the appropriate fee for insurance. The Federation of Independent Detectorists [FID], founded during 1982, gave a near equivalent choice, but in 2014 after thirty-two years the Federation found itself under new management and they incorporate insurance within their membership. Another group are the Metal Detectives Group (2022), who display thirty-eight entries, which constitute their Terms and Conditions, including three more points worthy of a mention as they are relevant to both this paragraph and previously mentioned topics: Bullet Point 5, *Detectorists must have a finds pouch*, Bullet Point 6, *Detectorists must use headphones*, and Bullet Point 14, *All detectorists must have insurance*; the latter stipulation can also be found in the club rules of Weekend Wanderers (2022). No advice is given, in this publication, as to which insurance or indeed which organisation or governing body to become a member of, as only guidance and information are offered with the anticipation that interested parties carry out the necessary research before purchase. Some groups, such as Metal Detectives and Weekend Wanderers, do not supply insurance but state that it is compulsory for any detectorists taking part on any of their digs to hold insurance to participate, and both groups request

A Metal Detectorist's Guide, Designed for Archaeologists

that any and all their membership must also be current members of either the NCMD or FID, who incorporate metal-detecting insurance as part of their membership. The recommendation is for all metal detectorists to carry insurance, which is usually a prerequisite on club and rally attendances and a definite must-have accessary for an individual detectorist, as it would be difficult to obtain a permission without presenting an up-to-date proof of liability insurance. Up-to-date insurance will need to be presented when working, paid or not, on any site under the jurisdiction of construction companies, archaeologist-run sites, private surveys, and commissions, not just out of courtesy but as a precondition of attendance. As with any official document, careful reading of every page concerning the Schedule, Summary of Cover, and Terms and Conditions is an absolute must and understanding all the insurance small print is essential; just because the whole document may involve near thirty pages, there is little excuse for not reading all of it. There are associated codes of practice with all the governing bodies, which are all straightforward and contain a multitude of what should be general practice, some possibly included as precautionary rather than instructive. Common sense is not all that is required, and again it cannot be stressed enough that correct insurance is a must and organisers are, hopefully, routinely checking that all participating detectorists are holders of the necessary documentation.

Chapter 4

An Archaeologist's Guide Designed for Metal Detectorists

This chapter is written purely as a field archaeologist. Not to discount all the specialist factions of the profession, but to concentrate on the personnel who would, in the main, be in the category of archaeological employees who, during an average day's work, a detectorist would encounter. The actual process of archaeological investigation is very different from that of a detectorist, and the aims of a professional archaeologist are governed entirely by written briefs and a methodology that is strictly employed but could often be shackled by and governed by both tradition and the purse. There is of course a brighter side to archaeology and that is found in the utopia of both research and community-led archaeological excavations, which undoubtedly bring much-needed smiles to the unfettered few. These research projects endeavour to attract community involvement as part of the funding process, and are more likely than commercial/construction-related projects to employ the services of both amateur archaeologists and metal detectorists. In the following pages the field archaeologist and their procedures, methods and mindset will be discussed to enlighten the detectorist; which should in turn give a better understanding of both archaeology and archaeologists. To note, this publication does not attempt to offer any sort of an archaeology course or even an introduction to archaeology, but to enlighten each faction by way of a guide to the activities of each faction. The discussion will also look at the academic side of archaeology, which is performed and practised in universities and private establishments and in principle, away from the frontline, and it is this area of the archaeological profession that tends to dictate and influence procedures and ideologies that may be not only somewhat dated but also insular in practice. A question asked many times with reference to metal detectorists is, w*hy do they go out in all weathers?* The regular answer is, *'for pleasure and enjoyment'*, just as other activities such as potholing, sky diving, swimming in muddy ditches

An Archaeologist's Guide Designed for Metal Detectorists 163

and swimming in freezing waters are also questionable but some people do enjoy the participation. A field archaeologist possibly experiences pleasure and enjoyment but also gets paid for the privilege, and like a detectorist no doubt a big smile ensues on the rare occasions that something of beauty is unearthed. Now, a thing of beauty is indeed in the eye of the beholder. As an example, the renowned archaeologist Phil Harding would possibly go weak at the knees uncovering a well-crafted flint arrowhead, while others would be skipping heartbeats as they held an Edward III (1344–1346) gold Noble. For me as an archaeologist, there is nothing better than a well-cleaned and drawn unmortared stone wall, and as a detectorist, believe it or not, it's not the find but any signal that indicates a non-ferrous object that gives that all-important hair-tingling buzz. The old adage all that glitters is not gold springs to mind, no doubt a reference to the Prince of Morocco's remark, '*all that glisters is not gold*' from the Merchant of Venice, by William Shakespeare (RSC, Act 2, Scene 7), and is true to most archaeologists and metal detectorists alike, but gold would of course be somewhat of a bonus and would undoubtably force a grin if not a smile on the weather-beaten face of both practitioners.

4.1 The equipment of a field archaeologist consists of trowels various, tape measures, metal pegs, six-inch nails, string, plumb bobs, gloves, small saw, pruners, pencils, pens, pens waterproof, pencil sharpener, eraser, drawing board, gridded planning frame, spirit level, camera, notebook, Swiss penknife, helmet, goggles, ranging poles, finds bags various and protective clothing, to name but a few, and they would be personally owned by the archaeologist. With regard to helmets, there have been occasions where different sites allocated different colours to others, so if you do not own a full collection of white, orange, black and blue helmets, wearing the correct one is essential. Burton-Hughes (2020) informs us that Personal Protection Equipment [PPE] Regulations covered the wearing of hard hats and a new colour-coding system was introduced that enabled the construction industry to match colour to status, and that standardisation duly assisted health and safety issues concerning status identification problems. The resulting nominated four colours for helmets worn by site personnel are listed below by High-Speed Training (2020), the colours for most of the construction industry, so depending on the role on any particular site, the correct hat must be worn.

White – Site Managers, Competent Operatives and Vehicle Marshals.
Orange – Slingers and Signallers.
Black – Site Supervisors.
Blue – All others and Visitors.

So, the equipment requirements of a field archaeologist are indeed varied and extensive but essential, as even a missing eraser, a forgotten tape measure or even a bulldog clip can cause considerable delays. Pre-site visit activities can match those of a surgeon's team instrument check before an operation. There are occasions, over the years, that come to mind, even though I would not consider myself a forgetful person, such as turning up on site without a trowel after cleaning three of them in my garage the day before or travelling twenty miles, on the excavator's day off, to draw the site with the wrong box of pencils. For the benefit of detectorists who have not delved into the art of drawing, the difference between an H2 or H4, which were left behind, and the Bs in the box I had brought is huge and totally unusable for the purpose required, so the result was a cup of tea and return home, and I did not return to the site that day. The archaeologist could be working on the same site for months, if not years at a time, especially when the site is a community-led dig, of which the longest that I personally worked on required attendance seven months a year for eleven years, and at research excavations where attendance covered shorter seasons of six to eight weeks and often for five years at a time. The commercial side of archaeology can be as short as a couple of days or even a number of hours carrying out watching briefs, making sure anything archaeological is not missed and investigated and recorded while a machine digs a narrow trench to lay cables or a pipe through archaeologically sensitive ground; often hours of boredom but an essential exercise. The larger commercial enterprises requiring scores of archaeologists are often treated both as a combination of archaeological investigations and research programmes and last for a year or two, covering new roads, tunnels, and even decades such as the HS2 programme of railway engineering, which according to a BBC (2021) news statement could easily reach the 2030s before finishing just the first of three links, and time extensions cannot be ruled out. More and more commercial explorations have the pleasure of the involvement or services of both community archaeological practitioners and metal-detectorist volunteers written into their instructions, but, as seen in Chapter 1.7, there is still a reluctance to advertise the fact that metal detectorists were used and the fact that both community excavations and commercial enterprises are guilty of that policy. Not all archaeologists carry all of their tools and equipment to a site, unless they have no idea as to the work they will be committed to undertake on any particular day, *id est* on days allocated to drawing excavated areas of a site, a limited assemblage of equipment would be carried such as: a one metre square planning frame and pegs, string, measuring tapes, pencils, erasers, roll or sheets of drafting paper, drafting board, masking tape, clips, trowel, plumb bob, folding ruler, all finished off by a wide-brimmed hat and a stout back. On another day taking levels would require dumpy level and tripod or more technical equipment, five-metre staff, ranging poles, waterproof notebook, etc. On some sites an individual field archaeologist could be expected to carry out all manner of work in a single day as needs must, and at times, especially on commercial sites where time means money, it would be essential to have access to any tools and equipment, so would be expected to bring or securely store everything but the kitchen sink. This is where there is a realisation that an experienced archaeologist relies on not only past experience but also the knowledge gained during countless hours of off-site learning. On large sites individual teams would take over specific work tasks, meaning that a field archaeologist could spend days or weeks on end on pure excavation duties while others solely record levels, do photographic work, or deal with small finds. So, the equipment for a field archaeologist comprises a very long list of must-haves and one begins to realise that an apt comparison for an archaeologist is a Swiss-Army Knife on legs; with particular reference to the report by Thomas Gaige (2011) of the world's largest example, the Wenger, which contains no less than eighty-seven tools incorporating more than 140 different functions, sounds just about right to me. Other equipment such as buckets, spades, mattocks, wheelbarrows are supplied by the employing company, which sometimes includes high-vis clothing. Archaeology, in normal circumstances, is indicative of a static location and reaching sites can sometimes be an exercise in stamina and determination, often some distance from parking areas, and carrying a large toolbox, rucksack of vital supplies, and any other equipment not supplied by the site management can be far from a pleasant undertaking. Even if a wheelbarrow was used to transport the equipment, which is a proven method on more easily accessible sites, it can be more of a hindrance than a help when a stile or small ditch crosses the pathway to the site. We may have, as archaeologists, or should possess, a certain awareness of shared tools such as spades, buckets, mattocks, and their care, which can differ from the treatment of cherished personal items, which are rarely loaned. There is a distinct possibility of an argument ensuing as to who or which department would take responsibility of ownership and actual operation of metal detectors, and there are a number of avenues yet to be explored in the world of archaeological pre-/post- or during the actual excavation process. To note, there are professional archaeologists who incorporate, as a piece of day-to-day equipment and an essential part of an archaeologist's toolbox, a metal detector, of sorts. If this piece of equipment along with accessories are contractor bought and made available to the workforce in general or by an allocated number of personnel, past experience is not a happy one. As personal equipment it would or should be cared for and treated with respect, but unfortunately, as a generalisation, items of shared equipment have a habit of deteriorating at an alarming rate, especially when batteries and small accessories are involved. A detector can be a valuable piece of equipment and I cannot envisage a member of the geophysics team sharing their equipment with a field archaeologist, or anyone else for that matter, who may on occasion require, by necessity, to use a metal detector. Having encountered an on-site metal detector that was held for general use, the machine could have been described as a detector but would not have been the envy of even a very young first-time detectorist. There are occasions when an excavation brief contains a proviso in the written instructions that a metal detector was to be used either or for both pre-excavation and during excavation, but there are rarely stipulations that the detector be an up-to-date version and fit for purpose, or indeed how often the machine is to be used, and no conditions of carrying out full or even partial surveys of the excavation site or surrounding areas. One would anticipate that the detector operator is sufficiently qualified to operate a metal-detection machine, but the only constitutional qualifier would be by experience. I have encountered professional archaeologists who have no academic qualifications in archaeology but either own or manage archaeological businesses, which by implication suggests that experience is a legitimate qualification; to note, I would expect that there is a very high percentage of personnel who are experts in their field, who you know and use, who survive by reputation rather than qualification. So, the best possible scenario, in an archaeological sense, is the engagement of an experienced metal detectorist who would alleviate any equipment custodial concerns by using their own familiar modern machines and accessories, leading to a comprehensive metal-detectorist's report.

4.2 Health and safety is a major concern for archaeologists and adherence to any guidelines when participating in any occupation, sport, pastime, or hobby is paramount. A professional archaeologist would carry the appropriate health and safety documentation as well as participating in any H & S training requirements, which would include individual contractor-specific H & S courses. Every part of an archaeological site is subjected to risk assessments, which are written instructions outlining any possible action or object that may cause injury or harm without due caution, and preventive procedures in place, and the documented outcome should be freely available. These risk assessments are under constant review and can materialise at a moment's notice, so, for archaeologists, an endless awareness of their surroundings and the activities of others is embedded in the thought pattern of the practitioner. An archaeological site is the proverbial 'accident waiting to happen' and the main objective of H & S is to act as both a warning and preventive by informing all parties involved of any and all hazards. Steve Roskams (2001, p. 85) offers a guide to what the contents of a risk assessment should contain: '*must identify foreseeable significant risks, be appropriate for the level of risk, enable the assessor to decide on action to be taken and priorities to be established, be compatible with the activity, remain valid for the period of work, reflect current knowledge of the activity*'. A more comprehensive and up-to-date guide is provided by the Health and Safety Executive (HSE), where all aspects of safety in the workplace can be perused at leisure, incorporating an eye-watering list of near seventy HSE-approved publications, Statutory Instruments and/or what are generally known as Approved Codes of Practices [ACOPs]. Not that all archaeologists are fully conversant with all contents of all of these publications, but would undoubtedly be aware of the accessibility of such as a relevant source of reference.

Health and safety, in practice, is not the sole responsibility of the employer but every person on-site, whether as an employee or visitor. A visitor should be made aware of procedures and risks and both employers and employees should ensure implementation of such. For many years I carried a Construction Skills Certificate Scheme [CSCS] card, which was awarded once the Construction Skills Health and Safety Test was passed; this card acted as a passport to sites and showed that the holder was knowledgeable in H & S procedures. To note, this scheme ends in 2024 (CSCS, January 23, 2023), so alternatives are being proposed, and anyone wishing to prove officially their accomplishments in the H & S programme will hopefully be offered alternative pathways. One of the formats to obtain a CSCS card was by qualification and the obligatory supervised computer-based H & S test. Another was by occupation, but in the past neither 'metal detectorist' nor 'metal detecting' was to be found listed under an occupation and still cannot be found, and it was recommended that metal detecting was classed under the occupation of 'archaeologist'. Hence detectorists working on sites either paid or as a volunteer are classed as archaeologists, which *is* a recognised occupation, but now qualifications, under the new system, may be a requirement. Interesting though that the rather extensive CSCS list of occupations does not even include geophysicist, and I suggest that a search of the list would uncover other anomalies. I have met quite a selection of geophysicists who have been professional geophysicists for many a year and consider that their primary occupation was not as an archaeologist, but offer their services as a geophysicist to archaeologists. As previously discussed, most institutions possess their own set of H & S instructions covering aspects of site safety, medical precautions, personal safety and welfare as well as insurance, which must be followed to the letter. One point to make, which in the past may have been used as an instruction, are the four words 'use your common sense', which is not a H & S instruction and no more than a personal request; the interpretation of common sense differs from person to person. That is to say that as an instruction it should be discarded, but as a practice, not ignored, and if in doubt, question before any action. All archaeological sites should contain an 'accident book' and access to a qualified first aider. Not to make light of the importance of health and safety in the workplace, but an anecdotal experience springs to mind when some thirty years ago, I dropped a pen in the site hut, bent down and recovered the item, stood up and hit my head on the first-aid box secured to the wall, resulting in an entry in the accident book.

4.3 Methodology of the field archaeologist and excavation techniques are literally written in stone. After the designated area is surveyed in, to the nearest millimetre, and depending on the size, from a square metre test pit to a six by four metre plot, the turf is ceremonially removed in perfect oblongs 300mm x 225mm x 50mm and stacked a couple of metres away from the trench edges, in alternating layers grass side down, grass side up, or as typically described grass to grass soil to soil. The resulting pile of turf resembles a well-structured wall and is built with a certain amount of pride and deliberation usually worthy of a photograph, and I am always happy to show my album of turf walls after a good dinner and a glass of something. If the excavation is any larger, which would be the case on most commercial sites, the area is subjected to geophysical exploration, which should highlight any areas of interest. These highlighted areas are then handed over to archaeologists to determine whether small trial trenches or larger-scale excavation is required, at which point further stripping by machine would depend on manpower and any indications of the depth of any identified archaeology. The normal procedure would be a series of machine-dug trial trenches for land with any indication of human activity found by desktop studies or from geophysics; land for construction use with no evidence of archaeology would be subject to wholesale machine stripping with the regulatory stockpiling of both topsoil and subsoils in readiness for reuse. Machine-opened trenches would now be investigated applying the traditional archaeological techniques using spade and trowel until archaeology is located, then trowelling by taking layers off millimetres at a time, in the process plotting, drawing, photographing, and dating structures and artefact recovery. Recovered finds are classed in one of two groups, bulk finds or small finds, both of which are placed into finds trays. If the find is of special interest, its exact location is plotted with what is called the X-Y-Z system, where X = West to East, Y = Height, and Z = North to South, given a place in the landscape, and then the artefact is called a 'small find' and placed into an appropriate finds bag with, on the outside, the site indicator and year, trench number, context number, small find number, type description function and materials, co-ordinates and the reduced level. In a trench, the above procedure is executed with ease by measuring from the trench edges, with the height of the artefact deduced by the use of a dumpy-level using readings from a fixed level called a Temporary Bench Mark [TBM] by placing a measuring staff on top of the TBM; that reading is called the Backsight, and adding the two together gives the height of the dumpy-level eyepiece. Now we have what is technically known as the Instrument Height [IH], then the measuring staff is placed on the artefact and that reading is known as the Foresight, which is then deducted from the previous total given the Reduced level. This reduced level is the height of the artefact; that formula is in precis TBM + Backsight =

IH − Foresight = Reduced Level; these figures would be entered into the Levels Book. The resulting small find is not an indicator of size but a title given, by archaeologists, that equates to the significance of an artefact, simply meaning that a small find would require special attention when reaching the finds department. As well as the details entered on the small find plastic bag, entries are also required in the finds book, from which the small finds numbers are taken in a strict numerical sequence, then details of the find are copied onto an individual small finds 'Record Sheet', which is a fuller account including a rough drawing, and then filed in the appropriate file. An archaeologist working on a commercial site may never see any find again, once it is placed into a finds tray, and there now emerges a certain understanding of just one possible pathway of resentment with the knowledge that a metal detectorist can cosset and admire a collection of artefacts gleaned, over many years, from the earth, even though not a single one would be worthy of the title of a small find, let alone a place in a museum. It is quite noticeable that a detectorist is not able to match an archaeologist for the amount of on-site recorded information, such as recording an artefact's find spot to millimetre accuracy by using the high-tech equipment of a total station. A concise example of the capabilities of a total station is given by GIS Resources (2022) when these machines measure with an accuracy in the region of single-digit millimetres. A detectorist would be pleased with the nearest three metres using basic apps; for a field 450 x 350 metres, that is not a bad result for an artefact that has been moved to-and-fro by the plough for hundreds of years, and of course highlights the fact that artefacts that are not in their primary contexts possess a certain fluidity in the landscape. A more accurate spatial positional measurement would be forthcoming for treasure finds, which in the main are already dealt with by archaeological departments, or for detectorists by FLOs from the PAS, and artefacts that fall into the newly created categories are fully explained by the NCMD [2023]. The result is a differentiation between the importance of some finds, which did not, in the past, meet the importance required for treasure finds, and some archaeologists' 'small finds', which will now find their way into one of the new categories, which will undoubtedly require a sub-category. Archaeology already uses treasure finds, small finds and bulk finds, and has space for small finds A and small finds B. Metal detectorists similarly use treasure finds, PAS recordable finds, bulk finds, and trash, so their extra category would be, conceivably, PAS recordable (A) and PAS recordable (B). This is a true indication that ordinary detectorist finds, regarded as not noteworthy, are of little use in the identification of human activity as the vast majority are not recorded because they are not worthy of archaeological classification as 'small finds'; in reply, neither are bulk finds of the archaeological excavations recorded in singularity but merely counted by type and thrown onto a pile in readiness for use as a back filler. This same category of finds, recovered by an archaeologist, would also be regarded as not worthy to hold the official title of something classed as a 'small find' – fragments of metal and modern trash – which raises a question: where are all the equivalent thousands, if not millions, of 'recordable' artefacts from the world of archaeological excavations that are hidden from historic and cultural researchers and members of the public? Definitely not on the PAS databases. This is a fundamental problem that is not easily answerable by the profession, and it is one that should perhaps be dealt with, with integrity, honesty and maybe heads bowed in acknowledged guilt and unequalled consequences. As mentioned earlier and just as a refresher, it is not my intention to offer a training manual for either archaeologists or detectorists, which would cover volumes, but enlighten the reader to the general activities, methodologies and processes involved in the practice of said occupations and hobbies. After stating that this is not a training manual, it must be pointed out that one of the main differences between an archaeologist and a metal detectorist is the technique involved in the art of finds recovery, which can be simply described as: an archaeologist scrapes and a detectorist digs, but not in the gardening sense, which gives a picture of a practitioner wielding a garden spade and digging large holes with piles of earth nearby. To explain, an archaeologist spends many years scraping with the obligatory tool of the profession, an archaeologist's trowel, and often develops admirable individual techniques producing level surfaces of the billiard table variety, and stonework, which was once covered in the mud and detritus of hundreds of years of both exposure and internment, that virtually gleams in cleanliness. A metal detectorist's method, both on a hobby dig or survey duties, employs the recognised technique: after accurately locating a find by using the non-invasive metal detector and employing a detectorist trowel to remove either a small core, roughly 100mm diameter, or on pasture a small square of turf cut on three sides so it can be lifted like the flap of an envelope and replaced with a seamless invisibility. On commercial sites where there are only archaeologists, all small finds in pasture and upper layers would have ended up on the spoil heaps out of context, with their historic evidence totally missed. The commercial sites that do use archaeologists and detectorists, in the main, only allow archaeologists to recover artefacts, once a signal is achieved and flagged, but, and a big but at that, the archaeologist scrapes the soil away millimetres at a time and creates at least a 200mm square, and with an artefact 100–150mm in depth would soon open a large hole, not to mention the time factor involved. Could the reason behind that practice be that an archaeologist is credited with the recovery of any artefacts located by metal detecting, so this procedure is therefore denying acknowledgement of finds recovered by a metal detectorist? With the realisation that in practice there could easily be more than 100 signals in an average field, the recovery process could take days in the hands of an archaeologist rather than hours with a metal detectorist recovering the find and placing into a finds bag with required site details, a finds number and depth annotated on the outside, and the finds bag placed next to the flag marking the find spot. X and Y position could be taken at leisure by the geophysics team. One of an experienced metal detectorist's greatest assets is their ability to undertake vast amounts of research, pre- and post-detection activities, research of the search sites and research of the artefacts rescued, which is indeed a lifetime's pleasure. A commercial field archaeologist possesses the knowledge that any finds recovered during a day's work are sent to the finds department, whose function is to clean, record, catalogue, and research, and unless the field archaeologists are also part of the finds team there would be little research undertaken once the day's work was done.

Having practised as both archaeologist and detectorist, one question that often arises is 'which do you like best?' My answer is always the same, 'both in the field', with a leaning towards community archaeology and the diversity of commercial metal-detecting survey work, and both when it comes to finds identification and conservation, dissemination, and research. Working with people who wish to learn and a realisation that that had been achieved is often all the satisfaction needed for a good day's work, and that is rarely achievable on a commercial site where the vast majority are trained employees working to a strict schedule. With the knowledge that using a metal detector on site, even if you are a qualified archaeologist who considers the item a necessary piece of archaeological equipment, there will most likely need to be an insertion in the WSI or even permission of the site's landowners for its use. These days there appears to be an increasing number of archaeological businesses and institutions that take advantage of the skills of metal detectorists and their equipment as a portal to the unseen, and more than often artefacts missed by archaeologists during excavation by whatever procedure are recovered by detecting spoil heaps. Metal-detecting surveys before excavation and/or development are now a little more commonplace but are quite often restrictive, i.e. to either spoil heaps or something similar in format to trial trenching, meaning metal detection of a small percentage of the total excavation area. Unlike trial trenching, where the trenches are placed in areas of archaeological anomalies identified by geophysics or previously recorded on sites and monument publications. Whereas archaeology may well be located by trial trenching, the science of small finds location requires a more delicate approach using specialist equipment preferably operated by experienced, dedicated operatives. The latter comment does not necessarily refer to either amateur or professional archaeologists who use metal detectors purely to accommodate WSI and other planning instructions, and is in fact geared towards a metal detectorist with the relevant knowledge and benefit of personalised equipment.

On an archaeological site, commercial or otherwise pre- and post-excavation metal detecting can be a little complicated as there is no guarantee that the use of such equipment is automatically allowed. On more than one occasion while excavating, it was felt advantageous to use a detector as a piece of technical equipment and even though bulldozers, spades, mattocks, dumpy levels, and magnetometers were all employed, the landowners forbade any use whatsoever of metal detectors, even on spoil heaps, which was unfortunate. Most times the commercial archaeologists are not the landowners, so either land-owning construction companies or local authorities governed by various WSIs and planning applications shy away from metal detector use, and even if allowed the machine is most often used with apparent reluctance.

4.4 Qualifications and metal detecting is a question not of intelligence, but more of circumstance and need. Those who require enlightenment of the methods and operation of a metal detector in so doing master the technicalities of successful detecting using even the most programable instruments. The pathways leading to an acceptable level are freely signposted and can be found emanating from a selection of sources, such as the multitude of instruction videos easily accessible via modern media or the helpful detectorist in the field. The skills required are honed to near perfection by practise, perseverance, and purpose; the provenance of which does not require a diploma (if indeed one was available) upon the study wall to enjoy the hobby. On the other hand, there are those out there who wish to, almost forcefully, grade, meld and incorporate the metal-detector hobbyist into something that they, the hobbyist, does not require or need. There are thousands of amateur archaeologists throughout the UK who are not being literally forced to undertake the academic pathway; the majority only wish to experience their most enjoyable hobby by participation, although there are numerous academic courses available, in all manner of doctrines associated to archaeology, all producing several levels of qualification. But in the world of metal detecting, knowledge and skill are the only form of a qualification and the proof is definable by work ethic and results. Monitoring by peers is not an option in the hobby, but if any bad practice is noticed guidance would be forthcoming from fellow practitioners, as would happen among archaeologists. Every metal-detectorist club has an apt set of rules, but there are no official bodies that a detectorist must stand before and prove their skill before participating in their chosen hobby unless they have acted inappropriately or dishonestly, in which case club officials and/ or their chosen national body will act accordingly. But to prove a level of skill before a committee to entitle anyone to enjoy a hobby would be at the least questionable. One of the largest participant hobbies in the UK, is fishing, something that I was personally fond of. As a hobby it requires skill, knowledge, dedication and adherence to any laws and rules, but what would happen if someone suddenly set up an association of fishing that required members to go before their peers and be interrogated to see if they could cast in a predetermined manner and identify the bubbles of a feeding tench in the morning mist, and if they did pass the interrogation of the peers be forced to join and pay for the privilege to enjoy their legal hobby, which, by the way, like metal detecting, also requires relative permission of the owners of the angler's search area and could also require a fee? Most, if not all, archaeological units do not possess the necessary skills and knowledge to comment on, monitor and record the performance of an experienced metal detectorist, but the metal-detecting community have been using the metal detector for some six decades, in which time one would have thought that the archaeologist and archaeology would have adopted the new technology with open arms, yet sixty years on there still appears to be a self-denial by perhaps turning their proverbial noses in an upright pose to said machine.

Perchance archaeological academia is truly against the machine and take a certain umbrage to those who enjoy the pleasures of rescuing artefacts from a near predetermined fate. Pick up the 'evil wand', I say, and master the mysterious beast, and breathe in the forbidden pleasures of truth and enlightenment in the knowledge that the 'wand' is the way and the path to fulfilment. There is not one mention that I can find against the use of various ground-penetrating machines that can highlight stone structures, areas of metal working, lead-lined coffins, ditches, etc. without the use of an archaeologist's spade, but to confirm dating evidence there is a need to dig, on a commercial site usually by large excavation machines.

There was, for detectorists, a glimmer of a training course roughly five years ago run by a newly formed organisation, the aptly named Association of Detectorists [AOD], which, on paper, sounded very promising. The outcome, at the end of a set of academic courses, was the possibility of receiving some sort of qualification. Or at the very least, a step on the pathway to a form of recognition such as a passport of knowledge, rather than a competence of operation, which would allow a metal detectorist to work on a commercial site alongside commercial archaeologists. The first one-day introductory course was held at Rewley House, University of Oxford (2018) and consisted, in the main, of topics concerning archaeological methods and practices, as one would suspect with a course title of '*Metal Detecting for Archaeological Projects, An Introduction*', and including such things as constructing a Harris Matrix. The organisation in question was set up as the Association of Detectorists [AOD], known also as AofD, by business entrepreneur Keith Westcott. In an article submitted by Kate Geary (2019) covering the CIfA conference, the AOD won the Training Award with '*Metal Detecting for Archaeological Projects, An Introduction*'. It was not long before the AOD implemented another project as a feasibility study with the intent of forming a second group, the Institute of Detectorists (IOD), which unlike the AOD would be open to membership. The Project Advisory Board was seen to consist of twenty-one members, but rather surprisingly twenty of them were from either archaeological, historical, agricultural, heritage or academic institutions, with the single indication of metal-detectorist involvement being the project instigator, AOD. Found on the same web page, the AOD (2023) states, categorically, that '*with a balanced number of advisors from the detectorist community and the heritage sector, The Institute of Detectorists Project …*', but as stated above, apart from this feasibility study by the association there does not appear to be any other metal-detecting organisation or representative on the Advisory Board. The list of advisors along with other information can be viewed at https://detectorists.org.uk/about/, where even the largest and most respected of metal detectorists' representative organisations, the National Council for Metal Detecting (NCMD), is ominously absent. The list could be printed here but this could, in my opinion, be classed as a vilification of the AOD, which is not intentional, and an enlightening of the facts is intended as I feel that the reader would benefit from the study of the full article provided by detectorist.org.uk. The AOD or AofD, which are one and the same, appears to be a well-marketed enterprise, which does not possess any members, as membership is not on offer. It received a grant of near £50,000 from Historic England (2020) to back the feasibility study by the AOD to ascertain if the formation of an Institute of Detectorists (IOD) was a viable possibility, with the study planned to reach fruition in 2021. The results of the feasibility study (Historic England Research Report Series (2021, 46/2021)) have now been finalised with the production of a document covering 122 pages and it is recommended that interested parties read this document, presented as Part One, Part Two and Part Three, slowly and carefully to understand not only the recommendations but also acknowledge the implications for the hobby of metal detecting as a whole. The initial idea from the AOD was welcomed by members of the Advisory Board, which consists of a cleverly chosen/invited group of stakeholders representing, in brief, archaeology, landowners, history, heritage and the environment. Of note, there is not one representative on the list for the 30,000-plus members of the metal-detecting community, and the AOD does not have a single detectorist who has joined as a paid member, nor is there any provision for membership on their website, although in its defence there is a mention of various focus groups that contain anonymous non-members interested detectorists, but at the very least the AOD portrays a rather misleading title when no metal detectorists are able to join. The AOD/AofD has created what some have called '*a cause of concern*' as well-respected numismatist and author Peter Spencer (December 2020) alludes and follows up in the following year with '*IOD The Hidden Agenda*' (Spencer (March 2021)), which offers an extended insight into not only the concerns of a knowledgeable Peter Spencer but also the telling comments from both the founder of the AOD and the honest replies of various institutions, all followed by a selection of some passionate hobbyists.

The Feasibility Report Results can be read online (Historic England (2021)) which comprises a document of three parts amounting to 122 pages outlining the Report's objectives, compiled by Keith Westcott (2021), founder of the AOD, with the intent of forming the additional IOD and also under Part One (2.1 Aims and Objectives 2.2, Q3. p. 10) something called The Detectorists Foundation. So, we now have three organisations: an existing AOD with no membership availability backed by stakeholders, of whom none are metal-detectorist organisations; the pending formation of the IOD, which will be open to membership but supported by non-detectorists and requiring archaeologically based courses and qualifications to become part of a structured institution; and The Detectorists Foundation, which will become an *'asset linked body'* to the AOD and IOD. The Detectorists Foundation gives no indication that even a single detectorist will be on the board of the foundation or even hold a prominent position in either the AOD or IOD organisations, even when all three clearly state, rather conspicuously, the word 'Detectorist' in their relevant titles. There could easily be a separate heading in this publication, specifically directed at the contents of the Feasibility Report (2021), but instead highlights of just a few of the insertions are required with the anticipation that it is recommended that the whole 122 pages of the Feasibility Report (Westcott, 2021) are left for the readers to read, digest, form their own opinions, and act accordingly. It is felt that from the outset there is a confusing, intentional or not, mix of titles of the proposed institute, which by interpretation the meanings purport to completely different intentions for which the following headings are entered for the benefit of the reader. The 'Feasibility Report', the full title of which is 'Historic England Research Report Series – 46/2021. 7851 The institute of Detectorists, Feasibility study for the proposed development of an institute for metal detecting Compiled (2021)'. The purpose of the document does explain that it was for the development of an *institute for metal detecting* (2021 p. 3), but on the same page The Project Name and Historic England Reference gives 7851 The Institute of Detectorists Feasibility study for the proposed development of an *institute for metal detectorists*. To clarify, on the following page under 'Executive summary', it quite categorically states that the feasibility study was made possible with the support of Historic England (HE) for the proposed development of an *'institute for metal detecting'*; the support was in the way of a near £50,000 grant that enabled the study; again, the proposed institute for which (HE) supplied the funding is named *Institute of Detecting* (2021 1.1.3, p. 8). Forward to the Option Review (4.1.1, p. 18) has a mention of the feasibility study reviewing the viability of setting up an *Institute of Detectorists*. The report compiled by K. Westcott (2021) and presented to Historic England, which provided funding for one institute, has now become four different proposed institutes: (1) Institute of Detectorists, (2) Institute for Metal Detectorists, (3) Institute for Metal Detecting, and (4) Institute of Detecting. All of these carry their own interpretation as to what is implied, which are quite different and a little unfortunate, especially in a document of such apparent importance, which would leave not only the readers a little bewildered but also the eminent stakeholders more than a little bemused as to which organisation they (the stakeholders) are supporting. The report is not only directed at metal detectorists but also points out some glaring failures by the archaeological profession, which highlights an apparent longstanding programme of lack of regard for portable antiquities (artefacts) during the excavation processes (p. 30 of the report refers 6.3, 6.3.1, 6.3.2). One can only hope that, collectively, the Council for British Archaeology (CBA), Chartered Institute for Archaeology (CIfA), Association of Local Government Archaeological Officers, Federation of Archaeological Managers and Employers, who all appear on a list of Project Advisory Board members and who collectively represent archaeology in practice and forethought, act accordingly to the statement of the Feasibility Report (Westcott (2021, 6.3.2 p. 9)). From the outset the content appears to be not purely metal detectorist oriented as the archaeologically connotative induction clearly raises its head with an assertive statement informing us that 'responsible detecting' refers specifically to the concept of 'archaeological responsible detection', i.e. 'do not destroy stratified deposits' (Feasibility Report (2021, p. 9)). This does not state that metal detectorists damage stratified deposits but that *'there is a potential of damage'*, but omits to inform the reader that this potential is most likely less than being struck by lightning as an extremely large percentage of finds discovered by metal detectorists are from topsoil, well out of reach of normal rural stratified archaeological structures, especially on arable land. The AOD report (2021) informs that the results of their survey rely upon a total of 684 individual replies, whose content contained some details about their background. Out of a fairly conservative estimate of between 30,000 and 35,000 active detectorists, the replies to the survey are at around 2% and surely in no way a representative figure but merely a very tentative guide.

The Feasibility Report (2021, section 4.4, p. 19) informs that a suggestion of creating a new hobbyist group for responsible detecting was overwhelmingly discounted by the stakeholder group of archaeologists, historians, and heritage-related organisations, who were more inclined to steer all metal detectorists towards recognised academic qualifications. The following statement (2021, 6.3.1) reflects the objectives of the association to actually become an educational and research association that *'will be of benefit to the general public'*, a term frequently used by stakeholders when referring to metal detectorists without actually mentioning metal detectorists. A number of interesting and most informative comments can be found in the Feasibility Report (2021) when referring to archaeological methodology and expertise in the use of the now essential metal-detecting equipment when used on an archaeologically active site, suggesting that the lack of use is due to either inexperienced archaeologists or the unavailability of a metal detectorist. The latter comment is a little hard to comprehend as there are thousands of experienced metal detectorists across the length and breadth of the country. The exact wording encountered in the Feasibility Report (2021, section 6.3.2) may offer the reader a different interpretation: *'most archaeological sites do not use metal detectors due to lack of experienced archaeologists or the unavailability of relevantly educated users'*; whatever is meant by *'relevantly educated'* is unexplained and to whom it was addressed, either to the archaeologists or metal detectorist, is a matter of conjecture and can only be explained by the AOD. The Feasibility Report (2021) continues with the rather telling comment *'Result is that many artefacts lay undiscovered and later destroyed by construction equipment'*, which speaks for itself. The first excuse that most archaeological sites lack experienced enough archaeologists to undertake the activity is to me not valid, but rather a blatant admission of an inadequate training programme by the archaeological establishment; concerning what is now an essential piece of archaeological accessory and the use of a metal detector is, questionably, the main rescue technique for small metal artefacts, and is in no way an excuse for ignoring the importance of artefacts located in the uppermost layers of topsoil, and the whole section implies that the metal detector was, and in various quarters still is, treated as a form of unmentionable vulgarity. So, reading between the lines, one can only presume that a certain amount of venom is directed not at the actual metal detectorist, but at the machine itself, the 'metal detector', although Professor Suzie Thomas (2009) offers a learned comment: *'Metal detector users are at best a major nuisance*'; venom indeed. On reflection, the formation of the AOD, IOD and the possibility of further education, courses and membership income, etc. was a tangible enterprise, but for whose benefit? Archaeological and historically based education is already available to the masses, with a multitude of courses lasting single days, weekends, and longer, which encompass various levels including certificate, diploma, and degree, waiting for anyone interested in such enterprise and all voluntary, and as most experienced metal detectorists are already employed and treat metal detecting as a legal hobby there could be a sense of feeling rather threatened by uncalled-for restrictions relative to academic achievement. Not to project an anti-educational attitude, as education is, I believe, a never-ending function of existence, but should not become a compulsory prerequisite to practise what is in reality a truly pleasurable and educational hobby in itself. If the professional archaeologist wishes to use the equipment as part of their profession, that is completely different as there would be an element purporting to proof of accomplishment in the skills and techniques to operate in accordance with any health and safety regulations.

4.5 Finds, removal, care, recording and sampling

On most archaeological sites the finds are dealt with by dedicated finds personnel and an equally dedicated finds department, and all the excavating field archaeologists need to do, during excavation, is to place any ordinary finds into bulk finds trays, which are always nearby. More important finds are called small finds and dealt with immediately by taking XYZ measurements (see page 129) and given a finds number and maybe if required photographed *in-situ* always with a scale, recorded and bagged with an appropriate tie-on waterproof label annotated with full details. Any finds that can be used diagnostically, but not classed as a small find in their own right, can also be given a small finds number. As an example, on one particular Roman excavation, several hundred fragments of roof tiles, mostly small, were recovered but some showed deliberate markings or a good example of a type of cut-away or an *in-situ* fixing nail; these would be kept and catalogued as a small find that could then be used in a reference collection and subsequently as a learning tool. Small finds are also annotated with all the details required that can then be used to link the artefact to not only to the find spot but also the site. Concerning 'small finds', an archaeologist would regard the position in a context of these more important and recordable artefacts as the most essential piece of evidence, for reasons of dating and interpretation. For recording purposes, the metal detectorist would aim to narrow a small find down to a maximum three-metre square in the landscape and log the depth to the nearest centimetre. As far as recording small finds, a metal detectorist would do no wrong by copying the archaeologist by using these ready-holed tie-on waterproof tags, which can be purchased for less than a penny each, of which I have my favourite brand. The entry on the tag for an archaeologist's finds tray should include the site code, date, context number, small finds number, XYZ co-ordinates, and short description as to function and material. The small finds number is also entered into the small finds book with a fuller description, along with a sketch, XYZ co-ordinates and the small finds number entered on the relevant context sheet. Depending on site working practices, the finds department personnel would deal with all the paperwork and recording, which in turn leaves the field archaeologist to continue with the job of excavating. For a commercial archaeologist, the year would most likely be sufficient instead of a full date, unless there are possibilities of a continuity of excavations on the same site. The archaeologist would also include the same details on a separate label if the artefact was classed as a small find, and put the small find and label into an individual bag, which would have the same details written on the outside plus a small finds number. The number of a small find is always given sequentially and obtainable from the aptly named 'small finds book', and only then, under the supervision of the person who has direct control and responsible for allocation of numbers. I have witnessed the results of the chaos caused when a group of small finds were given numbers on a piece of paper but not written down in the small finds book. A metal detectorist's finds pouch would act the same as an archaeologist's finds tray, and to treat any small finds the same as an archaeologist would be of a benefit to all, with small deviations in so much that the site would now be the name of the farm, field name, nearby village or even a self-allocated field number with an acceptable grid reference. The inclusion of more than a basic description along with a standardised recording system would be more than an acceptable process and an essential skill to be learned and practised as an instinctive procedure. The last statement referring to 'skill to be learned' could be a little misleading as the majority of detectorists are likely to possess knowledge of how to record a find, but a bit more dedication to duty would be of great benefit to all. An individual detectorist working on their own permission, in the main, would have developed a good catalogue technique and a superior recording system along with an excellent knowledge of the historical, heritage, and environmental importance of not only the permission but also of the surrounding area. Club and rally meetings consist of tens, hundreds and even thousands of detectorists covering numerous fields, sometimes miles apart, and on the larger rallies they would most likely be unfamiliar with the area, let alone the fields being searched. Unfortunately, this could lead to an insular mindset only interested in the recovery of artefacts with no regard for the historical or heritage interest. Then again, one wonders if a commercial archaeologist at the end of a hard day's excavating thinks about the wider environment instead of the obligatory shower, meal, and refreshment. So, it appears that both an archaeologist and a detectorist concentrate on the job in hand, unless the archaeologist is working on either a research or community excavation or the detectorist is involved with a research or community survey or on their own permission, and maybe only then knowledge and a need for interaction with the local community would become a cognitive practice.

The next department to handle the freshy excavated finds is the finds team, one of the most popular areas favoured by local volunteers and often a place of active conversation, and where initial finds reach a conveyor belt of a well-drilled operational activity. For ceramics, with the deft use of toothbrushes, a bowl or two of clean water and tender wooden picks at the ready, the team remove any mud and soil by no immersion washing, placing the finds usually in a fresh tray duly labelled and lined with newspapers to dry. There are numerous find types and all are dealt with by a number of methods according to their material, and it would be of benefit to a metal detectorist to take note of the different methods of cleaning and care of all types of finds as no doubt when metal detecting on their private permissions or club outings finds other than metal do appear. Once natural drying has been accomplished, all finds are examined for dating purposes and the bulk finds are subjected to sampling, and a small percentage are kept for research; any small finds are dealt with by the finds team with examples drawn, photographed, recorded and written up. The bulk finds are then subjected to sorting, weighing, counting, recording, and sampling; sampling refers to picking out any type of a bulk find and keeping back an example for the purposes of either forming, or adding to, a reference collection and marked as a small find. On a normal site, any find that is important enough

An Archaeologist's Guide Designed for Metal Detectorists 183

to require conservation will be dealt with by the allocated Finds Supervisor, who would in all likelihood not be a conservator but would prepare the artefact for transfer to a qualified conservator. What is left can be mountains of recorded but now unwanted bulk finds that no one requires; museums are not dustbins, nor for that matter in any position to store hundreds of broken Roman roofing tiles, many thousands of pottery sherds and tonnes of ruined building stone. Museums have for many years suffered from a lack of storage space and quite often been limited to accepting only the more lucrative notable artefacts that perhaps would result in an increase in viewing customers or added to archived collections. Archaeological units, commercial enterprises, research, and community-led excavations would make provision for disposal of finds during the planning processes. Where all of these archaeological artefacts (bulk finds) are now, which must total in weight thousands of tonnes, is a matter of conjecture. This is only one way to deal with the vast majority of finds that are categorised as bulk finds, but the methodology described above only relates to research excavations often governed by universities or local societies and history groups, mostly under guidance of, not necessarily a professionally qualified archaeologist, but hopefully a very experienced amateur archaeologist with access to the knowledge and know-how of the County Archaeologist and the contact number of the nearest FLO.

It is a very rare occurrence that the general public has any form of access to finds or even finds reports emanating from commercial sites, and this gives the impression that commercial-led excavations and investigations generate 'black holes' into which finds are not readily available to the general public or the PAS. Commercial archaeologists would handle both bulk and small finds rather differently by transferring the finds to a post-excavation processing facility. A percentage of the larger contractors take advantage of the willingness of local history groups to answer the call for 'involvement' as many contractors are given instructions during planning stages to include public involvement and are under obligations to provide that service, and most likely expect the same unpaid service from metal detectorists who are, as discussed earlier, rather unfortunately classed as 'members of the public', when convenient, *id est* when a detectorist strays from the proverbial *straight and narrow* they are given the title of metal detectorist by the media and academia and never called a member of the public, but when instructions dictate that members of the public are to be incorporated into either commercial archaeological investigations or when academia and the hierarchy of archaeology use the term 'members of the public', it again becomes the unwelcome epithet of metal detectorists.

Some food for thought as there are, apparently, some metal detectorists who would love to work on archaeological sites, something that is readily available on sites that require said detectorists in whatever capacity, but to this aim individuals stand much less chance than a *bona fide* club of being invited to perform their magic. It would appear that archaeology as a profession needs metal detectors rather than metal detectorists, much more than metal detectorists need archaeologists. The millions of artefacts destroyed annually by archaeological practices could be eradicated in one simple move: train and supply field archaeologists in the operation of metal detectors as part of the general curriculum, as usually in the first year all manner of techniques and equipment operation are mastered or at the very least experienced. There may be opposition to training archaeologists in the use of a metal detector as part of the general archaeological learning programme, but this opposition would possibly not emanate from a metal detectorist or from the metal-detecting community, who would welcome the proposal. The content of the last sentence would alleviate the need for the archaeological profession to search the country for *relevantly educated users* (Feasibility Report in Historic England (2021, 6.3.2)) and in compliance would undoubtedly save both financial expenditure, which would otherwise have been used to pay experienced detectorists to attend on site, and also save thousands of lost artefacts from destruction and give a huge opportunity to rescue millions of historic artefacts that would otherwise be lost or damaged by existing archaeological excavation and pre-excavation techniques.

Conclusion

The aims of this publication were to search for the roots underlying the discontent between archaeology, both as an occupation and an institution, and the now, firmly established, art of metal detecting. In doing so, highlighting the ideologies, expectations and demands of both the antagonists and the protagonists, their flaws, their strengths, and in the process offer an unbiased strategy for reform, leading to an amicable conclusion.

By far the science of archaeology, when compared to metal detecting, possesses the longest lineage of practice, from the ancient grave robbers, through renowned antiquarians searching for wisdom and enlightenment, to the era of the great collectors and treasure seekers who, in the name of archaeology, furnished vast private collections and most of the museums throughout the world, which in recent years are now the cause of ever increasing waves of persistent major repatriation claims. Modern archaeology, in the main, is now virtually married to the construction and transport industries, which offer long-term contractual commitments leading to maybe a much-needed, almost a resurrection or revival of budding archaeologists in a profession that may be not so glamourous as it used to be. The ever-decreasing number of universities who offer archaeology as a subject and the larger research excavations probably suffering as a result means that archaeology does look a little less romantic these days. However, as ever, it is always popular when presented on the small screen, usually by individual professional enthusiasts.

Metal detecting as a hobby has steadily grown and is now well established. It supports not only 30,000-plus practitioners but also a multitude of supporting industries and businesses, which humorously enough, include quite a number of archaeologically associated academics who have relied on the results of the endeavours of thousands of metal detectorists who have freely contributed well over 92% of entries to the success of the Portable Antiquity Scheme.

The persistent use of 'members of the public' as a reference to metal detectorists has for many years been a 'bone of contention' and may seem rather a petty argument, but one that should be treated as a very annoying itch and hopefully acted upon by the users, who appear to be from the higher echelons of academia and archaeological institutions, who resolutely appear to 'look down upon' and are determined to antagonise metal detectorists. Hopefully, a very slight change to openly giving 'credit where it's due' will do away with this 'thorn in the foot' scenario, and those concerned could be brave enough to swallow those irritating references and call a metal detectorist a metal detectorist; for that matter, the ball is well and truly in the court of those who condescend.

With regard to acknowledgement of the use of and benefits of metal-detectorist contributions on archaeological excavations, the CBA Reports went a long way to highlighting both the non-use and non-acknowledgement of metal detector use, whether by experienced detectorists or an archaeologist on live excavations. One can only admit that that study was indeed a revelation of significant proportions and a subject that can easily be monitored in the future, but the information gleaned by exploring near 2,000 CBA reports covering a span of twelve years (Spackman (2023, pp. 71–82, this publication) shows there is a lot to be learned concerning the use of or indeed admission of using metal detectors and/or metal detectorists as an aid to the archaeological processes.

There are inherent faults, deep set, in the doctrines and methodologies of archaeology that unfortunately need to change, not only to move with the times but also to survive as an institution. As we have shown, archaeology has taken many hundreds of years to evolve from grave robbers, treasure seekers, collectors of antiquities to develop into a respectable profession that appears to have reached another turning point along its once flamboyant path. Much time and energy has been spent pointing fingers towards new technologies; particularly noticeable was the constant attempts to prohibit the metal detector and its operators. In the early days, the metal detectorists mimicked the treasure seekers and collectors of the archaeological ilk, leading to the same goals in rescuing and recording of artefacts and apparently encountering the same enthusiastic, often mesmerising excitement of the hunt. So are the metal detectorists not just using the archaeological pathway as an example for historical exploration as treasure seekers and collectors? It would appear that the archaeologists are complaining about the presumed behaviour of the metal detectorists, with a form of self-denial that the archaeologists have acted in exactly the same manner for many centuries.

What is to be done, when some archaeologists are under the impression that metal detectorists do not record their finds, as a metal detectorist should? Indeed, if that were the case, let it be rectified. Let us mention, yet again, that more than 95% of recorded finds that have been entered on the PAS database are from the metal-detecting community, and that according to some archaeologists is not enough, but surely that is an excellent beginning for the recording of small finds.

The vast majority of metal detectorists just want to get out in the fresh air and enjoy their hobby without having to produce a qualification in archaeology; forcing detectorists to become archaeologists is not the answer.

It is apparent that some metal detectorists' practices need a little attention and continuity of action, mostly within the finds record-keeping department, essentially where detectorist finds and find spots are entered. The guidance and encouragement to report all 'small finds' to the PAS, or other recognised national databases, should be provided by club and rally organisers, who at the moment rely on the goodwill of their membership to act responsibly. From this study, it is apparent that there are indeed unknown millions of finds that are unrecordable by definition due to the age of the artefact, its significance, preservation, or fragmentation; this is where keeping concise records of these trash finds could assist future researchers as the majority of trash found by detectorists emanates from our modern era; at the moment, a metal detectorist is destroying the historical record of the future, *id est* in 300 years' time searchers and archaeologists will be declaring that people of the twenty-first century did not lose anything and a 'Dark Age' for finds declared, because the detectorist removed all the trash from the land and did not record them, or for that matter neither do archaeologists or the members of the public.

It is also apparent that archaeologists and archaeological institutions have in the past and still in the present day discard millions of tonnes of bulk archaeological finds as part of their general working practices, and that is not counting the systematic destruction of the uncountable small finds that could have been saved from certain destruction by blatantly disregarding the need for total detection, not just a percentage, of land earmarked for construction, and employ the services of the master of recovery, the metal detectorist and their ground-breaking high-tech machines. That simple transition in working practices, coupled with the essential use of technological advances, would leave the metal-detecting hobbyist to enjoy their legal rite of participation in a pleasurable activity. Or of course if archaeology as a profession is truly unable to use and accept the use of metal detectors, I can easily arrange for small, dedicated teams of metal detectorists to be available at short notice, not as volunteers but paid professional metal detectorists, who will give a full professional service of small finds recovery, plotting, recording, identification, and reports.

As an indicator that suggests, at the very least, a reluctance to employ the use of either a metal detector by existing archaeological staff, or a metal detectorist, or indeed a reluctance to admit the use of a detector or detectorist, see the results of the CBA Reports and extracts study by Spackman (2022, 1.7, this publication). It is not an intention of this publication to suggest that financial outlay dictates the thoroughness and levels of finds recovery from the realms of archaeological exploration, meaning not just excavation, but to point out that by not using metal detectors in all areas available for finds recovery, many thousands, perhaps tens of thousands, of finds and small finds would be and most likely were for centuries missed, and this questions the integrity of past and current archaeological working practices.

For whatever reason, the archaeological profession and the construction industry appear to be ignoring not just the benefits of, but also a commitment to the saving of historical and cultural artefacts from a fate of complete eradication, resulting in irreplaceable information.

This publication has drawn on the historical development of both archaeology and metal detecting and their working practices, and offers a brief but informative narrative to enlighten the reader to the state of play, with a realisation that there will always be the odd bad apple in both barrels and there will be those few who will not budge the proverbial 'inch'; unfortunately, that sort of stubbornness on the odd occasion perhaps lives in the hearts of those in high places.

The situation may be alive and fluid, but definitely not dead and buried. Hopefully, this publication at the very least illuminates whatever problems exist and stirs the many into constructive action that results in a satisfying *très magnifique entente cordiale.*

Bibliography

Chapter 1.
Addyman, P.V. and Brodie, N., 2002. Metal detecting in Britain: Catastrophe or Compromise? *Illicit Antiquities: The theft of culture and the extinction of archaeology* pp. 179–184.
—— (2009). Before the Portable Antiquities Scheme. In, Thomas, S. and Stone, P. G. eds.
—— (2009), *Metal Detecting & Archaeology*. Woodbridge: The Boydell Press. Paperback Edition 2017, pp. 51–62.
Adkins, L. and Adkins, R. (1982). *The Handbook of British Archaeology*, London: Constable 1998 edition.
Aitchison, K., German, K. and Rock-MacQueen, D. (2020). *Profiling the Profession*. Landward Research Ltd. Licence CC BYSA4.0. Available at: https://profilingtheprofession.org.uk/1-1-size-of-uk-archaeology (Accessed: 7 September 2022).
Allen Archeology, www.allenarchaeology.co.uk/our-projects. (Accessed: 13 April 2022).
Arnold, G. (2008). 'Leintwardine, Dark Lane, Herefordshire' in Payne-Lunn, S. (ed.) *West Midlands Archaeology. 51,* Worcester: CBA West Midlands. p. 18.
Attfield, B. and Davies, A. (2019), 'Edgcote, Trafford Bridge Farm.' in Crank, N. (ed.) *South Midlands Archaeology, 49,* Milton Keynes: CBA South Midlands Group. p. 87.
Association Metal Detecting Sport, AMDS. (2022). Available at: www.amds.org.uk. (Accessed: 9 October 2022).
BBC, (2021). When Will HS2 Open. www.bbc.co.uk/news/uk-16473296 (Accessed: 10 January 2023).
——- (2021). Lincolnshire Pendant is Millionth Archaeological Find by Public, www.bbc.co.uk/news/uk-england-lincolnshire-59607288 (Accessed: 23 January 2022).
Bailey, G. (1992–2011). *Detector Finds*, Volumes 1–7, Witham: Greenlight Publishing.
Bailey, M. (2021). Museum Returns Ancient Gold. Available at: www.theartnewspaper.com/2021/victoria-and-albert-museum-returns-ancient-gold-ewer-to-turkey (Accessed: 18 October 2022).
Barford, P. (2016). 'Portable Antiquities Collectors and an Alter Archaeology of Viking England' in *Acta Archaeologica Pultuskiensia Vol. V ('meetings at the Borders): Studies Dedicated to Professor Wladyslaw, Duszko*. Popielska-Grzbowska, J. and Iwaszczuk, J. (eds,) pp. 31–46).
Barker, P. (1997). *The Techniques of Archaeological Excavation,* London: Batsford Press Ltd.
Barton, T. (2019). 'Milton Malsor, Rail Central'. In Crank, N. (ed.) *South Midlands Archaeology, 49*. Milton Keynes: CBA South Midlands Group. pp. 71–72.
Beesley, A. (1841) The History of Banbury: Including Copious Historical and Antiquarian Notices of the Neighbourhood London: Nichols and Son.
Bland, R. Chadwick, A. Ghey, E. Haselgrove, C. Mattingly, D. Rogers, A. Taylor, J. (2020). *Iron Age and Roman Coin Hoards in Britain,* Oxford: Oxbow Books.
Bolton, A. (2017). *50 Finds from Warwickshire, Object from the Portable Antiquities Scheme.* Stroud: Amberley Publishing.

Boon, G. C. (2000). Part III The Finds III.1, in Fulford, M. and Timby, J. *2000. Late Iron Age and Roman Silchester. Excavations on the site of the Forum-Basilica 1977, 1980–86.* London: Society for the Promotion of Roman Studies. pp. 127–179.

Bord, J. and Bord, C. (1982). *Earth Rites, Fertility Practices in Pre-Industrial Britain.* St. Albans: Granada Publishing.

Brannlund, L. and Howard, A. (2013). *Lambs. Philpots Quarry,* https://legacyreports.cotswoldarchaeology.co.uk/content/uploads/2015/04/770012-Philpots-Quarry-Report-final.pdf (Accessed: 18 July 2022).

Brent, J. & et al (1862, 1863). *Archaeologia Cantiana, Kent Archaeological Society, (Vol. V. and VII)* London: J. Tayler & Co.

Brindle, T. (2009). 'Amateur Metal Detector Finds and Romano-British Settlement: methodological case study from Wiltshire' [online]. Available at: http://trac.org.uk/pubs/TRAC2008_53-72 (Accessed: 6 October 2022).

Britannica, The Editors of Encyclopaedia. "Thomas Howard-2nd-earl-of-Arundel." Encyclopaedia Britannica" Available at: https://britannica.com/biography/Henry-Spelman. (Accessed: 12 September 2022).

—— The Editors of Encyclopaedia. "Sir Henry Spelman". Encyclopaedia Britannica. Available at: https://britannica.com/biography/Henry-Spelman. (Accessed: 6 October 2022).

—— The Editors of Encyclopaedia. "William Camden". Encyclopaedia Britannica, 28 April 2023. Available at: www.britannica.com/biography/William-Camden. (Accessed: 4 May 2023).

British Academy, (2022). Professor Sir Barry Cunliffe Fellow British Academy. Available at: www.thebritishacademy.co.uk/fellows/Barry-Cunliffe-fba (Accessed: 22 June 2022).

British Museum, (1963). British Museum Act, Section 5. Available at: www.legislation.gov.uk/ukpga/1963/section/5 (Updated 1 September 1992). (Accessed: 4 August 2022).

—— (2022). https://www.britishmuseum.org. Great Russell Street, London. WC18 3DG

Buckard, J. (2010). 'Ludlow, Horsehides Field, Middleton. Shropshire' in Payne-Lunn, S. (Ed.) *West Midlands Archaeology 52,* 2010 Worcester: CBA West Midlands. pp. 20–22.

Burke, J. and Walker, C. (2013). 'Hartwell, School Lane'. In Horne, B. (ed.) *South Midlands Archaeology 43, Milton Keynes*: CBA South Midlands Group, p. 37.

Burrows, B. (2008). 'Perry Barr, Wellhead Lane'. In Payne-Lunn, S. (ed.) *West Midlands Archaeology. 51,* Worcester: CBA West Midlands, pp. 104–105.

Cambridge Dictionary (2022). Cambridge University Press [Online]. Available at: https://dictionary.cambridge.org/dictionary/english/general-public?q=General+Public (Accessed: 17 May 2022).

Carter, S. (2022). *CIfA, Chartered Institute for Archaeologists. Annual Review 2021–2022.* Reading: CIfA.

Chadha, Ashish. "Vision of Discipline", Journal of Social Archaeology, 2.3(2002): 378–401. www.academia.edu/21392661/visions_of_discipline_Sir_Mortimer_Wheeler_and_the_archaeological_method_in_India_1944_1948. (Accessed: 4 January 2022).

Clark, A. (ed.) (1990). *Seeing Beneath the Soil, prospecting methods in archaeology,* Reprinted 2001, Constable & Charles, London: Routledge.

Collins English Dictionary (1991) 12th. edn. 2014. Glasgow: HarperCollins Publishers.

Construction Skills Certificate Scheme. Available at: www.cscs.uk.com (Accessed: 14 December 2022).

Cotswold Archaeology, www.cotswoldarchaeology.co.uk (Accessed: 11 April 2022).

—— (2010). Sherborne, M40, Junction 15, (Longbridge) Bypass, Warwickshire, in Payne-Lunn, S. (ed.) *West Midlands Archaeology 52,* Worcester: CBA West Midlands, pp. 58–59. (Accessed: 18 July 2022).

Bibliography 191

Council for British Archaeology (2022). Available at: www.archaeologyUK.org.
Crank, N. (2019). *South Midlands Archaeology 49, Milton Keynes*: CBA South Midlands Group.
Crummy, N. (1983). *Colchester Archaeological Report 2: The Roman small finds from excavations in Colchester 1977–9*. Colchester: Colchester Archaeological Trust Ltd. Reprinted 1995.
—— (2012). In. Gilmour, Oxford Archaeology East. Land East of Kettering, Archaeological Report. 1408. https://eprints.oxfordarchaeology.com/2922/1/XNNEK12_report_1408_V2_full_LR.pdf (Accessed: 27 July 2022).
Cuddeford, M. (1992). *Identifying Metallic Small Finds,* Ipswich: Anglian Publishing.
Cunliffe, B. (1973). 'Charlton, Hants, The Evolution of a Landscape', *Antiq. Journal* LIII, Part II, 173–179.
—— (1988) *Greeks, Romans & Barbarians, Spheres of Interaction*, London: Guild Publishing.
—— (1994). (ed.). The Oxford Illustrated History of Prehistoric Europe. Oxford: Oxford University Press. Reissued 2001.
—— (2012). *Britain Begins*, Oxford: Oxford University Press.
DEFRA Construction Code of Practice for Sustainable Use of Soils on Construction Sites. www.defra.gov.uk. (Accessed: 9 January 2022).
Dennis, H. (2022) Channel 4, *The Great British Dig, History in Your Garden.* (Series 2, Episode 5) Available at www.channel4.com/programs/the-great-british-dig-history-in-your-garden/72396-005 (Accessed: 14 October 2022).
Department for Culture, Media and Sport. DCMS. Available at: www.gov.uk/government/publications/draft-treasure-act-1996-code-of-practice-3rd-revision (Accessed: 3 May 2023).
Dobinson, C. and Denison, S. (1995). *Metal Detecting and Archaeology in England*, English Heritage and Council for British Archaeology, London, and York.
Dorling, P. Pryor, F M, and Ray, K. (2010). 'Hope-Under-Dinmore, Dinmore Hill Excavations, Herefordshire', in Payne-Lunn, S. (ed.) *West Midlands Archaeology 52,* Worcester: CBA West Midlands, pp. 9–10.
Dugdale, W. (1656) *The Antiquities of Warwickshire, illustrated.* Reprint. Vol. 1. Online: Gale ECCO Print Editions.
Edwards, C. (2013). Sandy, Station Road, Bedfordshire. In Horne, B. *South Midlands Archaeology, 43,* Milton Keynes: CBA South Midlands Group. p. 12.
Eyers, J. (2012). 'Yewden Roman villa, Hambleden', in Horne, B. (ed.) *South Midlands Archaeology, 42, Milton Keynes:* CBA South Midlands Group, pp. 13–14.
Farrell, C. and Isman, Serge. (2021). *Jesus College first global institution to return a Benin Bronze to Nigeria. VARSITY,* 29 October 2021. Available at: www.varsity.co.uk/news/22330 (Accessed: 29 October 2021).
Fischer, H. (2023). 'Foreword, The Portable Antiquities Scheme Annual Report 2021' *Treasure Hunting* (January 2023) pp. 51–96
Fisher, I. (2019). 'Northampton, Barnes, and Becks Meadows, In Crank, N. (ed.) *South Midlands Archaeology, 49. Milton Keynes:* CBA South Midlands Group, p. 83.
Foreman, S. (2018). *'Channel Tunnel Rail Link Section 1',* (dataset) York Archaeological Service (distributor) https://doi.org/10.5284/1000230 (Accessed: 7 February 2022).
Franey, J. (2022). 'Pro-Russian Official Admits Putin's Forces Looted Remains 18th Century Prince' Daily Mail [Online]. Available at: www.dailymail.co.uk/newa/article-11363551/ (Accessed: 28 October 2022).
Frere, S. (1967). *Britannia, a history of Roman Britain.* 4th edn. London: Book Club Associates.
Fulford, M. and Timby, J. *2000. Late Iron Age and Roman Silchester. Excavations on the site of the Forum-Basilica 1977, 1980–86.* London: Society for the Promotion of Roman Studies.

Geake, H. (2020). 'Time Team's Helen Geake, On Archaeology vs Metal Detecting', DigNation 18. YouTube. 35:51. 05/04/2020. (Accessed: 4 May 2022).
Gethin, B. (2008). Warwick, Banbury Road. In Payne-Lunn, S. (ed.) *West Midlands Archaeology 51*, Worcester: CBA West Midlands, p. 81.
—— (2010). Warwick, land south of Tollgate Cottage, Banbury Road, Warwick, in Payne-Lunn, S. (ed.) *West Midlands Archaeology 52*, Worcester: CBA West Midlands, p. 61.
Gibbon, K, F. (2022). 'Citizen Activists Want Nepalese Art Back', *Cultural Property News*, January 2022. [Online]. Available at: https://culturalpropertynews.org/citizen-activists-want-nepalese-art-back/ (Accessed: 28 March 2022).
—— (2022). 'Russia's War Against Ukrainian Culture', *Cultural Property News*. August 2022. [Online]. Available at: https://culturalpropertynews.org/russias-war-against-ukranian-culture/ (Accessed: 10 October 2022).
Gilmour, N. (2012). Kettering, Land East of Kettering, Phase A. In Horne, B. *South Midlands Archaeology, 43*. Milton Keynes: CBA South Midlands Group, p. 46.
—— (2012). *Oxford Archaeology East, Land East of Kettering, Archaeological Report. 1408.* https://eprints.oxfordarchaeology.com/2922/1/XNNEK12_report_1408_V2_full_LR.pdf (Accessed: 27 July 2022).
—— (2016). *Jigsaw Cambridgeshire Best Practice Users' Guide. (Version 2) A Basic Introduction to Archaeological Excavation*, www.jigsawcambs.org. (Accessed: 11 June 2022).
GOV.UK. (2012). Planning Practice Guidance. Available at: www.gov.ukgovernment/collections/planning-practice-guidance (Accessed: 10 January 2022).
GOV.UK. (2012). National Planning Policy Framework. Available at: www.gov.uk/guidance/national-planning-policy-framework/updates (latest update, 2021) (Accessed: 8 May 2022).
Grant, J. Gorin, S. and Fleming, N. (2001). *The Archaeological Coursebook, An Introduction to Themes, Sites, Methods and Skills*. 3edn. 2008. Abingdon: Routledge.
—— (2001). *The Archaeological Coursebook, An Introduction to Themes, Sites, Methods, and Skills*. 4edn. 2015. Abingdon: Routledge.
Greene, K. (1983). *Archaeology An Introduction*, London, B. T. Batsford Ltd. Third Edition Fully Revised and reprinted. 1995. London: Routledge.
Hacket, A. (2022). Are Archaeologists Destroying Britain's Heritage? *'The Archaeology and Metal Detecting magazine'* December [Online]. Available at: https://archmdmag.com/metal-detecting/ (Accessed: 14 December 2022).
Hamerow, H., Hinton, D. A., and Crawford. (eds.) (2011). The Oxford Handbook of Anglo-Saxon Archaeology. Oxford: Oxford University Press.
Hammond, A. (2021). *Benet's Artefacts of England & the United Kingdom*, Fourth Edition. Coggeshall: Greenlight Publishing.
Hammond, B. (2014). *Benet's Artefacts of England & the United Kingdom*, Third Edition. Coggeshall: Greenlight Publishing.
—— (2015). *Benet's Medieval, Artefacts of England & the United Kingdom*, Witham: Greenlight Publishing.
—— (2016). *Benet's Roman, Artefacts of England & the United Kingdom*, Witham: Greenlight Publishing.
Hancock, G. (1995). *Fingerprints of the Gods, A quest for the beginning and the end.* London: William Heinemann Ltd.
Heaton, M. (2011). *Commissioning and control of archaeological works in development projects.* www.thenbs.com/knowledge/commissioning-and-control-of-archaeological-works-in-developments-projects (Accessed: 3 October 2022).

Bibliography 193

Higham, N. J. (1993). *The Kingdom of Northumbria. AD 350–1100*. Stroud: Alan Sutton Publishing Ltd.

Hirst, K. Kris. (Updated 1 October 2018). Understanding Context in Archaeology. Available at: www.thoughco.com/context-in-archaeology-167155 (Accessed: 10 October 2022).

Historic England, (2009) *The Nighthawking Survey*. Downloaded PDF. https://historicengland.org.uk/image-books/publications/nighthawking-survey/ (Accessed: 9 March 2022).

Hodgson, N. (2015). *Roman Corbridge, Fort, Town and Museum*. London: English Heritage.

Hogg, I. and Edwards, C. (2012). Sandy, Station Road, Bedfordshire. In Horne, B. *South Midlands Archaeology. 42*. Milton Keynes: CBA South Midlands Group, p. 3.

Horne, B. (2012). (ed.), *South Midlands Archaeology*. CBA, South Midlands Group.

—— (2013). (ed.), *South Midlands Archaeology*. CBA, South Midlands Group.

Hunt, L. (2019). 'Daventry, Mickle Well Park', in Crank, N. (ed.) *South Midlands Archaeology, 49*. Milton Keynes: CBA South Midland Group, p. 92.

Ingham, D. and Williams, A. (2019). 'Hanslope, Land off Long Street Road, Buckinghamshire'. In

Crank, N. (ed.) *South Midlands Archaeology. 49*. Milton Keynes: CBA South Midland Group, p. 48 Iona Research Group (2018) Available at: https://ionaresearchgroup.arts.gla.ac.uk/index.php/2018/05/07/day-1-de-turfing/ (Accessed: 21 March 2022).

Irving, S. (2013) The Repatriation of Ancient Artefacts. https//warwick.co.uk/fac/cross_fac/iatl/reinvention/archive/bcur2013specialissues/irving (Accessed: 18 April 2022).

Jesus College Cambridge, *Professor Lord Colin Renfrew*. Available at: www.jesus.cam.ac.uk/people/lord-colin-renfrew-scd-fda (Accessed: 4 June 2022).

Jigsaw Cambridgeshire. (2016). Available at: https://jigsawcambs.org/Images/Introduction_to_Archaeological_Excavatian.pdf (Accessed: 5 May 2022).

Jones, C. (2019). 'Irthlingborough, Nene Business Park, Northamptonshire'. in Crank, N. (ed.) *South Midlands Archaeology, 49. Milton Keynes*: CBA South Midlands Group. p. 82.

L-P Archaeology (2022), www.lparchaeology.com/about/offices/London/ (Accessed: 14 May 2022).

Laing, L. and Laing, J. (1982). *The Origins of Britain, Britain Before the Conquest*. St. Albans: Granada Publishing Limited.

Laing, M. (2013). Treasure from the soil: treasures in the stores? An analysis of the success of the Treasure Act 1996 in meeting its public benefit remit. Available at: www.academia.edu/9090223/ (Accessed: 12 June 2022).

Lane, R. (2016). *Guide to Good Recording Practice*, Historic England. https://historicengland.org.uk (Accessed: 19 April 2022).

Leslie, I. and Luke, M. 2019. 'Sandy, Potton Road. Bedfordshire.' In Crank, N. (ed.) *South Midlands Archaeology, 49, Milton Keynes:* CBA South Midlands Group, p. 24.

Lewis, M. and Burrow, S. (2022) 'Managing/Meeting Finders Expectations and the PAS', *'AMDS Times, Christmas Special Newsletter'* December, Available (by subscription) at: www.amds.org.uk/members-only (Accessed: 2 December 2022).

Lewis, M. (2013). '*Portable Antiquity Scheme records one millionth find*', https://finds.org.uk/news/story/260 (Accessed: 14 April 2022).

—— (2015b). Treasuring Our Past: Portable Antiquities and Treasure Strategy 2020. London: British Museum.

—— (2016) *A Detectorist's Utopia? Archaeology and Metal-Detecting in England and Wales*, in Aspects of Non-professional Metal Detecting in Europe, De Gruyter Open Archaeology 2016; 2: 127–139.

Lorizzo, E. 'Treasure finders praised for generous gesture of waiving right to reward', *Belfast Telegraph*, 14 December 2021. www.belfasttelegraph.co.uk/news/uk/treasure (Accessed: 14 April 2022).

Loubet, A. cited in Sabisch, A. *The Deus Handbook*, Siloam Springs: P&L Publishing. p. 6.

Luke, M. and Phillips, M. (2012). Burton Latimer, Higham Road, Northamptonshire. In Horne, B. *South Midlands Archaeology, 42*. Milton Keynes: CBA South Midlands Group, pp. 23–25.

Luke, M. and Barker, J. (2019). *Albion Archaeology Monograph. 4. A Romano-British Settlement and Cemetery at Higham Road, Burton Latimer, Northamptonshire*. Bedford: Albion Archaeology.

MacGregor, Arthur, (2001), *The Ashmolean Museum. A Brief History of the Institution and its collections*. London: Jonathan Horne Publications London.

Macpherson, L. (2019). Profile of Jason Sandy, in, *The Chiswick Calander*. Available at: https://chiswickcalendar.co.uk/jason-sandy-treasure-hunter-of-the-thames-profile/ (Accessed: 1 November 2022).

Mann, A. and Vaughan, T. (2008). 'Bullingham Lane, Bullinghope'. Herefordshire, in Payne-Lunn, S. (ed.) *West Midlands Archaeology 51*, Worcester: CBA West Midlands, pp. 9–11.

Manisse, P. D. (2019) 'Thame, The Elms'. Oxfordshire. In Crank, N. (ed.) *South Midlands Archaeology, 49.*, Milton Keynes: South Midlands Group. p. 137.

Marshman, I. James (2016). Making Your Mark in Britannia, an investigation into the use of signet rings and intaglios in Roman Britain. University of Leicester. Thesis. https://hdl.handle.net/2381/37527.

Marzinzik, S. (2011). 'Anglo-Saxon Archaeology and the Public', in Hamerow, H., Hinton, D. A. and Crawford, T. (eds.) *The Oxford Handbook of Anglo-Saxon Archaeology*. Oxford: Oxford University Press, pp. 1025–1043.

Mason, P. (2009). 'Ryton-On-Dunsmore, former Peugeot Factory, Warwickshire', in Payne-Lunn, S. (ed.) *West Midlands Archaeology 52*, Worcester: CBA West Midlands, pp. 57–58.

Matthews, K. (2021). 'Billionaire hedge fund manager surrendered £53m worth of stolen antiquities', *Independent.ie*. (Dublin edn), 7 December 2021. Available at: www.independent.ie/word-news/us-billionaire-to-return-stolen-antiquities-worth-53m-41126641.html (Accessed: 22 October 2022).

Michaels, T. (2019). 'Toll Bar Road, Islip', in Crank, N. (ed.) *South Midlands Archaeology, 49, Milton Keynes:* CBA South Midlands Group. p. 74.

Moore, M. (2020). 'Magdala Ethiopian Treasures' https://matadornetwork.com/read/stolen-artifacts-museums/ (Accessed: 9 October 2022).

Morris, M. (2019). *Fieldwork Guide, A quick guide to archaeological excavation. (Version 1)* http://leicsfieldworkers.co.uk. (Accessed: 9 March 2022).

—— (2021) *Fieldwork Guide, A quick guide to archaeological excavation. (Version 2)* http://leicsfieldworkers.co.uk (Accessed: 9 March 2022).

Murawski, P. G. (2000). *Benet's Artefacts of England & the United Kingdom,* First Edition. Ely: Paul G. Murawski.

—— (2003). *Benet's Artefacts of England & the United Kingdom,* Second Edition. Ely: Paul G. Murawski.

National Council for Metal Detecting, NCMD. Available at: www.ncmd.co.uk. (Accessed: 27 April 2021).

National Council for Metal Detecting. NCMD, (2023). *Update of Treasure Act 1996*. Available at: www.ncmd.co.uk/wp-content/uploads/2023/05/20230503-paag-treasure-changes.pdf. (Accessed: 24 June 2023).

Naylor, J. (2004–7). Vikings and Anglo-Saxon Landscape and Economy Project. www.ashmolean.org/people/john-naylor. (Accessed: 2 July 2022).

—— (2021). *50 Finds of Early Medieval Coinage from the Portable Antiquities Scheme*. Stroud: Amberley Publishing Ltd.

Naylor, J. and Standley, E. (2022) *The Watlington Hoard, Coinage, Kings and the Viking Great Army in Oxfordshire, AD 875–880*. Oxford: Archaeopress Publishing Ltd.

Onions, C. T. (ed.). (1966), *The Oxford Dictionary of English Etymology*, London: Oxford University Press. Eleventh edition 1985.

Oxford Archaeology. (2009) *Night Hawking Survey*, Available at: https://documents.pub/document/night-hawking-survey.html?page=1 (Accessed: 2 April 2022).

PAS, Conservation Advice for Finders (Online), Available at: https://finds.org.uk/conservation/index (Accessed: 14 January 2023).

—— (2022). 'Portable Antiquity Scheme' *British Museum*, [Online], Available at: https://finds.org.uk (Accessed: March 2021).

—— 'Research Programs', Available at: https://finds.org.uk/research. (Accessed: 23 October 2022).

Payne-Lunn, S. (2007). (Ed.) *West Midlands Archaeology 50*, CBA West Midlands.

—— (2008). (Ed.) *West Midlands Archaeology 51*, CBA West Midlands.

—— (2010). (Ed.) *West Midlands Archaeology 52*, CBA West Midlands.

Pearce, J., and Worrell, S. (2015) Detecting Roman Britain: 'The Portable Antiquities Scheme and the study of provincial material culture' In: Anales de Arqueologia Cordobesa 25–26 (25 Anniversary Volume) 19–48.

Pearce, J. and Worrall, S. (2020). 50 Roman Finds: From the Portable Antiquities Scheme. Stroud: Amberley Publishing.

Pelling, M. (2021) Digging up the Past, Contested Territories and Women Archaeologists in Eighteenth Century Britain and Ireland. Available at: www.youtube.com/results?search_query=catherine+downes (Accessed: 17 February 2022).

Perring, D. (2003) Gnosticism in Forth-Century Britain: The Frampton Mosaics Reconsidered. *Britannia*, vol. 34, 2003, pp. 97–127. *JSTOR*, https://doi.org/10.2307/3558541 (Accessed: 23 August 2021).

Petch, A. (2005). *Augustus Henry Lane Fox Pitt Rivers*. history.prm.ox.ac.uk/collector_pittrivers.html (Accessed: 27 July 2022).

—— (2005). *English Artefacts Purchased for the Founding Collection and Pitt Rivers Museum, 1884–2008*. Available at: https://web.prm.ox.ac.uk/england/englishness-english-purchases-artefacts-intr..html (Accessed: 2 August 2022).

Phillips, C. (1996). *Jewelry From Antiquity to the Present*. London: Thames and Hudson.

Portable Antiquities Scheme. [PAS] Available at: finds.org.uk. (Accessed: 2 September 2021).

Porterfield, C. (2021). *Europe's Museums, Collectors Are Returning Artifacts To Countries Of Origin Amid Fresh Scrutiny*. In *Forbes, Newsletter* 27 October 2021. Available at: www.forbes.com/sites/carlieporterfield/2021/10/27/europes-museums-collectors-are-returning-artifacts-to-countries-of-origin-amid-fresh-scrutiny/?sh=100456ba675b. (Accessed: 3 November 2021).

Potter, T. W. (1983). *Roman Britain*. London: British Museum Press.

Rail Central (2018) 'Rail Central, Milton Malsor, Northamptonshire' *Archaeological Mitigation. Draft Written Scheme of Investigation.* Microsoft Word. Available at: MIMA_WSI_mitigation_2018070706_v1_CFA.doc (planninginspectorate.gov.uk) (Accessed: 9 August 2022).

Redesdale, R. (2008). *Foreword*. In: Thomas, S. and Stone, P. G. eds. (2009), Metal Detecting & Archaeology. Woodbridge: The Boydell Press. Paperback Edition 2017, pp. IX-X.

Renfrew, C. and Cherry, J. F. (eds) (1986). *Peer Polity Interaction and Socio-political Change.* Cambridge: Cambridge University Press.

Renfrew, C. (1987). *Archaeology and Language, The Puzzle of Indo-European Origins,* London: Jonathan Cape Ltd.

—— (2000) *Loot, Legitimacy and Ownership,* London: Gerald Duckworth & Co. Ltd.

Renfrew, C., and Bahn, P, (eds.). (1991) *Archaeology: Theories Methods and Practice,* London: Thames & Hudson. Third edition 2000.

Richards, G. (2010). 'Nuneaton, Weddington Road, Warwickshire', in Payne-Lunn, S. (ed.) *West Midlands Archaeology 52,* Worcester: CBA West Midlands, pp. 53–54.

Riddler, A. and Sewert, R. (1994). Some Further Guidelines on Finds Retrieval Methods, in Site manual of Museum of London Archaeology Service, MOLAS. London: Published with the assistance of the City of London Archaeological Trust. Third Edition, reprinted 1995. First Edition 1980. www.colat.org.uk/_assets/doc/mol-site-manual-third-edition, PDF.

Roberts, A, (2021). *Digging For Britain,* Rare Television MMXXI for BBC iplayer. www.bbc.co.uk/player/episode/m0013dx6/digging-for -britain/ (Accessed: 4 May 2022).

Robinson, T. and Aston, M. (2002). *Archaeology is Rubbish, a beginner's guide,* London: Pan Macmillan Ltd.

Roskams, S. (2001). Excavation, *Cambridge Manuals in Archaeology,* Cambridge: The Press Syndicate of Cambridge University Press.

—— (2001). General site safety, Excavation, *Cambridge Manuals in Archaeology,* Cambridge: The Press Syndicate of Cambridge University Press. pp. 82–89.

Sabisch, A. (2018). *The Deus Handbook.* Siloam Springs: P&L Publishing. www.sabischBooks.com.

Salway, P. (1981). *The Oxford History of England, Roman Britain,* Oxford: Oxford University Press.

Sandy, J. (May 2022). 'Moat Larking the Tower of London'. In *Treasure Hunting.* Coggeshall: Greenlight Publishing, pp. 31–37.

—— (June 2022). 'Moat Larking the Tower of London'. In *Treasure Hunting.* Coggeshall: Greenlight Publishing. pp. 56–64.

—— (August 2022). 'Moat Larking the Tower of London'. In *Treasure Hunting.* Coggeshall: Greenlight Publishing, pp. 41–47.

—— https://chiswickcalendar.co.uk/jason-sandy-treasure-hunter-of-the-thames-profile/ (Accessed: 11 July 2022).

Scollon, M. (2021). 'From Scythians to Goths: 'Looting' Russia strikes gold digging up Crimean Antiquities', 4 July 2021. RFERL.org. [Online]. Available at: www.rferlorg/a/crimea-archaeological-treasures-russia/31339510.html (Accessed: 1 October 2022).

Shapwick Roman Coin Hoard (2000). Available at: www.nhmf.org.uk/project/shapwick-roman-coin-hoard (Accessed: 11 January 2021).

Shawyer, E. (2013). 'Swalcliffe Lea, Roman Settlement'. In Horne, B. (ed.) *South Midlands Archaeology 43.* Milton Keynes: CBA South Midlands Group, pp. 58–60.

Shopland, N. (2005). *Archaeological Finds, A Guide to Identification.* Stroud: Tempus Publishing Ltd.

—— (2006). *A Finds Manual, Excavating, Processing & Storing,* Stroud: Tempus Publishing Limited.

Simpson, C. (2022). 'Elgin Marbles Repatriation Campaign see British MP's Flown to Greece in Lobbying Effort', *Telegraph,* 10 October 2022 [Online]. Available at: www.telegraph.co.uk/news/2022/10/01/elgin-marbles-repatriation (Accessed: 10 October 2022).

Smith, J. F. H. (2022). *William Stukeley Antiquary 'Father of British Archaeology'*. Available at: www.stamfordcivicsociety.org.uk/uploads/1/2/9/9/12990/william_stukeley.pdf (Accessed: 5 September 2022).

Society of Antiquaries of London, (2022). *History, Enlightenment Origins.* Available at: www.sal.org.uk/about-us/who-we-are/our-history (Accessed: 9 September 2022).

Spackman, P. G. (2016). *An A-Z of 1001 Fieldnames and Their Interpretation* (*Etymologically Referenced*) Witham: Greenlight Publishing.

—— (2019). *The Adventures of Jonathan, Tales of Life, Love and Morality*. London: Austin Macauley Publishers Ltd.

—— (2023). *Archaeology Versus Metal Detecting, The Cause, and the Cure*. Barnsley: Pen and Sword Publishing.

Spencer, P. (2022). 'One Millionth Find Recorded at PAS'. Available at: https://detectingfinds.co.uk/one-millionth-find-recorded-at-pas (Accessed: 11 November 2022).

Steinmann, A.E. (2019). *Genesis, An Introduction and Commentary*. Westmont: Intervarsity Press.

Stevenson, A. (2014). Artefacts of Excavation, the collection and distribution of Egyptian finds to museums, 1880–1915, Journal of the History of Collections 26(1): pp. 89–102.

—— (2016). Conflict antiquities and conflicted antiquities: Addressing commercial sales of legally excavated artefacts. Antiquity, 90(349), 229–236. Doi:10.15184/aqy.2015.188.

Stone, D. (2019). 'Chalgrove, Land Adjacent to Irton House' Oxfordshire. In Crank, N. (ed.) *South Midlands Archaeology, 49*. Milton Keynes: CBA South Midlands Group. pp. 107–8.

Taylor, T. (1999). *The Ultimate Time Team Companion, An Alternative History of Britain*. London: Channel 4 Books.

Tharoor, K. (2015). 'Museums and Looted Art: The Ethical Dilemma of Preserving World Cultures'. 29 June 2015. *The Guardian*. Available at: www.theguardian.com/culture/2015/jun/29/museums-looting-art-artefacts-world-cultures (Accessed: 24 October 2022).

Thomas, S. and Stone, P. G. (eds.) (2009). *Metal Detecting & Archaeology*. Paperback edn. (2017) Woodbridge: The Boydell Press.

Treasure Hunting. (May 2022). *'Moat Larking' the Tower of London, Day 1*. Coggeshall: Greenlight Publishing.

—— (June 2022). *'Moat Larking' the Tower of London, Day 2*. Coggeshall: Greenlight Publishing.

United Kingdom Detector Finds Database, UKDFD. Available at: ukdfd.co.uk/pages/guidelines.html (Accessed: 19 November 2022).

University of Leicester Archaeological Unit, [ULAS]. Available at: https://le.ac.uk/ulas (Accessed: 9 March 2022).

Watkeys, D. (2012). 'Fleet Marston, Wayside Farm'. In Horne, B. (ed.) *South Midlands Archaeology 42*, Milton Keynes: CBA South Midlands Group, p. 21.

Wheeler, M. (1963). 'Introduction', in Wood, E. *Collins Field Guide to Archaeology*, London: Collins.

William, G. and Naylor, J. (2016). *King Alfred's Coins: The Watlington Viking Hoard*. Oxford: Ashmolean Museum University of Oxford.

Williams, M. and Brennan, N. (2013) 'Banbury – Land to the East of Southam Road'. In Horne, B. (ed.) *South Midlands Archaeology 43, 2013*. Milton Keynes: CBA South Midlands Group.

Wood, E. (1963). *Collins Field Guide to Archaeology*. London: Collins.

Wyatt, S. (2021). 'Tower of London Moat Detecting of Spoil', 2021–2022, Monday, 20 December 2021. Available at: https://finds.org.uk/database/rallies (Accessed: 16 July 2022).

Wyman, B. and Havers, R. (2005). Bill Wyman's Treasure Islands Britain's History Uncovered, Stroud: Sutton Publishing

Wyman, B. (2014). 'Bill Wyman's detecting Discoveries: Flint Tools Gallery'. Available at: www.billwyman.com/2014/07/bill-wyman-detecting-flint-tools-gallery (Accessed: 1 November 2022).

Chapter 2

AAAS, American Association for the Advancement of Science. www.alexandergrahambell.org/?msclkid=e78899e0ab6a11ec8b2a7e7a0c62c769.

Addyman, P.V. and Brodie, N., 2002. Metal detecting in Britain: Catastrophe or Compromise? *Illicit Antiquities: The theft of culture and the extinction of archaeology* pp. 179–184.

Allison, C. '*Crawfords Metal Detectors UK*'. Available at: www.crawfordsmd.com (Accessed: 2 May 2022).

Amos, J. (2022). 'Four arrested after being caught metal detecting at Ancient Monument' *East Anglian Daily Times*, 14 October 2022. www.eadt.co.uk/news/crime/suffolk-arrests-at-ancient-monument-9329876 (Accessed: 16 October 2022).

BBC, (2014). Gilbert, William (1544–1602/3) www.bbc.co.uk/history/historical_figures/gilbert_william.shtml (Accessed: 21 March 2022).

Britannica, The Editors of Encyclopaedia. "Peter Peregrinus of Maricourt" *Encyclopaedia Britannica*, [Online] www.britannica.com/biography/peregrinus-of-maricourt (Accessed: 12 May 2022).

Byard, A. (2013). Metal Detecting as Ploughzone Archaeology: Available at: www.academia.edu/9728059/metal_detecting_as_ploughzone_archaeology (Accessed: 14 January 2022).

Collins English Dictionary (1991) 12th edn. 2014. Glasgow: HarperCollins Publishers.

Ciocca, L. (2013). 'Interview with Alain Loubet'. Available at: www.amdtt.it/2013/exclusive-interview-with-alain-loubet-ceo-and-chief-designer-xp-metal-detectors/ (Accessed: 3 February 2023).

Cook, G. '*Rodney Cook Memorial Rally*', www.rodneycookmemorial.co.uk. (Accessed: 31 May 2022).

Crawfords Metal Detectors UK. 'Accessories'. Available at: www.crawfordsmd.com/metal-detecting-accessories (Accessed: 10 January 2023).

Crompton, Bruce. (2018). Combat Dealers, *Battle of the Bulge*. Series 4, Episode 4, Quest TV, Channel 12 Freeview. Produced by Wag TV. Aired 24 June 2022.

Current Archaeology (2019). '*The Chew Valley Hoard*' in Current Archaeology, Issue 356, 3 October 2019.

Detectival, (2022). Available at: https://Detectival.com (Accessed: 9 September 2022).

Dibner, B. 'Luigi Galvani' *Encyclopaedia Britannica* www.britannica.com/biography/luigi-galvani (Accessed: 17 August 2022).

'Digging for Treasure' (2022) *Digging for Treasure*, Series 1, episode 1. ITV 5, Television, 26 August 2022. Available at: www.facebook.com/archmdmag/ (Accessed: 14 September 2022).

—— (2022) *Digging for Treasure*, Series 1, episode 2. ITV 5, Television, 2 September 2022. Available at: www.facebook.com/archmdmag/ (Accessed: 14 September 2022).

—— (2022) *Digging for Treasure*, Series 1, episode 3. ITV 5, Television, 9 September 2022. Available at: www.facebook.com/archmdmag/ (Accessed: 22 September 2022).

—— (2022) *Digging for Treasure*, Series 1, episode 4. ITV 5, Television, 16 September 2022. Available at: www.facebook.com/archmdmag/ (Accessed: 22 September 2023).

Draper, M. (2022). 'Wiltshire pair due in court for illegal metal detecting', *Facebook*. Available at: www.facebook.com/archmdmag/ (Accessed: 27 November 2022).

Evans, S. (2015). 'University Don Who Faked Archaeological Digs to Pocket £240,000 of Lottery Money is Jailed for 6 years' *Mail Online*. 23 September 2015. Available at: www.dailymail.co.uk/news/article-3246180/ (Accessed: 19 November 2021).

'Galvanometer' *Collins English Dictionary*, (2014) 12th edn. Glasgow: Collins, p. 795.

Garrett, C. Garrett Metal Detectors, https://garrett.com/our-story (Accessed: 4 April 2022).

Garrett Metal Detectors (2022) https://garrett.com/our-story/history (Accessed: 9 April 2022).

Garrett, C. *Garrett Memorial Hunt*. Available at: https://garrett.com/garrett-memorial-hunt-2023. (Accessed: 17 January 2023).

Gray, Andrew. (2008). *Lord Kelvin: An account of his scientific life and work*. London: J. M. Dent & Co.

Hicks, W. M. (1881). "On Toroidal Functions" Philosophical Transactions of the Royal Society of London vol 172. The Royal Society, 1881, pp. 609–52. www.jstor.org/stable/109363. (Accessed: 22 March 2022).

Hicks, W. M. (1890). *Elementary Dynamics of Particles and Solids*. New York: Macmillan and Co.

Historic England, (2009) *The Nighthawking Survey*. Downloaded PDF. https://historicengland.org.uk/image-books/publications/nighthawking-survey/ (Accessed: 9 March 2022).

History.com Editors, '*Alexander Graham Bell*', published by A and E Television Network. Available at: www.history.com/topics/inventions/alexander-graham-bell (Accessed: 27 August 2022).

Hodgson, N. (2015). *Roman Corbridge, Fort, Town, and Museum*. London: English Heritage.

Ingram, N. (2022) Email to Peter Spackman, 20 January.

Joan Allen Metal Detectors. Available at: joanallen.co.uk/brands/fisher/.html (Accessed: 2 July 2021).

Kuepper, M. (2022). 'Thieves Steal Hoard of Roman Treasure' *Mail Online*. Available at: www.dailymail.co.uk/news/article-11516671/thieves-steal-hoard-roman-treasure (Accessed: 8 December 2022).

L-P Archaeology (2022), https: www.lparchaeology.com/about/offices/London/ (Accessed: 14 May 2022).

Mastin, L. (2020). '*Carl Friedrich Gauss*' Available at: www.storyofmathematics.com_gauss.html/_(Accessed: 1 March 2022).

Metal Detectives, (2022). *Terms and Conditions and Code-of-Conduct*. Available at: www.metaldetectives.co.uk/index.php/ (Accessed: 1 October 2022).

Michell, J. "John Michell." Famous Scientists. Famousscientists.org. 20 April 2018. Web. 8/3/2022 www.famousscientists.org/john-michell/ (Accessed: 9 March 2022).

Morrison, R. (2013). '*Jersey hoard is world's largest' Celtic coin discovery*'. Available at: www.bbc.co.uk/news/world-europe-jersey-22846664 (Accessed: 10 October 2022).

National Army Museum (NAM) Lieutenant J. S. K. Kosacki. Available at: https://collection.nam.ac.uk/detail.php?acc=1999-07-14-1 (Accessed: 22 March 2022).

National High Magnetic Field Laboratory, MagLab, https://naionalmaglab.org/education/magnet-academy/history-of-electricity-magnetism/pioneers/williamgilbert (Accessed: 22 March 2022).

NCMD, (2023). *Update of Treasure Act 1996*. Available at: www.ncmd.co.uk/wp-content/uploads/2023/05/20230503-paag-treasure-changes.pdf. (Accessed: 24 June 2023).

Nolan, S. (2013). 'Raider of the Lost Vases' *Mail* [Online]. Available at: www.dailymail.co.uk/news/article-2333461/ (Accessed: 2 August 2022).

O'Grady, P. (2002). *Thales of Miletus, The Beginnings of Western Science and Philosophy.* Abingdon. Taylor and Francis Publishing.

Orsted, H. C., Jelved, K, et al (1998). *Selected Scientific Works of Hans Christian Orsted.* Princeton New Jersey: Princeton University Press.

PAS, (2022). 'Portable Antiquity Scheme' *British Museum*, [Online]. Available at: https://finds.org.uk (Accessed: 15 March 2021).

—— (2022). Code of Practice. Available at: https://find.org.ukgettinginvolved/guides/codeofpractice (Accessed: 16 March 2022)

Pearce, J., and Worrell, S. (2015). Detecting Roman Britain: 'The Portable Antiquities Scheme and the study of provincial material culture' In: Anales de Arqueologia Cordobesa 25–26 (25th Anniversary Volume) 19–48.

Regton, Metal Detectors. https://regton.com. (Accessed: 3 April 2022).

Robinson, T. and Aston, M. (2002). *Archaeology is Rubbish, a beginner's guide,* London: Pan Macmillan Ltd.

Rosen, F. (2016). *Murdering the President, Alexander Graham Bell and The Race to Save James Garfield.* Lincoln: Potomac Books.

Seitz, Frederick. (2005). Henry Cavendish: the catalyst for the chemical revolution. Notes Rec. R, Soc. 59:175–199. http://doi.org/10.1098/rsnr.2005.0086 (Accessed: 2 April 2022).

Shank, J. B. 'Andre-Marie Ampere' *Encyclopedia Britannica*, 31 March 2022, www.britannica.com/biography/andre-marie-ampere (Accessed: 4 May 2022).

Slack, E. (2022). *Great British History Hunters.* Channel 4 Television. More4, aired May 2022.

Smith-Rose, R. L. (1948). *James Clerk Maxwell 1831 A Mathematical Physicist of the Nineteenth Century.* New York: Longmans Green and Co.

Spackman, P. (2023). *Archaeology Versus Metal Detecting, The Cause, and the Cure.* Barnsley: Pen and Sword Publishing.

Tent, M. B. W. (2006). *Carl Friedrich Gauss: Prince of Mathematicians.* Natick: Ma. A. K. Peters/CRC Press.

Thomas, S. and Stone, P. G. (eds.) (2009). *Metal Detecting & Archaeology.* Paperback edn. (2017) Woodbridge: The Boydell Press.

Trainer, M. (2004) *The Patents of William Thompson,* World Patent Information, vol 26, issue 4, 2004, pp. 311–317. www.siencedirect.com/science/article/pii/S0172219004000651 (Accessed: 23 March 2022).

Treasure Hunting. (May 2022). *'Moat Larking' the Tower of London, Day 1.* Coggeshall: Greenlight Publishing.

—— (June 2022). *'Moat Larking' the Tower of London, Day 2.* Coggeshall: Greenlight Publishing.

UK Government. (1979). *'Ancient Monuments and Archaeological Area Act 1079'.* Available at: https://collections.org.uk/resource/ancient-monuments-and-archaeological-areas-act-1979/ (Accessed: 23 March 2022).

Weekend Wanderers (2022) *Club Rules.* Available at: www.weekendwanderersdetecting.com/general-4 (Accessed: 2 October 2022).

Welch, P. Weekend Wanderers Club. www.weekendwanderersdetecting.com (Accessed: 31 May 2022).

Welford, J. (2021). Michael Faraday 'One of the most important British scientists of all time' https://medium.com/@johnwelford15/michael-faraday-f4co24ec7da6 (Accessed: 5 March 2022).

Williams, L. Pearce, (1965). *Michael Faraday, A Biography.* London. Simon and Schuster.

Wilson, G. (2010). *The Life of the Honourable Henry Cavendish Including Abstract of His More Important Scientific Papers (1851).* London: Kessinger Publishing.

Wyatt, S. (2021). 'Tower of London Moat Detecting of Spoil', 2021–2022, December 2021. Available at: https://finds.org.uk/database/rallies (Accessed: 16 July 2022).

Chapter 3
Association Metal Detecting Sport, AMDS. (2022). Available at: www.amds.org.uk. (Accessed: 9 October 2022).
Drakon Heritage. (2022) '*PAS Conservation Advice For Finders*'. Available at: https://drakonheritage.co.uk/services (Accessed: 23 October 2022).
Federation of Independent Detectorist, Available at: www.fid.org.uk (Accessed: 1 June 2021).
Hobbs, R., Honeycombe, C. and Watkins, S. (2002). *Guide to Conservation for Metal Detectorists*, Stroud: Tempus Publishing Ltd.
Metal Detectives Group, Available at: www.metaldetectives.co.uk/index.php (Accessed: 11 October 2022).
MOLAS. Museum of London Archaeology Service. Available at: www.mola.org.uk/about-us (Accessed: 2 April 2022).
NCMD, (2023). *Update of Treasure Act 1996*. Available at: www.ncmd.co.uk/wp-content/uploads/2023/05/20230503-paag-treasure-changes.pdf. (Accessed: 24 June 2023).
National Council for Metal Detecting, NCMD. Available at: www.ncmd.co.uk. (Accessed: 27 April 2021).
NCMD, (2023). *Update of Treasure Act 1996*. Available at: www.ncmd.co.uk/wp-content/uploads/2023/05/20230503-paag-treasure-changes.pdf. (Accessed: 24 June 2023).
Portable Antiquities Scheme. [PAS]. Available at: finds.org.uk. (Accessed: 2 September 2021).
Rodgers, B.A. (2004). 'The Archaeologist's Manual for Conservation, A Guide to Non-Toxic, Minimal Intervention Artifact Stabilization.', New York, Boston, Dordrecht, London, Moscow: Kluwer Academic Publishers.
Sabisch, A. (2018). *The Deus Handbook*. Siloam Springs: P&L Publishing.
Shopland, N. (2006). *A Finds Manual, Excavating, Processing & Storing*, Stroud: Tempus Publishing Limited.
South, S. (2004). '*Forword*' in. The Archaeologist's Manual for Conservation, A Guide to Non-Toxic, Minimal Intervention Artifact Stabilization.', New York, Boston, Dordrecht, London, Moscow: Kluwer Academic Publishers. pp. vii-viii.
Treasure Act, (1996). Revised (2023). Available at: www.gov.uk/government/publications/draft-treasure-act-1996-code-of-practice-3rd-revision (Accessed: 3 May 2023).
Watkinson, D.E. and Neal, V. (1998) *First Aid for Finds*, Lavenham: The Lavenham Press Ltd.
Weekend Wanderers (2022) *Club Rules*. Available at: www.weekendwanderersdetecting.com/general-4 (Accessed: 2 October 2022).

Chapter 4
AOD, Association of Detectorists. Available at: https://detectorists.org.uk. (Accessed: 7 March 2022).
BBC. (2021). When Will HS2 Open. Available at: www.bbc.co.uk/news/uk-16473296 (Accessed: 10 January 2023).
Burton-Hughes, L. (2020). Hard Hat Colour Codes In Construction: what do they mean? Available (Online) at: https://www.highspeedtraining.co.uk/hub/hard-hat-colour-codes-in-construction/ (Accessed: 27 February 2023).
Approved Codes of Practices, 2023 (ACOPs). Available at: www.hse.gov.uk/legislation/legalpublications.htm (Accessed: 23 February 2023).

Construction Skills Certificate Scheme. Available at: www.cscs.uk.com (Accessed: 14 December 2022).

Geary, K. (2019). '2019 Training Award won by Keith Westcott for the Association of Detectorists'. Available at: https://www.archaeologists.net/news/2019-training-award-won-keith-westcott-association-detectorists-1556528179.

Gaige, T. (2011). *Protool reviews, Professional Tool Reviews For Pros. [Online]*. Available at: www.protoolreviews.com/wenger-16999-giant-swiss-army-knife/ (Accessed: 3 May 2023).

GIS Resources. (2002). GIS Resources, A Knowledge Archive. Available at: https://gisresources.com/total-station-and-its-applications_2-in-surveying/ (Accessed: 3 March 2023).

Health and Safety Executive. *Health and Safety Legislation – laws in the workplace*. Available at: www.hse.gov.uk/legislation/ (Accessed: 17 February 2023).

Health and Safety Executive. Available at: www.hse.gov.uk. (Accessed: 11 February 2023).

Historic England (2018) 'Grant to Help Set Up New Body to Support Metal Detectorists'. Available at: https://historicengland.org.uk/whats-new/news/grant-to-support-metal-detectorists/ (Accessed: 8 March 2023).

Historic England (2020). Statement about the Institute of Detectorists feasibility study. Available at: https://historicengland.org.uk/whats-new/features/institute-of-detectorists/ (Accessed: 7 March 2023).

Historic England (2021). The Institute of Detectorists: Feasibility Study for the Proposed Development of an Institute for Metal Detecting. Available at: https://historicengland.org.uk/research/results/reports/462021?searchType=research+reports&search=46%2F2021 (Accessed: 7 March 2023).

National Council for Metal Detecting, NCMD. Available at: www.ncmd.co.uk. (Accessed: 27 April 2021).

National Council for Metal Detecting. NCMD, (2023). *Update of Treasure Act 1996*. Available at: www.ncmd.co.uk/wp-content/uploads/2023/05/20230503-paag-treasure-changes.pdf. (Accessed: 24 June 2023).

Roskams, S. (2001). General site safety, Excavation, *Cambridge Manuals in Archaeology*, Cambridge: The Press Syndicate of Cambridge University Press. pp. 82–89.

Royal Shakespeare Company. The Merchant of Venice. Available at: www.rsc.org.uk/the-merchant-of-venice/about-the-play/famous-quotes (Accessed: 22 August 2022).

Spencer, P. (2021). '*IOD The Hidden Agenda*'. Available at: https://detectingfinds.co.uk/iod-the-hidden-agenda (Accessed: 1 January 2022).

Westcott, K. (2021) *The Institute of Detectorists: Feasibility Study for the Proposed Development of an Institute for Metal Detectorists*. https://historicengland.org.uk/research/results/reports (Accessed: 24 December 2022).